George

With Love,

Dad & Mom
Christmas '73

THE YEARS
OF THE
FOREST

Helen Hoover

THE YEARS
OF THE
FOREST

pen-and-ink drawings by Adrian Hoover

  ALFRED · A · KNOPF   NEW YORK   1973

THIS IS A BORZOI BOOK
PUBLISHED BY ALFRED A. KNOPF, INC.

Library of Congress Cataloging in Publication Data:

Hoover, Helen, date. The years of the forest.

1. Natural history—Minnesota. 2. Nature stories. I. Title.
QH105.M55H64 1973   500.9′776′75   72–11022
ISBN 0-394-47538-0

Manufactured in the United States of America

FIRST EDITION

TO MY HUSBAND
with thanks
for the happiness
he has brought me
during the past
forty-odd years

CONTENTS

ACKNOWLEDGMENTS

As I look back through the years, I realize that so many people—editors, book reviewers, reporters, photographers, old friends and new—have helped me in one way or another to write this book that I cannot possibly name them all. Thus, I limit my personal thanks to Miss Winnifred Hopkins, a friend-by-mail of long standing, who sent me my letters to her that I might use them to refresh my memory; to Thomas Roberts, managing editor of *Humpty Dumpty's Magazine*, and Alvin Tresselt, who formerly held that position and is now a vice-president of Parents' Magazine Press, for sending me copies of letters written to Mr. Tresselt over a number of years; and to Gary C. Brown, a university student, from one of whose letters I quote in the Epilogue.

I have referred to feature stories about Ade and me, and to their illustrations, published in the *Minneapolis Star and Tribune*, the *St. Paul Pioneer-Press*, and the *Duluth News-Tribune*. I have also referred to or used parts of early articles published in *Audubon, Canadian Audubon, Frontiers, Nature,*

Minnesota Naturalist, Organic Gardening and Farming, and *Gourmet.*

I am especially grateful to Defenders of Wildlife for tear sheets of my quarterly feature, "Wilderness Chat," from their *Defenders of Wildlife News,* and to Thomas Y. Crowell Company, publisher of *The Long-Shadowed Forest,* and Alfred A. Knopf, Inc., publisher of *The Gift of the Deer,* for a few paragraphs from these books which I have used because they are part of this story, too, and I am sure I could not write them better than the first time.

Last, but far from least, thanks go to my agent and editor for their patience through the long time I needed to get this book ready for them, and to my husband for the illustrations and his kindness in ignoring my fits of uncertain temper during the early days, when I was sure I would never find a way through the underbrush of the past to the present.

H.H.

FOREWORD

This book is a sort of summary of the sixteen years that followed our hectic first year and a half in the North Woods. It might even be thought of as a record of our progress, and to show how tortoiselike this was, I have used in both text and table of contents the items from a list of things-to-do, scribbled by my husband shortly after we bought our log cabin.

It was easy to write *A Place in the Woods,* which covers the short period of time mentioned above, because I had written down events and conversations as they occurred, with a faint idea that these notes might be useful some day. When I turned the notes into a book, I eliminated numerous uproars of little interest and let a few symbolic but real people with fictitious names represent many people, that I might not flood the book with characters.

After the fire in Ade's work building that closed that period for us, I was too busy with urgent work to keep notes. So I have searched the Hoovers' combined memories, old records and letters, and my early writings for the order of events. If I have confused it anywhere it is not in any important way. I have employed the same device for people as before, except that I have used real names for Gladys Taber and persons already named in the acknowledgments; also, Awbutch appears as herself.

Because our close association with the life of the forest has led us to know members of the more highly evolved species as individuals and to recognize all animal life as related to us, even though very distantly, I have used "it" and "which" only for nonsentient components of our wild world.

Since there was nothing temporary or theoretical about our life away from civilization, I hope that such comments as I have been able to make from our experience will help those who want to save both the good earth and its life—human, other animal, and plant.

part one

THE
INNOCENT
YEARS

1956 | *cut wood*
install wiring
clear brush and paths
clear trash
running water
make a living

———— It was early afternoon near the beginning of May when I sat by the lake on a pink granite slab the size of a small room, looking through the clear water at the gray and green and brown of the submerged rocks, and at a crayfish, poking his claws tentatively from a hiding place between the stones. A giant water bug departed at speed. Maybe he had seen the crayfish and was taking precautions. A school of tiny fish flirted by, and out from the shore there was a plop and a series of expanding rings where a big fish had broken the surface. I was amazed, as I always was, at the adaptations that made it possible for so many creatures to live comfortably through the bitter winter in the water under the ice.

I sprawled flat on the stone and dabbled my fingers in the water. It was still very cold, and the deepest, richest blue I know. As it rippled its way from the Minnesota shore to the low hills of Canada that rose from its far edge, it turned to indigo and grew even darker. There was no sound until a loon laughed, a cheerful *ho-ho-ho-ho* that will always mean northern waters to me. Above the hills, black-green with spruce and browny-gray with bare aspen tops, the sky was pale. It darkened gradually to deep azure at the zenith, where little clouds like bunny tails lay motionless. I sat up, shook the drops from my fingers and rubbed the cold from them.

———— The ice had gone out only a few days earlier, and there were remnants of it beneath overhanging sections of the bank. Dirty-white patches of snow lingered in the forest where sunlight did not reach—under the swirled roots of cedars, beside boulders dropped by glaciers long ago, on the north side of our log cabin, where the rusty barrel stove we used as a winter freezer stood.

Spring was here, though, in the early breakout and in the air—damp and soft and scented by the earth, which was already warming in the sun. The pussies on the willows were a month old and looked bedraggled. Soon slender pale-green leaves would replace them, and the fat buds on the red-berried elder would be fanning open. By the middle of the month, barring a return of winter's cold, grasses and daisies and yarrow would be tall enough to hide the low wood violets, thick with buds almost ready to open and show their small white or blue faces. The misty sprays of the horsetails would be sparkling with dew in the mornings, and the fiddleheads of the ferns would uncoil almost while I watched.

Already the red squirrels were through with their amorous chasing through the pines and spruces, and mothers-to-be, showing smooth red summer fur where patches of their gray winter coats had fallen away, were carrying grass and leaves to secluded nurseries. A crow, back from the south since mid-March, swooped over, circled, and flapped away, cawing an alarm.

The forest year had begun.

Somewhere in the warming time, after the hardships and

lethargy of winter, these natural years begin, full of rising life and a surge of what, in men, would be called optimism or hope. In wild creatures it comes as naturally as breathing and does not have to be called by any name. It is a manifestation of the earth—in my case, of the forest—which to me has as much personality as any human. Man-made standards of good and evil are unknown to it, and its innocence and strength are such that it has given Ade and me understanding, compassion, and tolerance by merely surrounding us and allowing us to watch its activities. From it we learned that the calendar year belongs exclusively to the world of men and that the forest year starts, as does that of a field of corn, with the stirring of its seeds.

I came out of my dreaming and saw that the still-low sun had passed its highest point. Ade would soon be back from his six-mile round-trip walk for the mail, and such a hardworking husband would be hungry.

I stood up, stretched, and noticed a crack starting across the middle of the slab on which I had been sitting. How long would it take for the endless wash of water, the freezing and thawing, to break the great piece of granite? I felt cool wind and looked down the lake to see a broad, gray cloud-front slowly moving in from the east. Nature was making little changes everywhere—in the weather, the bedrock, the surroundings, myself. As I walked up the path to the log cabin I wondered if I would still be here when the granite broke in two.

———— I pulled open a deep, heavy drawer under the kitchen counter and looked through the few cans remaining from last fall's shipment of groceries. The choice for lunch seemed to be limited to a lone envelope of dehydrated vegetable soup. There was also, behind the cans, an abandoned mouse nest. I emptied the drawer, and in removing it from the cabinet to take outside for washing, and drying in the sun, I noticed that a crumpled piece of paper had been caught behind it. I smoothed it out and saw that it was one of Ade's many lists of things-to-do. I put the drawer on the doorstep, added water to the soup, set it on the back of the wood range, and went into the living room to sit by the window and read my find.

Clear brush and   *Install wiring*
    paths   *Running water*
Clear trash   *Inside toilet*
Remodel icehouse   *Clear small cabin*
Build dock   *Cut wood*
Lay hardwood floor   *Get another car*
Fix roof   *Make a living*
Finish inside   *Take a vacation*

The paper was brown on the edges, and I wondered when Ade had written the list. All but the last four of the fifteen items pertained to the log cabin, and none to the summer house. We had bought the log cabin as a vacation spot on our first trip to the area in the spring of 1954. Some months later we had made a second trip because Ade had been ill and needed to recuperate away from the cold-and-flu atmosphere of our home city, Chicago. We took over the adjoining summer cabin and land during that stay, not long before our sudden decision to remain permanently in the woods. There had been plenty of things to do at the summer house, so he must have made up the list on our first trip and before we bought the second house.

And there was no mention of the log cabin's soggy basement with a spring coming through one wall. We had discovered this shortly after we took possession, and it was less than a week later that a cloudburst almost washed the foundation from under us. For the umpteenth time I felt a wave of gratitude for John Anderson, the old-time builder who had filled the basement and saved the cabin for us. The list was probably Ade's first, scribbled even before we learned of the basement's condition. He could not have omitted that once he knew about it.

I read it through again. So far, not one thing on it had been completed as planned. It would be interesting to keep it as a measure of our progress.

I went to my desk and drew a line through "Build dock." A boat with no means of propulsion, not even oars, had come with the log cabin. The dock had become a hastily constructed skid when Sven Peterson, our very good friend who owned the Lodge two miles away, sold us an outboard motor cheap in the summer of 1955. Come to think of it, Sven and his wife Hilda should be back from Minneapolis to open up any day. It was a heart-warming thought.

I also drew lines through "Remodel icehouse" and "Lay hardwood floor." Ade had done a fine job on the icehouse, but as a fitting climax to a year and a half when near-catastrophes went by in a parade, the building had been ruined by fire on the first of the December just past. And as the hardwood for the floors had been in the remodeled icehouse, the fire had taken care of that, too.

"Cut wood" must have been tacked on when we were settling in for our first winter, and was still one of our more important chores. "Get another car" and "Make a living" had surely followed the collision on the snow-narrowed blind hilltop six weeks after our stay had become permanent. The accident had not only left us without transportation but had prevented Ade's getting to Duluth to sign a contract for art work, which in turn left us almost broke and with no income. "Take a vacation" could have been written in at any one of a thousand times when Ade must have felt as weary and nearly hopeless as I had.

My eyes followed a blue jay through the trees to the partly charred icehouse—now euphemistically called the work building—and I remembered how cold the lake had been when I knelt on its submerged rocks, filling buckets with which Ade had somehow managed to drown the flames, and of how hectic the following weeks had been.

Ade's drawing hand, sprained during the commotion when he slipped on an ice-glazed rock, had healed well except that his thumb was stiff and awkward to use. On the first Wednesday of January he came in, saying he had let a wedge slip in a chunk of wood he was splitting and caught his hand. "There's a flap of skin you'll have to trim off," he added. I looked and gulped. The flap of skin was an inch-and-a-half-long triangle, cut completely through and exposing the bones of his thumb. While I cleaned and stitched and splinted as well as I could, I wondered if the next accident would end his drawing days.

To cheer myself the next morning I washed the two dusty India-print throws we used on the worn armchairs that had come with the cabin. It was snowing, so I strung impromptu clotheslines inside and had the throws dry and on the chairs by evening. I then caught my toe on the edge of a warped floorboard and spilled two bowls of soup, one over each chair. I had to wash the throws again immediately, else our mice would smell the food and start turning them into lace during the night. While hanging them outside to freeze dry, I managed to wrench my back, which was almost recovered from a minor injury incurred while I was helping Ade put out the fire. By some wonderful process of illogic, I blamed Ade for all of this because he had set up the power plant whose exhaust spark had started the blaze. He, of course, laughed, which truly topped my day.

Two nights later I went out to check on Ade's pet rooster, the Crown Prince, and his majesty's two hens, Bedelia and Tulip, who supplied our eggs. I slipped on the icy doorstep, whacked the back of my head on the sill, and almost knocked myself out. This, however, fixed the back perfectly.

Things went smoothly enough after that, through the late snows and into the first small thaw, when we got a check from the fire insurance company. The building had been underinsured because Ade had improved it after we took out the policy, but the adjuster gave us all he could—a small nest egg but very exciting, considering our chronically moneyless state.

The sound of Ade's boots squelching in the spring mud brought me back to the present. Adding a heading, "Years to complete," to the list, I marked "1" after the three crossed-off items, put the list in the center desk drawer for future reference, and rushed to the soup.

When Ade opened the door and I saw his expression, I stopped, pan in hand. "What's wrong?"

He held out an opened letter, saying, "From Hilda."

I read: ". . . always was easier for me to take bad news after the ice was out so I waited to write you. Sven died very suddenly in January. The Lodge has a new proprietor and I will stay on in Minneapolis but hope to come to see you soon . . ."

Without a word we went into the living room and sat down. My eyes fell on the bush-line phone and I wondered how many times it would ring and I would answer, expecting to hear Hilda's voice, excited over a bit of news; how many times one of us would start to call Sven for advice before we remembered he would not be at his desk by the phone. I turned back to the letter and read on, aloud: "I understand there are many plans for updating the Lodge."

We looked at each other, recalling our friendly reception

there, our meal by the iron cookstove in the spice-scented kitchen. Out of our recollections of "updated" resorts we had visited while we searched for our place in the woods, we silently said good-bye to a precious time of friendship and of sharing.

I lay awake a long time that night, thinking of the past and hearing the east wind breathing, resting, breathing again through the trees and in the chimney. This kind of wind, along with the clouds that rode on it, meant a soaking three- or four-day rain. I recalled that the ancients had named four elements—Fire, Earth, Air, and Water—and decided that they were, in their way, right, because we are born of starlight and dust and sustained by air and water. I thought how wonderful it was that we can depend on the Fire of the sun to pour light and heat and the triggers of mutation across the vastness of space, and on the Earth's rotation to bring day and night and on its tilted axis to change the seasons, but how disconcerting that the movements of earthbound Air and Water are versatile and capricious, erratic and contradictory.

I let my mind wander to the winds that dry the sodden ground of spring and whisper through new growth, that howl as gales to topple dead timber. That carry the sound of real voices, and ghostly echoes that might be those of voices long gone. That frustrate and aid both the hunted and the hunter. That puff in the drouth and push in the clouds. My thoughts turned then to the water from the clouds, that is the savior of life and sometimes its taker. To rain roaring in torrents to wash debris from the earth and freshen the streams and raise the lake levels, or drizzling in silence to fur every leaf with silver, green the mosses, and soak the duff until mushrooms pop up like elves in big hats. Or pattering like the feet of many mice to sink into the soil and moisten the roots.

My mind went again to the wind, returning to steal the diamonds left by the rain. Drowsily I thought of the utter dependency of every living thing on Mother Earth, and drifted from my fantasy of jeweled leaves into sleep.

———— Ade and I stood together at a window in the morning and looked out on a dim and dripping world. There was no sound except the soft plop of water and the shrill love song of a toad. No guests came to our feeding area except two whiskey jacks, who picked industriously at some suet nailed to a bench under a cedar, their feathers as water-darkened and straggly as the landscape.

Ade sighed and stretched. "Glad the mail was yesterday."

"You could let it wait, anyway. Why walk six miles and drown yourself when you don't have to?" I looked at the partly painted ceiling and added: "There's plenty to do inside."

Ade glanced up at the slanting panels between the log beams and moved hastily toward his workroom, saying, "I'd better get at the new notepaper designs. If we're going to make any money selling it next fall, that is."

I squelched some impractical thoughts of a *House & Garden* kitchen and asked, "Do you need any supplies?"

He checked, then said, "Two reams of white paper."

"Fine," I said. "I can take that much out of the groceries."

I walked toward my typewriter and he settled at his drawing board.

After the long soaking rain, the forest basked in warmth and moisture. The clearing turned green as if by magic. The air moved gently, caressingly. The days were punctuated by the small sounds of ants dropping from the cabin ceiling. This set us to looking frantically for a possible nest in a log or beam until we discovered a small opening in a roof peak where they entered from the outside. They were females, winged when they left their nest, each capable of starting a new colony if she found a rotten or water-softened piece of wood she could bore into. They lifted in thin clouds against the robin's-egg-blue sky, scattered, and as their short time of flight ended, dropped to earth again. Some pattered onto our roof, and outside the windows the air glistened with the iridescence of their discarded, falling wings.

The bird songs grew fewer as they nested, and not many animals came near the house because they, too, were preparing for their all-important task of bearing young. But the *chip-chip* of the red squirrels was there for company, and a pileated woodpecker came, with his vivid red crest and shining black back, to drum his mating call on a hollow cedar tree. He drummed and listened, drummed and listened, until from afar a faint drumming answered him. He and the bird I assumed was his mate-to-be talked back and forth on the hollow trees, cackling now and then, moving nearer to each other, and then were silent.

The mosquitoes and black flies were out in full force, ready for their coming task of fertilizing the flowers, and they bit so ferociously that we gave up on outdoor work. I cleaned in corners that had not looked dirty during the dim winter days but were disgraceful when the sun came through the windows. Ade settled to the task of filling the knotholes in the floor. Carl Johnson, the former owner of the cabin, had covered them with pieces of tin can. In winter these transferred cold inside and were covered in the mornings with frost, whose moisture, lingering under any floor covering, would eventually cause dry rot in the floor boards. Knots taper. If these boards had been laid with the large faces of the knots upward when possible, they would not have dropped out. As it was, Ade had to cut tapered plugs for every one of them, crawl through a foundation ventilator and under the house to fit the plugs as well as he could, and then nail a piece of wood across each on the underside of the floor to hold it in place. One day he sat down to rest and commented: "It wouldn't be so hard to do things here if we didn't always have to rebuild something before we can get started."

Early in June, Ade went up the hill after lunch to get oil for the lamps and came back with Ernie Witmanski. I could not have been more surprised and delighted. Ernie was a young engineer at the ball-bearing factory where I was production metallurgist during the final year of World War II and for three years after. We had been friends then, in the shop and the lab and the drafting room, such good friends that there was no strangeness to bridge when he appeared in the woods after an eight-year separation.

We had a gay and noisy reunion full of "Do you remember . . ." and "I still hear from . . ." and "Whatever became of . . ." With that over, I suddenly wondered aloud what he was doing in the woods, and Ade followed with "How did you find us?"

"I've a troop of Boy Scouts with me. I brought 'em back from a canoe trip this morning. To the Lodge . . ." His voice died, he glanced at the ceiling, ruffled his yellow hair, opened and closed his mouth twice, and turned red under his tan.

I gaped. Self-consciousness in Ernie was incredible. "Whatever's the matter with you?" I asked.

"I—I wouldn't want to hurt your feelings . . ." He looked from Ade to me and back again.

This, too, was incredible. "I'm really a very touchy type," I said with scorn, and Ade merely snorted.

"Well . . . okay then. I went into the lobby and saw 'Hoover' on one of the mailboxes. I didn't have any idea it was you and Ade, but—maybe you remember—once we were gassing out by one of the screw machines and you told me you'd spent the first third of your life in a small town, the middle third in a big city, and you wanted to spend the

last third in the wilderness. I thought of it when I saw the
name and asked a couple of people if you might be my friends
from Chicago. One of 'em said it wasn't likely—that you were
a couple of kooks who claimed to be an artist and metallurgist. And the other one laughed and said, 'The guy has cooties
in his beard.' "

He stopped because Ade was doubled up with laughter. I
managed to say, "I wondered why you didn't mention it—
the beard, I mean," before I joined Ade.

The picture that grew in my mind was hilarious. This was
the second summer after Ade had lost his razor blades and I
had persuaded him to let his beard grow. And how it grew!
It was waist-long, thick, and untrimmed, giving Ade the appearance of a biblical prophet in a windstorm. And this was
the time of the "beat" generation, with bearded young men
drooping over guitars and sad, disheveled young women mop-
ing around in "death-wish" black. My endless navy-blue shirts
and pants must have been near enough. The contrast between
the beats and us, both forty-six, puffing about at full speed to
keep alive, would tickle me for years.

We finally recovered enough to ask who our press agents
were, but we could learn only that they were a man and a
woman, Ernie's descriptions not being graphic.

"I did set 'em straight," he said.

"That doesn't mean anything," Ade said. "How many people do you know who'll go to the trouble of correcting a
wrong impression they've given out? It'll die out some day
and it won't make any difference, anyway."

Later, as Ade walked up the steep path with Ernie, I stood
on the doorstep wondering why you can tell the exact truth
about yourself, but if it is out of the hearer's experience or
is something he does not expect, he will not believe a word
of it. Ernie's revelation explained many small mysteries,

though, such as the behavior of a man Ade had met on the road when he went for mail and who said, "Come over and see us—but you don't have a car, do you?" Ade was wrong in saying it would make no difference. Out of my girlhood years in a small Ohio town, I knew that it would, and just how we would be affected we could only wait to see.

Then I noticed that there was no movement around the old bench we used as a bird and animal feeder. The bird songs and squirrel talk were stilled. There was a sense of waiting that told me that, in spite of a hyacinth sky with flotillas of puffy white clouds, a storm was coming. I hurried to bring in half-dry socks and shirts that might be blown off the clothesline, and Ade, also touched by the atmosphere, came running down the path to move tools to shelter.

The storm, the year's first of the summer pattern, came just after the sun dropped behind the hills. Rays spread in a vast fan above the hummocks and domes of the lead-gray clouds advancing from the west. Lightning forked above the hills and the light momentarily turned a dead fir top into a spike of goldenrod. The rain showered gently at first. Then the light failed and the rain gave way to hail that rattled on the roof and slashed at the earth. It passed in a few minutes and I opened the door to a scent as clean as that of new-mown hay—the aromatic, mingled perfumes of the juices of leaves cut by the hail. The little balls of ice lay in glassy piles and blue jays dropped down to eat them like candy.

Such weather told us that the warm season had come to stay and that it was time to move the chickens to summer quarters.

Their winter home, slope-roofed and tarpaper-covered, had heater and fume vent devised by Ade from an old railroad lantern and some stovepipe, a double-glass window that would not frost and so gave them a limited view of the snowy woods, and a perch. However, it was very small, and though it could be kept warm at forty below, it did not even give them enough room for good wing stretching.

Chickens being unpredictable, Ade opened their door only part way when he was ready to move them. The Crown Prince fell onto the ground, picked himself up with dignity, flapped his wings, and began to make coaxing noises to the hens. Tulip followed him after a cautious survey of the mysterious outside. Bedelia sidestepped to the far end of the perch and tucked her head firmly under a wing. When Ade opened the door fully to reach in and pick her up, she shot past him and flew to a branch overhead, where she exploded into frenzied squawking. The jays and squirrels added screams and chatter to her alarm, Tulip showed signs of joining Bedelia, and the Crown Prince looked uncertain.

"Grab Tulip," Ade said, picking up the Prince, who settled on his arm, ready to leave hen management to us and enjoy what might come next. I caught Tulip, taking the precaution of getting my right arm over her wings and my left hand around her feet. She thanked me by pecking my knuckles.

"You take 'em next door," Ade directed, settling the big rooster on my other arm. "I'll nab Bedelia."

I walked slowly through the woods, smiling at the way they turned their heads from side to side like tourists catching a scenic view as they drove by. I released them in the big run, wiremesh covered as a protection from hawks, that Ade had built adjoining one of the summer house outbuildings that had been their first home. We had bought month-old chicks the previous spring from summer people named Greenfield, with the thought of keeping a small flock for meat and eggs, but had given up the notion in the fall because we knew we could neither eat chickens we had reared from their hatching nor properly protect more than our three pets against the winter cold.

Hideous squawls announced the approach of Ade and Bedelia. The Crown Prince, much alarmed, dashed at the fence and tried to find a way to go to the rescue until Ade appeared and let the beleaguered hen fly through the gate into the run. Peace descended as all three investigated the filled water and feed containers, then began to scratch eagerly in the dirt.

They were black Minorcas with a touch of some other breed. They had jet feathers, darkish beaks and feet, yellow eyes, a decorative white spot below the ears, and scarlet combs and wattles. Tulip and the Prince, even though they were dusty from their winter confinement, were beautiful. They were large and gracefully formed, and their combs were spectacular. Tulip's hung down on one side like the half of the flower from which she was named. The Prince's stood almost straight up, was four inches tall, and had such long and graceful points that it reminded me of a crested helmet. Bedelia was a poor relation in the matter of appearance. She was small, much underslung, with a haphazard comb and an expression that ranged from alarm to that of someone who smelled something that had been forgotten in the refrigerator. She was originally—and appropriately—named Hysteria, but her expressions were so like those of a woman I had once known that I renamed her for the lady. On the credit side, she laid bigger white eggs than Tulip, maintaining her eccentricity by crowing instead of cackling to announce her accomplishment. It was not much of a crow but was recognizable, and made an interesting duet with the Prince's crowing when she decided to join in at dawn.

"I wonder if they remember this place," I said, watching Tulip walk up a ramp to a small closed door into the building

that was their coop. She stood, fidgeting, then looked fixedly
at us.

Ade laughed. "She does, anyway. She's reminding us that
a well-bred hen does not lay an egg in public, and that the
nest where she laid her first pullet egg is inside."

He pulled some grass for nest-box padding and went into
the coop to open the small door for Tulip.

Once they were comfortably settled, we moved ourselves,
trotting back and forth for a day and transferring such necessities as food, typewriter, blankets, and books to the summer
house. The move let Ade work on the log cabin unhampered
by the activities of daily living. It was also a stimulating
change for both of us because the summer house had large
rooms, high ceilings, big light-filled windows, knotty pine
walls, a double fireplace, a bright kitchen, our good furniture,
and a screened porch for relaxing.

I typed on the porch when it was warm, inside by a fire
when it was chilly, and in all weathers except pouring rain
spent some time in the old forest between the cabins. This
kind of forest—untouched, remote, majestic—whispers of
creation and the timeless things—life, death, eternity, and
time itself—that we so often forget when we lose sight of
our place in the scheme of nature. I wandered under the
high, green roof, looking down at mossy mounds that covered
long-fallen trees and up at scrolled bark on mighty birches;
smiling at young saplings, fresh and green and taking advantage of patches of sunlight. In the evening the spaces between
the trees at the forest's edge were like great, arched doors,
and when moonlight touched the pillarlike trunks the openings between became portals, black-curtained to hide the mysteries beyond.

The garden and cleared area south of the summer house
were flooded with sunlight—and with a dismaying amount
of growth that had sprung up where I had cleared debris

from the fern beds the previous spring. Hidden beneath the layer of decaying vegetation, raspberry runners had awaited their chance and now thrust up vigorous, brightly leaved canes, which would crowd out everything else if not removed. (Gloves or no, I have never pulled out raspberries without getting my hands full of their little stickers.) The cleared area, which we had not examined closely when we bought, was growing up in a tangle of grass, with scattered bluebead lilies and many half-buried patches of bunchberry. The clusters of greenish-yellow lilies and the metallic-blue fruits that follow would be lovely all summer above their waxy leaves, and the white blooms of the bunchberry, much like those of their relative the dogwood, would open just above low, dark leaves and later produce nosegays of scarlet berries. Mr. Larimer, the former owner, had kept the clearing scythed down, but there were more of the wild flowers than the summer before, and if this was any indication, all we had to do was wait for the native flowers to crowd out the alien grass. (This worked, by the way, and some years later the whole bit of ground was covered naturally and beautifully.) Removing raspberries and transplanting sweet williams from the summer house paths to the yard of the log cabin would keep me busy enough through this, and probably more, summers—if I were going to do any writing.

One morning I yanked at a tough cane buried in moss at the top of a low stone wall that separated the garden from the lower ground beside the house. The whole mass came up, to reveal a horrified chipmunk staring up at me from an unroofed tunnel. Hastily I smoothed back the moss and its pad of earth, went for bread to put on the wall for the disturbed tenants of the burrow, and retired inside the kitchen window.

The small householder poked her nose out from a mossy crack between the stones of the wall some five minutes later. A striped face followed, then a plump body with lengthwise black-and-white stripes, a richly shaded reddish rump, and a grayish tail. She climbed—or perhaps I should say levitated —to the top of the wall and patted down the displaced pad of moss. Then she went to the bread, sniffing, patting, examining this strange material. She tasted, liked, ate two pieces, and carried the rest home, seeming to vanish against the surface of the wall, so well did the moss hide the burrow entrance.

Within a week, bread on the wall had attracted too many chipmunks for me to supply with homemade bread, so we took corn from the chickens' supply and left it on the flagstones between the kitchen door and the stone wall. Soon the chippies hurried to the new food, but fled if they heard us near. We could hardly keep the kitchen door closed all summer to please the chipmunks, so I began to stand motionless outside after I distributed the food. This was acceptable in a short time. Then I moved my hands a little, and later walked about very slowly. Finally I sat with corn in my hand and my fingers resting on the stones. After reconnaissance, a daring individual ventured to take some of this corn and beat a hasty retreat. Within a few days the adventurer and what must have been all his relatives and friends rushed to the door whenever Ade or I went out and sometimes one hopped onto a boot toe to look up in a most appealing way.

Once acquainted with our corn, the chippies found openings under the run fence that let them reach the chickens' feed pan. At first they cleaned it out at night—they must have stored several pounds of corn—then one hopped into the pan by day. The Crown Prince was watching from the far side of the run and strolled over to investigate. He bent down and the chippy sat up so that they were almost beak to nose, staring at each other with something like wonder. I held my breath because the rooster, whose foot was as tall as the sitting chipmunk, would surely kill or seriously injure the little animal if he pecked only once. Instead he seemed pleased—maybe

he thought this was a baby chicken—and made pleasant cluck-ing sounds when the chippy resumed his cheek-pouch stuffing.

When the red squirrels got wind of the corn supply by the kitchen door the peace was sadly disturbed, so I left corn outside the front porch, which was near the tree homes of the squirrels. However, since they are year-round feeders, while the chippies retire for the winter, this meant many trips from the log cabin through deep snow to supply the squirrels at the feeding place they had learned to depend on during the summer.

The squirrels entered the run only when the big birds were in their coop, usually at dusk after the chickens had settled for the night. One mother-to-be made regular evening visits to the feed pan, and after delivery, brought her twins with her until she took them into the trees to learn, among other essentials, how to find natural food. The squirrels' caution was justified, because the hens did not have their lord and master's tolerance for little creatures who ate chicken feed.

In the early years of our woods life, we got perishable food by mail from the Village, and in September of 1956 our grocer sent us a large sack of mouse-damaged peanuts in the shell. The chipmunks were as nearly belligerent over these as such amiable little animals could be, their battles being limited to noisy squeaking. At first they took them shell and all, then discovered that one might remove the shell and cram many more nuts into one's cheek pouches. With faces stuffed until they resembled cartoons in old-time ads for toothache remedies, they depleted the supply. Then they started on corn again. It might be the worst winter ever, for all they knew, and they worked very hard to take home everything edible and light enough to carry.

The little red squirrels, about twice as long and four times as heavy as the chipmunks, make a hundred times as much confusion and noise. They are as effervescent as champagne and as sputtery as strings of firecrackers. The only daylight hours when we did not hear their arguments over territory or food, or the soft twittering of one of them gathering goodies all alone, were those that preceded a storm. They deserve top rating as entertainers.

The chipmunk youngsters stayed out of sight until they could hardly be distinguished from the adults, but by July there were squirrel children everywhere, some very young and all so smoothly coated, so wide-eyed, so full of play. They hopped stiff-legged sideways, forward, backward, the last with little success and numerous hasty attempts to balance. They crept under grasses, flat to the ground, rumps wriggling, tails twitching, until they could leap out at a brother or sister and roll and wrestle in the duff. I once saw triplet sisters playing "train," the front paws of the rear two tight around the hind feet of those in front, while they hopped ahead with many falls and readjustments. As a method of progress it was a failure, but it looked like lots of fun.

One of these three grew up to be Squiggles, who got my vote for Wilderness Mother of the Year several times. Her first litter of three was born near the log cabin in the roof of the storage building, and she reared them to be the fattest, liveliest youngsters one can imagine. She spent many hours training them to defend themselves. She exhibited the signs of rage and warning, jumped at the selected pupil, rolled him over, and ran. He then "attacked," and she went through the motions of fighting without actually touching him. After their lessons, the babies went through the whole scheme of attack and defense, pattering with their hind feet, thrashing their tails, and finally "attacking" each other but plainly without intent to harm.

Once, when a second female came to the pile of corn where Squiggles sat, she withdrew, and the newcomer, a feisty mother of almost-grown twins, settled to eat near Squiggles's young daughter. One of her brothers ran up a tree and hung head down to chatter a warning. Then he and the second brother slipped around through cover until they could attack this invading female from both sides, while the sister stood firm by the corn. When they leaped at the adult, she dodged expertly and moved about two feet away from her first position. This was repeated several times, but with different members of Squiggles's family taking different parts, while the strange mother squirrel dodged but did nothing of an offensive nature. My guess is that the youngsters were serious, the mother squirrel deliberately avoiding them, but any conclusion is doubtful.

Some years later one of Squiggles's children got inside the log cabin and became confused and terrified. He jumped frantically at the window glass and was in great danger of injuring himself. While we were trying to catch him, Squiggles dashed in the open door, sat up in the middle of the kitchen and made soothing squirrel talk. It took several minutes for the panicked youngster to hear and recognize her voice, but when he did, he ran to her and she patted him, played with him, then led him back to his outdoor world.

She was very friendly with us, and was one of the first of many squirrels to beg for graham crackers and take them from our hands. The only time I saw her express rage was when Ade, in closing the door, accidentally caught the right front paw of one of her youngsters, who had climbed up and was hanging by both paws from the top of the door. The little female screamed, a dreadful cry of pain, and dropped whimpering to the ground. Squiggles, almost covering the little one, stormed at Ade, who stood miserably in the doorway.

When the youngster stopped whimpering, her mother moved aside to let her limp away. She went straight to a piece of cracker lying on the ground and tried to eat it. As squirrels have no thumbs and hold food between their forepaws, and her injured paw seemed too sore to use, she had difficulty. Then she braced the cracker between her left-hand fingers and right foreleg and ate as though her shock, discomfort, and disability were forgotten. It is unlikely that squirrels can consciously dwell on misery, and so react instinctively to recover their normal outlook. How different from humans, who may make a to-do about a scratch—who may even enjoy making the most of it.

We saw that she could move the paw and its fingers slightly and so was not seriously injured, but Squiggles sat firm on the step, sputtering if Ade so much as twitched. He offered her a cracker, but she looked at him without moving, tight with distrust. He talked softly to her, and after more than half an hour she came to him and took the cracker, as if she finally understood that he had not meant to hurt her child.

As Squiggles grew older, she enjoyed naps, lying flat across a log like a small rug. The first time I saw this I thought she was sick or injured, until a second squirrel came near the log, minding his own business and hopping along in a leisurely manner. Apparently Squiggles thought one's sunbath should be taken in complete privacy, because she leaped from the log, chased the startled intruder up a tree, and came back to lie down on another log. She had no sooner relaxed and closed her eyes than a very young squirrel hopped past the log. Squiggles flashed into action, but skidded to a stop when her young opponent stood to do battle. She faked a few blows, then turned and ran, moving just fast enough to keep ahead of the pursuing youngster. Only after the young one had returned to the yard, looking very pleased at the outcome of his "fight," did Squiggles return and climb onto the log to resume her rest. Considering the way she trained her own young, it may be that she was giving this youngster a lesson in confidence.

One May, when she was seven years old, she produced a litter of five. She still nested in the storage building, but on the floor that year. When the babies' teeth were well enough developed, we left bits of cookie nearby, which they took into the nest for a squirrel version of eating crackers in bed.

Each child got his share of patient and thorough training, and in early July I saw her, very obviously pregnant again, but rolling amiably though clumsily with her well-grown family. Even while she was training the twins she bore about the end of that month, she still found time to attend to her first litter.

That August I walked through the woods to get some mushrooms, remembering a squirrel we had known earlier and named the Little Old Lady. She was stiff and slow, but always busy and friendly. I last saw her near our path to the road on a warm fall day. She popped from under the scarlet and gold of some brushy maple, chittered, popped back, and returned to sit up at my feet, holding in her mouth half of a white mushroom fully seven inches in diameter. I have always hoped she lived long enough to eat her handsome delicacy after it had dried.

When I reached the mushroom patch, I found that the mycelium had moved under the duff and now extended in a straight line, and that the first third of the line of mushrooms had been cut and capped, the middle third had been cut only, and the last third was still standing. While I stared at this orderly harvesting, Squiggles came from behind a tree, lay down on some of her capped mushrooms, and looked up at me as though to ask me, *please*, not to take her food. Ade and I had canned beans for supper and liked them.

A month later she and her seven gathered pine and balsam cones and stored them in several middens. She stopped storing earlier than usual and began to construct a winter nest of cedar-bark strips and the stuffing of an old pillow we supplied for her convenience. Her building site was a shelf in the woodshed, but it was only a single board, and so narrow that material kept falling away from the half-built nest. Ade nailed a wide board just below the shelf and put a slant-ing board from this to the wall so that she could pack her material under shelter, safe from leakage through the aging roof. She liked this arrangement, and made a round nest with a neat inner cavity and a small round door—a sort of hobbit house. I think she built there because she was old and finding it tiring to get food, and wanted to be near the cabin, which she knew was the source of corn and graham crackers.

Later in the fall we saw her, sitting outside her nest and looking at all seven of her children, who were eating corn in the yard. She drooped wearily, and her once-slim figure was ruined, but she had a contented look, touched with some-thing like pride.

There is no way to thank the Squiggleses of the earth for what they give to struggling humans, but perhaps we may pass to others some of the joy they bring us, if we extend kindness and love beyond our sphere.

———— By October, when we moved the chickens and ourselves from summer quarters, the transplanted sweet wil-liams had established themselves by the log cabin, and until heavy frost came, brightened the greenery with their endless variety and combination of white and pink and red flower heads. The knotholes in the cabin floor were filled, and Ade had added a touch by hammering protruding nail heads flush with the wood in the interest of our being able to cover the floor with something or other on some future day. The rasp-berries were gone from the summer house fern beds, and in spite of the prickling of their thorns in my fingers, I had typed and sold some articles. Ade's new notepaper designs had been patiently hand-cut on stencils, and I found time to address his advertising mailers while he was mimeographing and packing the paper for sale.

Once these were gone he marched me to the extra cabin, thereafter to be called the storage building, and dazzled my eyes with a view of its once heterogeneous clutter, now sorted neatly. For a moment I thought I could mark "Clear small cabin" from his 1954 list, then decided to be firm and wait until we had a way to remove the boxes of trash. In addition, Ade had split all the wood at the top of our path and some of that in the summer house carport, and stacked a generous supply near the log cabin. By and large, it had been a productive summer, Ade doing a lion's share of the producing.

———— Hairy and downy woodpeckers were busy around the woodpile, hunting insects and their eggs under the bark, so we asked the butcher to send up some suet with our next order. Ade hung a suet cage on one of the cedar trunks and the woodpeckers then breakfasted on suet, hunted in the bark during the day, and had a late suet snack before dusk. But we had forgotten the bears, who move so quietly and secretly that it takes a long time to remember that they are around all summer, whether one sees them or not.

A week after Ade hung the feeder, a young bear sniffed his way out of the brush and stood up under the tree. He could not reach the suet, so he hunched up the trunk, hooked his claws under the wire, and yanked the cage down. Cage demolished and suet eaten, he climbed high in the cedar, searching for more of this delicious fruit. Patiently he went from cedar to cedar, investigating each one, and he went out of sight, still combing cedars and hunting suet. Regretfully, because we sympathized with the little bear's search, we put

the repaired feeder aside until the bears had gone away to
snooze the winter through. Bears may look like teddies, but
as a game-warden friend once said to us, "Little bears grow
into great big bears," and great big bears neither look nor, if
they are annoyed or hungry or otherwise unhappy, act like
teddies.

At dawn the next morning we were awakened by a hubbub
of cackling and drumming. The woodpeckers wanted their
suet. Ade dragged himself out and hung up the feeder, waiting
half asleep until the birds had fed to bring it in. From then on
the first one who heard the birds went through this process
during bear time.

It was while Ade was making more of these feeders that
he got his beard tangled in the wire. While I laughed myself
to tears, he carefully disengaged himself and reached for the
scissors, saying, "I'm going to get rid of this right now, before I get hung up in the brush somewhere." He had himself
rough shorn when he remembered that he still had no razor
blades, which had to be ordered by mail and sent out from
town. Consequently it was near the end of October when he
finally emerged and I had a chance to see what he looked like.

It was then that his hair, uncut for months and well below
his collar, caught my attention.

"You could let it get a little longer and braid it, pioneer
fashion," I suggested.

"Or go across the lake and get Awbutch to cut it."

We went down to the lake and stood for a while by the
boat skid, looking at the kind of scene that does not come
often. The sky and the water were azure of identical color
density, and the water was completely still. The hills across
the lake, brilliant with the gold of late-turned aspen leaves,
were so perfectly reflected that a photograph would not have
differentiated between the real hills and their mirror-image;

and the sight reminded me that up and down are only relative on this space-borne bit of dust that is man's home.

More practically, Ade looked at the sinking sun and slid the boat into the water. As we moved toward the far shore, the reflection broke before us, shimmered, closed in blue-and-gold waves behind us, and a breeze began to bring down the leaves that made the equally transient beauty of the trees.

Awbutch was waiting as we glided in to her dock, and I marveled, as I always did, at her neatness—blue jeans unwrinkled, red shirt as fresh as if it had never been worn before, black hair perfectly in place. She caught our painter and tied us up with expert brown hands.

"Company's good today," she said. "Mother's out in the woods so I'm all by myself."

"How old is your mother?" I asked.

"Seventy-five maybe. I don't know exactly."

"Seventy-five? In the woods by herself?"

She laughed. "You forget. She's been in the woods all her life." She looked critically at Ade. "You wait." She went into her cabin and brought out a chair. "I'll cut your hair here. Your chin needs sun. It's whiter than the rest of your face."

While she worked with scissors, comb, and clippers, I thought that our old friends, even Ernie who had seen where we lived, would think it very strange that Ade should go by boat to Canada to have a Chippewa girl cut his hair in the sun. And thinking of Ernie reminded me that Awbutch was the first human being I had seen, barring Ade and tourists in distant boats, since Ernie's visit. And I had not been lonely. We were too busy with necessary things to think much about ourselves, which is the way it used to be with most people. They simply lived, as we were doing, and this was good.

Awbutch's voice brought me out of a half-doze.

"I'd ask you to stay for supper, but Mother said there's going to be wind on the water before dark. I don't know how she knows, but she does. You'd better go. You might knock a hole in your boat on those rocks by your house if you don't hurry."

As we moved out from shore we felt the slow rise and fall of the water ahead of the coming wind, and Awbutch's voice followed us. "I'll come and see you after the lake freezes over."

Ade waved, and I knew he was thinking, as I was, that we might see few people but we could not have better friends than those few.

———— We had been told of flying squirrels in the forest, even of one who had come to a feeding shelf outside of a lighted window one night, only to be picked off by a hungry barred owl. This led us to remove our shelves from window locations and put one shoulder-high just outside the log cabin door, where the wide eave gave some protection. Occasionally on dark nights we heard padded thumps on the roof, which we thought might be made by these squirrels as they glided to a landing, but it was not until early December that I saw one, and happily, close at hand.

My aunt had sent us the wherewithal for a Thanksgiving dinner, and we stretched the turkey until there was only a bony carcass to hang on a cedar trunk for the birds to pick and a large piece of browned skin, which Ade tacked to the feeding shelf by the door for anyone who might be interested, perhaps mice or woodpeckers or whiskey jacks.

We were reading one evening while snow whispered against the windows and piled up in Christmas-decoration fashion at the corners of the small panes. Ade put down *Plutarch's Lives* and went into the kitchen to rummage for something to eat. I piled *The Hound of the Baskervilles* on top of his book and moved past him to open the door and see how much snow there was. The fall had stopped, and the forest was lighted by that faint and shadowless glow given by moonlight filtering through high frost. I stopped short when I sensed movement on the shelf beside me.

The little animal sitting up and clutching the turkey skin tight to his furry breast was unmistakably a flying squirrel. His tail, thickly furred and like a flat plume, hung below the shelf edge, and I could see folds of fur at his sides. His enormous eyes were like shiny black moons, now filled with terror of me and of losing his greasy treasure. I backed inside and he seemed to vanish, so swiftly did he spring away. I caught the briefest glimpse of him inside the woodshed before I closed the door.

For a few evenings we put scraps of fat on the shelf for these animals, but stopped this after we found a lonely tail on the snow and spotted a barred owl, waiting patiently on a branch for another meal to arrive. Since the flying squirrel who had taken the turkey skin had found refuge in the shed, we decided to use the shelf in there as a lunchroom for him and his relations. We stocked it with bits of suet and broken graham crackers, which they found and ate that night.

It was not long before they accepted us and we could watch them by dim lantern light. Except for their shape, they were quite unlike the red squirrels. Their olive-brown fur was so thick it looked fluffy, and their furred gliding membranes, which stretched between fore and hind legs on each side, bunched when they sat and gave them a fat, wide-bodied look. They were quiet and soft-voiced, and when a number of them ate together they pushed and shoved without argument.

The sight of one by day was most unusual and meant that he was very hungry or had left the community nest in some other emergency. They did not even come to the shed in moonlight, but waited for the moon's passing to leave its dense shadows for their protection. On cloudy nights they arrived as soon as it was fully dark.

They nested high in the trees, probably in holes, but I had no idea where. I often felt the swish as one glided past me to swerve upward and land on a tree trunk, and knew that he had slid a long way on the air because there was no tall tree nearer than sixty feet in the direction from which he came. They do not "fly" in rain or snow or strong wind, as these could alter their flight direction and make landing dangerous. Once one landed on my head, probably because I stepped out with such timing that he could do nothing else. He clutched, and I can reliably report that his claws were as sharp as a domestic kitten's.

I think that their natural diet, about which not much is known but is thought to include a high percentage of eggs and meat, may contain more vegetable matter than some authorities believe. When we saw them going out into the open to eat corn from the bench where we fed red squirrels, we put corn on their shelf, and later, when we were able to buy special food for our animals, we gave them oatmeal. They came for this in large numbers, and ate what seemed to be great quantities for their size. It may be that they do not find as many seeds and related food in the wild as they would like, and so especially welcomed our grains.

They learned to beg for food as quickly as the daytime squirrels, and hopped onto our shoulders or waved their hands from the shelf to attract attention. They loved graham crackers and oatmeal cookies and settled in various locations to eat these morsels—behind the split wood, on a claw hammer hanging in the shed, under a board slanting from floor to wall, inside boots left out to be cleaned of mud and snow.

Handing food to them required the same precautions as when so feeding red squirrels and chipmunks, because although they all have wide side vision and partial front and rear sight for locating enemies, there is a space in front of their noses that is outside of their range of vision. When a young squirrel, used to the smell and taste of graham cracker, say, had one held for the first time to his mouth, he looked confused. He sniffed, finally opened his mouth and took the food, but had a bewildered look about him. If a squirrel happened to be in a hurry or was startled by something, he might take the food with a snap, and if I carelessly let a finger-tip extend beyond his cracker, he caught finger instead of food and his teeth left small holes like pinpricks. These bites were not painful and healed quickly, as the squirrels' teeth are kept clean. I might say, too, that I have never seen any squirrel or chipmunk showing signs of disease.

———— Shortly before Christmas the mail contained a big bill from the grocery. This was strange, because the store did not give credit. Instead, they sold books of coupons to people like us who did not often come to town, and when the book was almost used, sent a note with groceries so that we could buy another. It was worse than strange, because we had not ordered since Thanksgiving and the bill was dated December 8. There was nothing for it but that Ade should again walk to the Trail, take the portable phone usually attached to the bush line, toss a wire over the forestry phone line, and try to reach the grocery.

An hour later he returned, saying that someone—they could not remember who—had picked up the groceries for us. There were not enough coupons to cover the whole order, so they had made an exception and billed the remainder, but there was no way we could order from them in the future except by using the coupon books.

Someone had used our name and coupons to get free groceries and we could not afford to have this happen again.

"What'll we do now?" Ade wondered.

"We'll have to use some of the insurance money to pay the bill. I don't like it, but we can't let it get around that we're deadbeats. And we'll have to go without anything perishable, unless someone comes in and is willing, *if* he's going to town, to buy for us, pay, bring the stuff out here, and let us give him a check. That's a lot to ask."

"Yes. And nobody may come in. There's been nobody but Ernie since last winter. The oil man, of course, but he's too busy to do our shopping."

"We'll make do somehow. We've plenty of staples, and Bedelia and Tulip can be counted on for a couple of eggs almost every day. Thank God we've enough food for them." I heard a faint crowing from the chicken house. "It would be nice if the Crown Prince was a hen, too."

Ade sniffed. "It would be our luck that he didn't lay in cold weather."

On Saturday, December 22, we woke to the first heavy snow of the winter, and it was coming from the east, which meant it was heavier toward town. The mail came on Tuesday, Thursday, and Saturday from Labor Day until New Year's, but it could not come on this Saturday because the road was surely blocked. And Christmas was the following Tuesday—no mail then, of course—so any hope of receiving cheese or candy or the like from friends was dashed. I took stock of our supplies: a diminishing store of canned vegetables; plenty of margarine, baking powder, and yeast; enough coffee to last until spring if we were careful; some tea, brown sugar, chocolate, and powdered milk; one small can of salted peanuts; potatoes, flour, and sugar in hundred-pound sacks; smaller sacks of cornmeal, oatmeal, and dried beans; partially used cases of dry spaghetti and canned mushroom sauce; and, outside in the barrel-stove freezer, a little cheese, and part of a slab of bacon to go with our fresh eggs for Ade's lunches.

Trying to create a Christmas dinner out of these materials would be to use more than we should at one time and would emphasize that things were not exactly rosy. And nothing was going to turn up as it had the year before, when, after the fire, Awbutch's brother had come and invited us to have dinner across the lake with, as he put it, laughing, "those Indians."

On Christmas afternoon he had come with his car, which he parked on our side of the lake for trips to town, and drove us to the beginning of his tramped-down snowshoe track on the lake ice. We snowshoed across, and my progress was so slow that our guide could have started when I had three-quarters of the mile-and-a-half trip behind me and still been waiting for me when I puffed up to Awbutch's dock.

We had a glorious time. Awbutch and her mother, her brother with his wife and three children, her cousin and his mother, were all gathered in a big cabin to enjoy the day and the dinner, and to make sure that we did, too, by offering everything with the natural graciousness and hospitality that comes from the heart. When we walked back across the ice with frost stinging our faces under a moon like a dim window in the opalescent sky, we brought with us a memory that will always be one of our richest and happiest.

Bother a Christmas feast! We would do nicely without one. Ade's notepaper had done so well that he was almost out of stock and had been trying to find time between chores to ready some for the repeat orders that would surely come. He could do that, and I'd write something—and I'd better find a good subject. One that was interesting enough to keep my mind off roast turkey.

It was very late on Christmas Eve when I heard the faint howling of a wolf, and stepped out through the drift on the doorstep and into the still falling snow to listen. The sound came nearer as the animal moved along the Canadian shore

and reached a point directly across from me. There he
stopped, perhaps on the top of one of the snowy hills, and
his wild voice rose and fell, more like singing than howling,
beautiful and deep-toned, filling the night. As he moved on,
one long cadence lingered and faded, like the voice of the
wilderness saying "Noooooo-eeelll!"

When Christmas night came, cold and star-filled, Ade had
his pile of notepaper ready to sort and I had a Christmas
animal fable ready for final typing. Although it had the un-
popular wolf as its hero, I felt that I could sell my tale to some
juvenile magazine. It had been a good and satisfying day after
all.

————— January and February are the months of deep
winter in our forest, and in our early years most of the people
who lived there went on vacation, moved temporarily to the
Village, or holed up and complained of the long drag before
the first signs of the breakout. It was a time of deep silences,
periods of bitter cold, and in our case, of an increasing number of visiting birds and animals, all looking for handouts
because their natural food was frozen in or buried by the
deepening snow layer. We were hard pressed to find enough
for them, but we had plenty of flour and baked extra bread,
which most of them ate. Even our woodpeckers, when the
suet was gone and the ration of bacon grease grew less and
less, learned to peck at bits of bread and graham cracker.
Homemade bread does not make the best toast, so we went
back to an earlier routine of pancakes and brown-sugar syrup
for breakfast. I got very tired of this, so I added some cornmeal to the cakes, which gave them a better flavor and made
them stick to our ribs longer, but did nothing for their
lightness. (Corncakes without eggs or shortening resemble
leather if one does not beat the batter to the point of having a

paralyzed arm.) When the brown sugar grew scarce, I increased the amount of white sugar in the syrup, which lost in flavor, although it still gave us quick energy for a short time.

A pair of whiskey jacks were at the door every morning, waiting for their pancake, their softly shaded gray and black and white feathers fluffed against the cold. I cooked seven cakes: four for Ade, two for me, and one for the birds, the last served in quarters, warm from the iron skillet. I went out first with a piece of pancake on the palm of each hand. The birds came, one to a hand, and settled down to warm their feet on the cake while picking around its edges. Then each tore off a section and flew onto the woodshed roof to have breakfast. When my half pancake was gone, Ade went out with the last two quarters and the birds went through their routine again before flying away into the forest.

They are more often called gray jays, sometimes Canada jays, and we wondered about the name common in our area. Then a lumberjack Ade met on the road told him that their name in an Indian language was something like *wiskijon,* and a woodsman years before had called one who came to his cabin "Whiskey Jack." Awbutch told me that the Chippewa word for them is *quinguishi,* as nearly as I can spell it. The two names might be distortions of the same Indian word-sounds, since Chippewa and Ojibway are said to have developed from one Indian word.

Some people do not like these cheerful, friendly birds and think them piggish because they carry away more food than they can eat. However, other birds and some animals find the food the jacks have tucked away in the trees, and none of it goes to waste. And for some reason they have a reputation for being noisy, although they usually express themselves in soft whistles, and may beg in melodious warbling tones. Only when they are alarmed do they raise their voices in a ratchety

sound, much like that of the wooden rattles children used to
swing round and round to the aggravation of their parents'
ears. We enjoyed their happy company, especially because
they came all year to a source of food, except on very cold
days near the end of winter. Then they stayed with their
eggs or newly hatched young, in the nests they had prepared
when the snow was still deep on the ground.

It was on one such day that Ade came in carrying Tulip.
At my startled exclamation, he said, "Nothing's wrong. They
have no way to wear their beaks down inside their house and
the upper part is so long they can't pick up their feed. I'll
have to file 'em down."

Once her feet were firmly tucked between his knees and
her flapping wings partially restrained between his arm and
body, Tulip submitted to treatment, which was painless but
produced complaints anyway. I shall draw a veil over
Bedelia's performance, except to say that her feet had to be
tied and her wings confined in a straitjacket devised from a
towel and safety pins.

The Crown Prince, however, behaved like a gentleman.
He sat on Ade's lap making comfortable sounds as though he
knew exactly what was being done and why. He did not
object even when Ade trimmed his spurs, grown so long that
he locked them when he walked and occasionally fell down.
When the trimming was finished, our amiable rooster preened
the hackles Ade had disarranged and looked around as if to
ask what came next. I often thought the Prince would have
been a fine house pet—if chickens could be housebroken.

———— Because we felt the effects of our unbalanced diet
not only in hunger and weakness but in lowered resistance to
cold, we were thankful that we still had plenty of wood to

keep us warm in the worst weather. Part of it was aspen with the bark still on, and Ade brought short lengths inside, to stand near the airtight until the frost had melted and evaporated.

One day a sound like agitated leaves drew my attention to these log sections. The loose bark was being pushed vigorously from the underside and flakes were flying in all directions. Suddenly a common shrew popped from under the bark and darted to the top of the chunk, where, making a rapid clicking sound, he set about eating a fat, white grub. He was grayish-brown, a little more than three inches long, short tail and all, with a pointed nose, invisible ears, and jet-bead eyes. While he was finishing the grub, I discovered another shrew hunting under the loose bark, much too absorbed to pay attention to me.

I trotted through the snow to the woodpile and dug out three grubs, which I preferred to be eaten by shrews than accidentally roasted in the stove. Then I sat on the floor, held the grubs low in my outstretched hand, and waited. The shrews discovered the feast simultaneously. After a rush and a small but vigorous squabble, the victor dashed at the grubs and bumped his nose, a pale, shell pink on the bare underside near his mouth, against my hand. It felt cool. When he had taken the first grub and was eating it under the stove, the second shrew came over and selected his meal. For a moment he rested one hand, so like mine with its thumb and four fingers, on my palm and I wondered at the contrast between my huge hands and his fairy-size ones.

He moved away a few inches, settled to devour his dinner, downed it in minutes, and returned for the last grub. When he had eaten half of it, the clicking of his busy teeth stopped. He curled himself around the leftovers and went to sleep, a minuscule picture of repletion.

Ade had not yet been able to close all the cracks between the floor and the logs of the walls, so other shrews found their way inside. Some were the more often seen short-tailed species, mouse-size, with lead-gray fur, heavy bodies, the characteristic pointed nose, and very short tail. These small creatures are often feared because their saliva is venomous, but the quantity of poison is only enough to paralyze a mouse and is no menace to so large an animal as man.

Then there were the less often seen pygmy shrews, the smallest of the mammalian world, who look very much like the common shrews and cannot be surely identified without examining the teeth. I once saw a mother, no more than two-and-a-half inches over-all, carrying in her mouth a furred baby little more than an inch long, including the tail. While I was marveling at this tiny forest madonna, trying to imagine the delicacy of her child's bones and claws and whiskers, she discovered a piece of peanut on the floor, perhaps dropped there by a mouse. She rushed away, to return without her child and take the nut. I put out several more pieces and she took them all, running back and forth with incredible energy. It is no wonder that all species of these tiny creatures must eat voraciously to supply the energy needed during their short but active lives.

The common shrews were regular visitors during the rest of the winter. Aside from hastily skittering out of sight at loud noises and sudden movements, they showed no fear. We did our best to help them through the long cold with tidbits. Although their natural diet is made up of insects and any meat, fresh or deteriorated, they ate cooked oatmeal when nothing else was available. Later, at the beginning of the new forest year, when ants entered the house and half-inch spiders seemed to sprout from the cracks of the logs, our shrews made short work of them. Like all our wild neighbors, they made our lives better in their own special way.

———— One day in March Ade stumbled back with the mail as if he were in a trance and collapsed into the nearest chair. I gave him hot, sweet tea and made a sandwich with the last of our cheese. When he felt better, I told him that he must take something to eat whenever he went for mail, there being no sense in trying to save food and as a result risk his life in twenty-below weather just to get a half-dozen ads and perhaps some letters. He agreed, and we decided to ask our mailman to bring the mail on Saturday only all year.

I had been too slow, however, in noticing how the long treks through the cold were affecting him. A few days later he was hit by an attack of facial neuralgia, an excruciatingly painful and disabling illness that he had had on and off for years. No doctor had been able to do mor. than assure him that there was no discoverable physical cause nor anything wrong with his nervous system, and to suggest that he avoid overstrain. But how could he do that in the woods?

After five days the pain subsided enough for him to take some soup. Soon he fell asleep and I slipped out with the toboggan to get wood from the diminishing supply in the carport by the summer house gate. It was clear and very cold, with a pale sky and glittering snow. The whiskey jacks followed me through the forest along the path Ade had made bringing wood, then perched on the eaves of the carport to watch me pile the chunks on the toboggan. Since Ade was definitely getting better, I enjoyed my outing—until I started hauling the loaded toboggan back to the cabin. No matter how carefully I piled the wood, I could not get it properly balanced, and the whole thing upset every time I met a ridge in the snow. I have no idea how many times I piled it on, then repiled it, along the winding path. And when I stopped to rest by the summer house outbuildings, I saw that snow had packed on the chick wire that covered the top of the chicken run. The whole thing was very near the point of collapse. I tried to knock down some of the snow and found that it had packed and frozen into a hard block. I made the best time I could back to the cabin, stacked the wood in the shed, then got a hatchet and went back to chop the snow off the chicken run.

Next day Ade was able to eat solid food, although he was still pale, hollow-eyed, and weak. He was giving me a futile argument about being quite well enough to go to the lake for water when there was a knock on the door.

We hardly knew the man who came in after kicking the snow from his boots against the doorsill. He owned a fishing camp some distance away, and when he picked up his letters earlier in the day the mailman had remarked that Ade had not come for his mail.

"So I came to see if anything was wrong and I could help," he finished.

And help he did, bringing another toboggan-load of wood and filling every bucket and large container we had with water, after chopping open the layer of ice that had frozen over the hole during the days I was melting icicles.

After we had tea and bread and margarine, with Ade wrapped in a blanket to sit up in a big chair, the man left, saying that he would bring our mail next Saturday so that Ade could take time to rest and be sure he was fit for the long walk. Then Ade and I talked of the night during our first cabin winter when Jacques Plessis, a strong-bodied, big-hearted woodsman who was our staunch friend, had come to our cabin near exhaustion from a long trek out of the woods. Of how the man just gone had returned to us the help we had given Jacques. And of how there was this passing on of help in time of need, because there was always someone who, when he came on the little signs that all was not well, took the time to do whatever was needed.

The thought was as comforting as was the sound of the wind changing to the south, which told us that in the morning there would be drops of water for the birds and squirrels to drink, and the new year of the forest would soon begin.

<table>
<tr><td rowspan="6">*1957*</td><td>*cut wood*</td></tr>
<tr><td>**install wiring**</td></tr>
<tr><td>*clear brush and paths*</td></tr>
<tr><td>*clear trash*</td></tr>
<tr><td>*running water*</td></tr>
<tr><td>*make a living*</td></tr>
</table>

——— It was mid-May before the big snows had melted and the ground was thawed and dry enough for us to consider the garden we felt we needed. Ade was still shaky from his illness, and I found myself weaker than I had been the year before. We could blame much of this on our poor diet.

We picked out four spots, each of which got sun through the trees for a few hours at different times of the day. One we gave up at once because a spring flowed just under the surface and turned the earth into sticky mud. The others seemed fine, and we expected to clear them easily because the growth that had followed the bulldozing three years before was small and shallow-rooted.

We had not counted on the rocks. By the end of the month we had the plots reasonably free of all but small stones, and enough boulders piled up to make a long wall. We estimated that we had removed a ton and a half of granite. Then, since the cleared areas, without the stones, were eight inches lower than the surrounding surface, they filled with water every time it rained. Ade edged the plots with logs, dug channels at suitable corners, and arranged rocks from our handy supply so that we could drain the water as rainfall, plants, and seasons required.

We were making out an order for seeds when a hard freeze struck. Even the wild plants were blackened, and cold rains followed. It was almost July before we had weather normal for early June, and the growing season in our location is at best only about a hundred days. With one month gone and a cool summer forecast, we gave up the garden until the following year.

We also decided not to move to the summer house, because there would be little time when we could be comfortable there without fireplace heat, and this meant an extravagant use of such wood as we still had. Not moving meant that the chickens must stay where they were, within sight of us in case of a nosy bear.

"What if it gets really hot?" I asked. "They're too crowded in such a small house for warm weather."

"I'll make them a screen door," Ade said, "replaceable with the solid one if it gets cold or there's danger from animals."

He went to look for scrap material, I heard hammering shortly after, and before evening the new door was in place, with the chickens gathered behind it, enjoying the breeze and the view.

Warmer weather brought a blaze of dandelion blooms, so many that the ground in the clearing had an overall pattern of gold. Some plants grew so near the walls that light reflected from them to brighten the logs, and the flowers at the edge of the clearing cast a faint golden glow on the underside of the low evergreen branches above them. More practically, they supplied us with summer greens, and no delicacy of *haute cuisine* ever tasted better than those bitter but refreshing leaves. Our wild chives grew two feet tall. We sautéed their hollow leaves as a vegetable, they were as good as onions for flavoring, and when their purple flower clusters opened they were as attractive as any flower we might have planted.

Late one afternoon I went into the woods to see if the plant I thought was the tiny orchid called rattlesnake plantain was showing any sign of blooming. As I turned from the cabin I noticed that the tops of the balsams were spotted with brown. Probably an attack by foliage-hungry insects, but since it was high up and did not seem to differ much from any other such attack, and since they were common in any case, I thought no more about it. I went on to see that my special plant had a fine stalk of buds, and it was almost dark when I returned to the cabin. I wondered why Ade had not lighted a lamp. As I came in he said, too loudly, "I'm all right. Just a nicked finger."

It had not occurred to me that he was not all right, so this startled me and I went to him, picking up a flashlight on the way. He had grazed the side of his right forefinger with an ax, slicing away the skin from palm to tip. I lighted the lamp and got bandages and disinfectant.

"I was a little tired, so I started to chop with my left hand," he explained after I had fixed the bandage in place and was washing up the blood on his workbench. "I can use either hand . . ."

"So I see. And this is the second near-miss with that drawing hand. We're about out of wood and it's time to get an oil stove. Your hand is more important than the insurance money."

We sat late that night studying catalogs, because everything for winter had to be fitted into part of the small sum we had in the bank. After three evenings of planning, all was ready for me to write an order for the stove and such pipe as we did not have on hand, another for the paper Ade needed for his notepaper, and a final one for our winter groceries.

And we had managed to leave enough in the bank to buy the oil at bulk prices from the tank truck and get the necessary tank with, hopefully, some kind of balance, no matter how small.

As I watched Ade go up the path to take the orders to the mail on the next Saturday I felt a qualm of uncertainty. Had we made the right decisions? If we had not, we had done our best, and no one could do more. Then it occurred to me that the making of decisions is one of the backbones of freedom, that for this reason living free entailed more responsibility than being dependent, and that meant that no one who chose to be dependent—on a job or a government or friends or anything—and so avoided responsibility could be truly free. To me, this is the essential difference between "escaping" and choosing to live as reasonably independent a life as is possible in our specialized world.

Before our move to the woods, Ade and I worked for companies that made many decisions for us, and when we enjoyed vacations, they were a type of "escape" in that we put aside all but the most minor decision-making for the time. When we moved, we accepted the responsibility of making all the decisions on which our futures and indeed our lives would depend. Perhaps this is why I always felt a stir of annoyance when someone wrote, "How wonderful for you to have got away from it all!" as though our lives had become merely a long vacation. We had something more rewarding than that: the kind of freedom men dream of, based on the right to work out our destiny in our own way against whatever odds might be.

———— Late in August we were almost buried by boxes and bags when the freight truck brought stove, paper, and groceries in one delivery. It was so near evening that all we could do before the light faded was to get the cases of damageable goods inside in case of rain and stack them, leaving little aisles for moving around. It was like the dock of a warehouse, which was fine except that we had left no room to open the studio couch on which we slept. This meant hauling cases out of the way and closing the path we had planned to use in the morning for moving in the new stove, which waited under the eave by the doorstep. It was not until the next morning that we remembered we could have slept in the summer house and left the boxes where they were.

After I helped Ade carry the iron log-roller out of the house so that he could skid it down to the work building for storage, I stacked the cases of paper in the doorway between living and work rooms, leaving an opening above them for heat and air circulation. Then we brought in the oil stove, and he set that up while I put our few cases of meat, fruit, and vegetables on the floor behind the curtain that hung from the high shelf on the living room wall. To get a can from a bottom case, the cases on top had to be lifted off, and the davenport, which stood in front of the whole, had to be swung out of the way. Since there was no other place for davenport or cases, I concentrated on our good fortune in having the food.

The only leftover was a case of toilet paper, which took up most of the free space in the middle of the kitchen. I remembered that the former owner's private dump held dozens of one-pound coffee cans and all of them had lids, so were clean inside. I wire-brushed the outside rust away, washed them, then stacked them like the cells in a honeycomb on crosspieces in the privy. Each one held a roll of paper, conveniently at hand and safe from squirrels and mice, who popped in and out of the gaps between the logs as they pleased. Incidentally, since this paper was very inexpensive by the case, we used it in place of facial tissues and kitchen towels, and so saved on the cost of paper products and of soap we could not spare for washing cloth towels.

We dined sumptuously that evening on canned corn-beef hash, tomatoes, and wax beans from our new supplies, and felt considerable satisfaction in knowing that we had twenty-three more cans of hash and also twenty-four cans each of chili and pink salmon. We would eat a lot of spaghetti and pancakes, of course, and would have to stretch the vegetables as best we could, but the eight months before freight delivery began in the spring would not be entirely monotonous as to food.

Once fed and rested, I became entranced by the stove. After all, I had never lived with an oil stove before, and I could see hours of time freed for both of us.

"But why the little tank on the back?" I asked.

"For oil. What else? I'll carry it down from the big tank we'll set up near the road."

"Can't you pipe it in?"

Ade shook his head. "It would take around two hundred feet of pipe at twenty-five cents a foot. Besides, water condenses in oil tanks in a damp climate like this, with big changes of temperature. If a drop froze in a long line, you'd have the devil's own time finding where under three feet of snow and then thawing it. Carrying the oil won't be hard. I'll fill both cans when I go for something else and save trips."

"Both? I thought we only had one."

"We did, but I found an old one lying beside the road when I went for mail a while ago. It's sound, so I brought it home."

I thought fleetingly that salvaging cans from a dump or a ditch would have shocked me once, but no more. "Fine," I said. "Now all we need is a tank and some oil and we have the

essentials." I paused, struck by an uncomfortable thought.
"We still have enough wood for the cookstove, I hope. Trying to cook on that antique kerosene thing . . ."

"Enough for years. I'll chop some before winter, and it's
all split in half now, so don't worry about my hands."

"How about drafts between the logs? We'll waste a lot of
oil when the wind blows a gale across the living room." I
shivered in retrospect.

"I've plenty of oakum, but where are the leaks? You can't
find them now and I haven't time to do the whole cabin."

"Well, when we have our first cold snap you can see where
by the frost on the inside walls. You can chink when it gets a
little warmer."

Ade nodded. "That'll let me put some patching asphalt on
the worst of the roof leaks now."

———— It had been a happy summer, alive with birds.
Robins found nesting sites in the forest, and their cheerful
songs filled the air before the quiet time of nesting. A pair
of rose-breasted grosbeaks nested somewhere near the west
side of the cabin, and after a while I learned to distinguish
the male's song from the similar robin's. For some time after
they arrived, this pair came often to the little willows to
preen—the male strikingly handsome, with black back and
tail and white-barred wings, his deep-rose bib bright above
his white breast; the female modestly striped in shades of
brown, with brown-streaked white breast. They reminded
me of flocks of pine grosbeaks that had come to feed on
blown-down seeds the previous winter, the females so quietly
colored that they looked gray and the males' heads and backs
and breasts glowing with raspberry when they caught the
sunlight through the trees. Our bushes provided nesting
sites for numbers of chipping sparrows, who in late August

had brought their young to pick cracked corn from the paths outside the log cabin. The babies followed Mother, wings fluttering as they waited for her to drop a morsel into their open beaks. Gradually the mothers fed themselves more and their begging children less until the young ones began to try to pick up their own food. Soon only a few still begged, and these were ignored. When it was time for them to fly away for the winter, all the young were going about their feeding independently, saying *chip-chip-chip* in an irregular chorus with their parents.

I had been told that the hermit thrush was commonly heard in our forest, but I have not heard them here and think that the evensong of the olive-backed, or Swainson's, thrush might have been mistaken for the other, since the birds are much alike in appearance except for the hermit's rufous tail. The song of the olive-backed bird is built of rising tones, clear and thrilling, going away in a delicate spray of music. Whenever we could, Ade and I left our work and went out to listen to this until it faded with the light, and it always filled us with hope for better tomorrows.

There were more crows than usual, and it seems to me that they cannot be guilty of destroying as many songbirds' eggs and young as their accusers claim, since we saw both extraordinary numbers of young crows and young songbirds. I enjoy crows. They are clever and have a large vocabulary, and patient listening let me understand a few of their "words." I might not see the lookout high in the forest tree, but when I stepped from the cabin door and heard his sharp alarm, I knew that he had seen me and that any crow within sound of his voice would be wary of the human. There was another call that meant "hawk," and usually I could see the crows gathering around the perched broad-wing or sharp-shin to harry him until he flew away to some crowless place where he would be more likely to catch his supper.

A crow family of four ventured to come near the cabin for corn, and their strutting was very like that of a pompous lawyer who strolled every Sunday past the house where I was born. The youngsters were noisy, even before they left the nest, and I found something touching and appealing in the babyish squawls and squeaks in which they attempted to imitate their parents' emphatic *caw-caw*. Only the peeping of new-hatched chicks sounds as young to me as the voices of young crows, even though they may have grown as large as their parents.

The summer's highlight was the arrival of a porcupine, who waddled along as though utterly fagged. When I tried to approach, all signs of languor vanished as his frosty, black body turned into a quill-defended fortress, with added warning in a slapping tail and powerful teeth bared and gnashing. I knew he could not throw his quills, but he so plainly wanted nothing to do with me that I retreated, came out again with a piece of salted bread, then went back into the cabin. The quills settled into smoothness once he found the bread, which he ate slowly, as though to savor it as long as possible. I tried to coax him back with bread and salt, but was unsuccessful.

Porky was rare in the forest, perhaps because of his arch-enemy the fisher, perhaps because of some disease. He had his place. The cuttings he dropped from trees onto the snow as he fed in turn fed other animals, and his nibblings helped to thin stands of young trees. Ade and I would have welcomed his return, as one created to carry out his special functions in the living forest.

———— We went for one of our rare boat rides on a September afternoon, and were drifting home past the summer house when Ade, who was looking shoreward, blurted, "My God!"

I looked, but saw nothing. "What . . . ?"

"The oil truck on the road, going out. You can't mistake that bright yellow."

"Great day—the stove!"

We had been so absorbed in watching for porky that we had forgotten all about getting a tank and heating oil for the winter. If the oil man had stopped, we would have met him when we came from the dock, but he had not, because as far as he knew we had plenty of oil for light from the last filling.

"Will he be back up the Trail?" I asked. "We've got to have oil. To move the wood stove back and go after wood now—"

"The Lodge closed Labor Day, but the mailman told me that fellow from the East who bought the Greenfields' cabin is staying the winter. I'll walk over as soon as we get ashore and find out if he's getting oil later."

When he returned, he looked grim. Feeling the start of a chill running down my spine, I raised my eyebrows.

Ade pitched his cap across the room and dropped into a chair. "The man says he's heard the truck doesn't come up the Trail in the winter. He also says he'll sell us oil in cans at retail price. That's resort price—and high. *If* I take the cans up there and bring them back."

"But how . . ."

"In the boat till it snows. Then I can drag 'em on the toboggan."

"Up and down those hills? Heavens! He's got a car, hasn't he?"

"Sure—and a truck. And he goes past here every time there's mail." He paused, then: "He also said I can have an old can that's lying around somewhere. Then I can get fifteen gallons at a time."

"Very kind, I'm sure."

"I don't understand this," Ade said. "People don't ordi-

narily act like this. You'd think he was trying to put obstacles
in our way. We've never had any trouble getting along with
people, and I can't believe the ones up here are less accom-
modating than any place else."

"They aren't, but you've forgotten something. Over a
year ago Ernie told us we were kooks, and not a soul but the
man who came to help when you were sick and the oil man
has knocked at this door since. We've been too busy to
think about it, but we're different and therefore suspect, and
probably undesirable. People just don't move into the woods
the way we did. It's weird even to such of our old friends as
still write to us. We also have no visible means of support,
and plainly we haven't much cash. We'd have replaced our
wrecked car if we had. That piles it on and makes us really
suspicious characters."

Ade sighed. "I wonder what percentage of the world's
troubles come out of people being suspicious or afraid of
people who aren't like themselves. It's a good thing we don't
speak a foreign language."

"It's also a good thing we've no car. If someone carries off
the furniture from a closed cabin, it can't be us."

He stretched and grinned. "Ill wind and all that. Seriously,
though, maybe the guy needs the few bucks he'll make. I'll
walk the mail and use the boat only to get oil. There's enough
gas left for that, and some over. We can go easy on heat.
Watch the pennies, as if that's anything new."

"Oh, we'll manage, but you'll have a rough time hauling
that oil when winter's really dug its claws in. I can't help but
think of that neuralgia attack last winter." I thought a minute.
"The extra cost of the oil is going to cut into the money for
any food we might be able to get from town. We probably
won't eat any better than last year, so it behooves us to save
all the energy we can, especially you. I can get the water
every other time."

"No," Ade said decisively. "You are not to get water through the ice unless there's a real emergency. You don't have my long reach and you'd have to get so near the hole it could be dangerous. We'll ration the water and save some energy for both of us."

"Mmmmm. Once I read of a woman who divorced her husband because he was so tight he made her save the water from his boiled egg to make tea."

"I said ration, not reuse," Ade said indignantly.

I laughed and started dinner, thinking of how much I missed running water. I did from our first days in the woods and still do, but the difficulties of putting in a system that would be usable during the winter were so great that we vetoed it from the start.

Bedrock was very near the surface of our land. The frost line was three feet down. And if there had been any way for us to cut through the rock and lay the pipes below three feet, any surface shock would cause them to freeze. I have heard of pipes seven feet underground and carefully insulated by layers of straw and burlap that froze solid when a deer walked above them. Underground water systems that were ingeniously—and expensively—heated had frozen, and even running water froze occasionally at extremely low temperatures.

Ade brought his first cans of oil home over rolling water of a special lavender-blue we never saw except in the fall, past hills touched with the first fading of their green before the coming frost. The cedars were patched with brown and the chrome-green clusters on the pines were rusty with a selection of needles waiting to fall in the wind. A few daisies, white as the snow to come, swayed above yellowing grasses and the many-flowered stalks of wild asters were pale beside the blue of the sky. Ade hurried to finish the roof patching before the coming gray days of cloud and rain.

My begonias had spread from Hilda's little start to masses

of silken leaves and clusters of rosy flowers that overflowed
two containers, made by cutting a rectangular oil can in half
lengthwise. Every night I brought them in against the possibility of frost, every day took them out into the light, hoping
this would strengthen them against the long winter on a sill
the sunlight reached only for brief periods. I was eager for
the snow, but I also knew the encouragement green leaves
can give when the thawing days alternate with sleet and the
spring greening seems too far away.

A wind from the south whirled through the pines, bringing the needles down in clouds, and dropped the year's layer
of iron-ore-colored duff under the cedars. It was Indian
summer, when the squirrels and chipmunks paused in their
nest furbishing and seed storing to relax in the sun, and the
wild geese went high overhead, their cries like distant
trumpets, their trailing wedges both an inspiration and a
reminder that men are set apart from answering clarion calls
like theirs.

Then the rain came. The daisies bent their soggy heads
into the dying grass, the aster petals hung like wet fringes, and
the chipmunks stayed prudently inside, living on their stores.
Only the red squirrels went about as briskly as ever, their
bedraggled appearance not improved by mouths and paws
black with the sticky resin of the balsam cones whose seeds
they were enjoying. Ade and I, gratified that there was only
one small leak in the kitchen ceiling, went to work on the
notepaper mailer and had it ready to go when a north wind
cleared the sky and dropped the afternoon temperature to
thirty-eight. The next morning the flowers were blackened,
a few late keys whirled down from maples that showed their
first gold, and migrating juncos and sparrows dropped from
the trees like leaves to pick at scattered cracked corn. In the
evening the Hoovers had the fun of lighting their new oil
stove.

I marked "Cut wood" from Ade's 1954 list of things-to-do and added "3" under my column of years to complete. Then I erased the number and put "2" because the cutting really had ended in 1956 and we had not accomplished anything else on the list during that year. I looked at the scratched-off words with a deep satisfaction my friends of the outside world would have found puzzling. I could hear them: "Give up the romance, the friendliness of wood heat?" And my answer: "Fueling with wood is romantic, all right, but the logs don't bring themselves in nor the fires keep themselves going."

Most of the dead trees on our land had cunningly managed to be located well away from the cabin. The nearest was a great, windthrown pine, which supplied our first wood. Ade sawed the trunk into two-foot lengths; these sections were from two to four feet thick, pine is heavy, and we were about done in after we had dragged them to the cabin over as rough terrain as one might find on a supposedly gentle slope. Doggedly, Ade split the sections into stove-size chunks and stacked them near the door.

Shortly after this we were able to borrow a trailer and use this and our car to haul in logs already cut and stacked beside the Trail. Still later, when the car was useless after our crack-up, we met Jacques, who sent a man to us with more logs. There was still the sawing and splitting and stacking, but I helped Ade carry the chunks and life was easier without the long, hard drag through the woods.

When I lighted those friendly wood stoves, I learned that temperamental was too mild a term for them, at least in the hands of amateurs. The night heater, banked for slow burning with green wood from a newly fallen tree, took off when the wood dried, and almost set the cabin on fire. I need not spell out what would have happened if our house and clothing and food had burned on a subzero night with the nearest

shelter miles away. And the night fire had to be kept going
to prevent freezing of both the Hoovers and their food.

Adventure? Yes. Fun? No. Good experience? Sure—but I
loved our oil stove.

October was a good month. The days were bright-leaved
and warm, the nights frosty but not very cold, so that we
needed heat only a few hours a day and the oil lasted and
lasted. Freed of the burden of wood cutting and stove tending,
we filled increasing numbers of notepaper orders with ease.
Ade kept his stock ahead of the orders, and I wrote two
articles in response to expressions of interest from editors of
magazines new to me. Then skim ice began to form along the
shore as the nights grew colder and Ade took the boat, before he pulled it up for the winter, and had the oil cans refilled. Soon we heard the tap and sizzle of snow in the stovepipe and listened at night to the sound of breaking glass as the
thickening windowpane ice lifted and cracked with the
movement of the water.

The stove was very economical in oil used for the amount
of heat it gave. Even so, it was not long until Ade filled the
lamps and dumped the last of the supply into the stove tank.
He went for more but was gone such a long time that I
walked to meet him. The sun was so pleasant I did not need
my jacket. I skidded and almost fell as I started up the path.
No wonder he was taking his time. There had been enough
melting for the refreeze to slick the ground. When I reached
the road, Ade was coming down a steep hill, struggling to
brake his load so that he would not dump the oil into the
ditch. He stopped beside me to get his breath, said he could
wiggle the unspeakable and unsteerable toboggan down the
path better alone, and slid away. As I turned to follow him,
the man who had sold him the oil went by in his truck. I had
not seen him before, and was mildly surprised that he looked,
not like Count Dracula, but commonplace—peaked cap

pushed back on dark hair, ordinary features, medium weight and height as far as I could tell. He did not turn his head and I was glad. Maybe people *did* need each other in isolated places, but I was overjoyed at being ignored by this man and any more like him. True, there was danger in being more or less ostracized and as alone as Ade and I, but we would get along. It would mean watching health, avoiding accidents, making many adjustments we had never thought to have forced on us and which I could not foresee, but it would be worth it.

The next day I paid for my sojourn outside without a wrap by nursing an aching jaw and neck. A week later I was still nursing the ache, and I knew from the throbbing that I had an abscessed tooth. Just what was to be done I did not know, but I would not ask the man who peddled the oil to give me a lift to town. If the pain became unbearable or the infection showed signs of spreading, I could walk up to the Trail with Ade when he went for mail. The mailman would be glad to take me to town, and no doubt I could hitch a ride back the same day with some amiable truck driver, maybe a logger. That way I could avoid the expense of staying in town until the mailman made his next run.

A couple of weeks later Ade came back from a trip for oil, grinning.

"Jacques is up there," he said. "He says he'll stop by here in a couple of days."

"Did he see the oil cans?"

"No, or he'd have brought me back, of course."

"I'm glad he's here." Then I finally told Ade about the tooth. I shall omit the explosion that followed, especially because I deserved every word of it.

Three mornings later Jacques came whistling down the path, to stand smiling on the step, door-wide and almost door-high. While they had coffee, Ade told him about my tooth. He said nothing, only looked at me as though he would have liked to say something similar to Ade's earlier remarks. Then he put down his cup, said, "Get your coat," and walked out. I followed meekly.

We piled into the truck, and I realized that this was my first trip to town in more than three years. While Ade explained our social status and Jacques humphed at intervals, I settled to enjoy the ride.

The snow from the last fall had not been touched by the wind, and lay velvet-smooth on the branches that reached toward each other above the little road. Their shadows, softly gray-blue, rippled across the verges, dipped into the wheel ruts, stretched to join in a graceful curve on the ridge of snow that lay in the center of the right-of-way. Nowhere in the three miles to the Trail had two cars met and swerved to pass since the snow had fallen. We turned onto the road to the Village, and as we climbed a long, steep hill, I saw two giant spruces at the top, sentinels that had watched the way when it had been a foot trail, years before a white man had seen it.

Beyond the spruces the road was changed—widened, flattened, straightened—and a once-familiar bald-granite hilltop, slippery as ice when wet, was no more. Soon we were winding and dipping as I remembered, going over hills that seemed to drop into nowhere, held in our narrow path by the steep, snow-covered banks and the tall barriers of trees. Once Jacques slid to a stop and pointed at the woods. For a moment I thought he was showing me the high stump of a huge spruce, split off by lightning. Then it moved, and I made out a cow moose watching us from the shadows. He laughed at my startled yip. Wise in the ways of the forest, he knew that the great size of the moose was superb camouflage among the thick tree boles.

I tried to find the hill where we had had our accident, but

that part of the road had been bypassed by another widened section, and this led to blacktop plowed clear of snow—the section that was being bulldozed when we made our first trip up the Trail. It would be a loss when the old road was gone and with it the sensation of going into mysterious places, but the forest itself was not altered.

Though the trees along the improved sections might no longer touch snow-heavy branches from one verge to the other nor guide the traveler past vanished blind spots by the alignment of crowns visible ahead, the newly exposed forest edges were taking on the appearance of the old as small balsams sprang up. The forest depths stretched away from the man-made gashes as they always had. I remembered an aerial photograph of South American jungles that showed a faint line where a road built by the Incas had once carried their traffic. Some distant day this road might also be only a shadowy line in a sea of green.

We passed the small virgin stand of white pine that had encouraged Ade and me when we made our first trip into this forest, and I was still thinking about those early days when we pulled up in front of the dentist's office in the Village. Ade and Jacques went off to eat and shop while I faced the coming extraction with my usual craven attitude. This was exceptionally foolish, because the tooth was so loose that I hardly noticed its coming out.

We started back in the early dark of late November in the north, and except for noticing the way the headlights beamed into space on the old sections of road, showing nothing but the black-and-white tops of trees, I drowsed all the way back to the cabin.

The next morning I woke with a severe headache, and after stumbling around the cabin for a couple of hours, took Ade's advice and went back to bed. By evening I was hot and heavy-eyed with fever. After a prolonged search Ade found the thermometer, apparently mistaken for a ball-point pen and stored with them in the desk. It showed 104.5 degrees, and I thought it was damaged until I considered why my head felt so light and my thoughts wandered without making much sense. Even so, I knew that infection had spread from the tooth, but I was so confused that I could not recall the dentist's name, which Ade did not know, either. I did manage to write a note to the local doctor, explaining what had happened and asking for some suitable medication. The next two days were an ordeal of chills and fever, and when Ade came back with the mail he brought, not medicine, but a letter making an appointment at the doctor's office the next morning at eight o'clock. I must have been too sick to tell him we had no transportation.

I thought that this was the way it was in days almost forgotten when someone lay ill of a "fever," and prayers were said and spells were made, and some wise woman scraped a deer antler or gathered herbs to make a healing tea. And the fever went, or rose to unendurable heights.

Ade was frightened, but I was not. I lay there, as much under the control of natural forces as a tree in a gale. If my fighting power was the stronger, I would recover, as the tree might stand against the wind. If it was not, I would become part of the earth from which I came. Whether I went back to the earth the next day or on a day ten thousand days ahead was something I could not control, and so should not think about.

A week later, when I woke feeling hungry, I knew that I had gained an understanding and acceptance of death, and of the natural laws that govern the extent of life. The circumstances that opened my mind to this came from our isolation, but the knowledge came from the forest, where the transience of animals, plants, even the shapes of the rocks, is a constant reminder of the impermanence of all forms of mortality, and the steady renewal of life and growth affirms the unity and timelessness of the source of all things known to man.

———— A week before Christmas, when I was strong enough to walk through the snow, Ade escorted me to the lake, which was still open. It was such a pleasure to get out again; to see the grayish shadows on the snow in the woods and look through the trees to the white-blue sky, the slate-blue water; to watch the snow on the far shore slowly turning to gold in the rays of the setting sun. There was frost in the air, falling like sparse snow from nowhere, cool against my face. Almost at the moment of sunset the moon rose like a colorless sun behind the veiling crystals, and later the frost fell in thin platelets of ice that caught light from the moon and glistened like chips of the stars themselves. It was a wonderful welcome back to the winter woods I love so well.

Next day I went through the accumulated mail to see if my aunt had sent her Thanksgiving-dinner check, but she had not even written.

"It's odd," I said. "It would be like her to make it an annual special event."

Ade handed me a letter. "I picked this up two weeks ago. She's been ill—heart. Your uncle wrote that she's on the road to recovery."

"That's good news, anyway. I'll create from cans."

"Wait." Ade went out and came back to hand me a frosty parcel. "Two pounds of ground beef," he said proudly. "I put it in the barrel-stove freezer when we got back from town."

"Meat loaf!" I shouted. "We can have meat loaf for Christmas."

As he opened the door to return the package to its storage place he said, "There's always some kind of compensation."

He stopped with his mouth open, then: "It sounds idiotic, but I think of heaven as a pound of hamburger these days."

———— New Year's Eve came on still and cold. I dragged a carton from behind the curtain in the living room and sat on the bare floor, cleaning the neglected records we had brought from Chicago. We had given our player to a friend there because it would be useless here without power. I questioned the sentimental urge that had led me to keep the records and to unpack them without a sensible reason. Handling them only made me long for unobtainable music to celebrate the coming year. And we surely needed something to make the night festive. The best I could do for a midnight snack was a peanut-butter sandwich and half a hard-boiled egg each. If Tulip had not outdone herself and laid two eggs on the previous Sunday, we would not have had that much. Feeling nostalgic and a little depressed, I put the records away and sat by the window, watching the last light fade from the sky, hoping that perhaps a deer might move across the hill in the dusk.

Then I heard the unmistakable sound of an engine running. I pricked up my ears—it was not a car and there was no one near us, supposedly. I was about to call Ade, who was in the work building, when the whole cabin blazed with light. I was confused for a moment, then knew that he had finally managed to get the light plant working. I looked around the living room, discovering spider webs that had been concealed by the merciful shadows, then remembered Ade's list. I yanked open the desk drawer, and had just marked "Install wiring" from it while trying to think of something complimentary enough for Ade on this occasion, when he came in, all smiles. He reached past me to turn on our table radio from Chicago, which I had not noticed, although it took up much of the desk top. The radio began to admit rattles and howls. It was the most exciting static I ever heard.

When the aurora had ceased to cast its greenish glow on windows and snow, we began to pick up stations. We switched all over the dial, and were astonished that we could get New Orleans and North Carolina but not Duluth. News reports were not much different from those we had left behind three years before. Commercials, which once had been annoying, were now funny as we considered the utter unimportance of some of the things being touted. But music was still music, and as attractive to both of us as the pipes of Hamlin.

At eleven o'clock we heard the account of the ball coming down in Times Square and decided to follow the year across the country. At midnight it was Chicago, and the cabin was full of memories. An hour later it was Denver, and I never hear the station announcement from KOA without remembering that night of simple excitement in the woods. In spite of the food and strong coffee we were feeling the unaccustomed late hour, but I was determined to get a midnight broadcast from the West Coast. It was twenty to two when we got a whisper from Los Angeles, which faded at once. When two o'clock passed, I gave up and carried our plates to the kitchen.

"You know," I said as I put the peanut butter away, "if I could hear Louis Armstrong sing 'Blueberry Hill' I'd walk to town in my bare feet."

"You can do it tomorrow, then," Ade called. "Come here. Quick!"

I almost ran into the other room, to hear the well-loved gravelly voice coming faintly across the miles with the sentimental song that I always feel brings me good luck.

Just how lucky it was, I would rather not say. Anyway, six weeks later, the two articles I had written in October and which we had expected to pay our taxes and insurance, came back. One editor apologized because he had had one on the same subject in stock when I queried him, but had forgotten. The other said he had bought one on that subject before mine arrived, and now regretted this because mine was better. I rewrote them for other types of magazines and sent them out again, then started a true bird story that had begun the previous spring and continued through the year, but which needed an ending. I might never get the ending but, even so, I might find a use for the account some day.

———— On the first of March we had a heavy, soggy snow that came on a driving wind. Deep drifts and fallen trees blocked the road, and a cold snap followed the storm. It was a week before the plow came through, a week of rapidly diminishing oil, and Ade left to get more as soon as the road was cleared.

The snow scent that blew in when he opened the door was a refreshing contrast to the faint smell that lingered inside from the oil lamps. I stood outside, breathing deeply and watching Ade drag the toboggan up the path. Then I heard queer sounds from the chicken house—not crowing or clucking but more like a combination of both with an overtone of alarm.

I walked over and saw the Crown Prince at the window, turning his head from side to side as he watched Ade, and sounding more agitated than before. I opened the door. The rooster hopped out and came to stand at my feet, still watching the path and making definite sounds of alarm. I checked the hens, the heater, the feed, the water. Everything was fine, but the Prince was disturbed about something. I talked to him and smoothed his feathers until he quieted, then put him back inside. But he stayed at the window, looking toward the path, and was still there an hour later when I checked the birds again. As I turned to go in, he crowed, clucked contentedly, and left the window. I looked up and saw Ade at the top of the path.

I stood in the snow, wondering how a rooster felt when his protective instinct was frustrated by close confinement and both he and his hens were totally dependent on an alien protector. The Prince accepted anything that Ade did for him without resistance. His trust in me was considerable but less complete, which might result from my not feeding the chickens except when Ade could not. Did the Prince feel afraid when he saw the main source of his food and water walking away in the distance? I thought this might well be so, and resolved to go out when Ade went away in the future and "reassure" the Prince by letting him know that he and his charges were not being abandoned.

I was about to mention this to Ade, but he looked so discouraged that I went in and heated some coffee before I asked what was wrong.

"He's leaving until May," Ade said wearily. "I tried to suggest he might leave me a key to the lock on the oil tank, but he got in ahead of me. Said he was almost out. But the frost line on the tank shows it's half full. Maybe I haven't an honest face."

"Nonsense. He could measure the oil in the tank with a dip stick before he goes and when he comes back."

Ade shrugged. "Too true, but the fact is we'll get no more oil this winter."

We drooped in our chairs, staring at the wall. I thought with longing of the days when Hilda and Sven were near us—the two miles to the Lodge that had once seemed so long now seemed very short. They would have let us have oil, or wood, or would have suggested some alternative, like staying in one of their cabins. Suddenly I sat up.

"We've been going along with the idea that we've been

living an independent life, haven't we?" He nodded. "Well, the thought comes a bit late, but our independence has been a dependence on people who happened to be near."

"That's what everybody says—up here people *need* each other."

"That's true sometimes. But when something goes wrong we think first of asking for advice. It's a bad habit. When we had a fire we knew there was nobody around, so we put it out ourselves. From now on we think first of what *we* can do."

Ade sat up as abruptly as I had. "And the current problem is how not to freeze before it warms up." He thought. "First, let's consider the fuel we have left."

We still had some wood, but drifting snow had piled to the carport roof, and the wood was now so deeply frozen in that Ade doubted if he could break it free. Even if he could, it would be wet and hard to burn, and we would have the struggle of moving back the wood stove through the snow. But if we were very careful, we would have enough oil for low night heat. At least enough to prevent freezing our food. But there simply was not enough oil for daytime heat.

"It will help some," Ade said, "if we stop the drafts between the boards of this floor. Newspapers are perfect insulation, and there's a big stack of them the Larimers left in a shed next door. . . ."

"And those green shag rugs we dragged from Chicago can go over the papers. I know they'll catch more dirt than we think we track in, but they'll be warm."

"And the airtight's still set up and it'll burn anything. I've a lot of combustible trash piled up here and there. . . ."

"And there're those old clothes Carl Johnson left behind. . . ."

For the next weeks the airtight simmered and wheezed under its load of damp wrapping paper, torn boxes, moldy rags once intended for a braided rug—you name it. But you can get a lot of heat from an old overcoat, even if it is a good idea not to open the door oftener than necessary because the stink of the smoke from burning mildewed wool is appalling. I wondered that the animals, with such sensitive noses, could stand it, but they did, only sniffing and peering around now and then. We finally had to cut out our night heat in order to save some oil for our lamp, but nothing froze except the potatoes, and we did not think this too important because we still had plenty of flour and spaghetti. The freight would start running in May and we could order potatoes then.

It sounds simple now, but we were constantly plagued by uncertainty. New snow fell. The temperature seemed fixed below freezing. We were delighted to get rid of the trash and make good use of it, but always there was an underlying quivery feeling because we wondered if we might have to start burning furniture, as has been done by people without fuel in an isolated place. The days, though, were brightened by signs of warmth to come.

In mid-March, the promise of spring flapped overhead and squawked *caw-caw-caw.* Not long after, the crying of gulls drifted to us on a breeze from the west. Somewhere in the narrows between our lake and a bay to the north, fast-moving water had defeated the ice, and the gulls had come to fish in the riffles. The next day there were chipmunk tracks outside a hole in the snow that covered the bank of our drainage ditch. I put corn near the hole and the next day the chippies were dashing back and forth from their burrow, prudently storing corn.

It was early April when a few slate-colored juncos came, and then the sparrows—tree, white-crowned, white-throated, Harris's—and with them a starling and two little brown birds I could not identify. It was some time before I realized that they were female house sparrows. As a supposedly competent observer I felt deflated, but perked up when I remembered that I had seen none since we left Chicago, and that Chicago sparrows are a uniform dust color, even the male's black bib being hidden by dirt. The deep woods is not house-sparrow country, but I wished that they would stay. They are cheerful and lively, and I wanted to see how they would get along with our local birds, some of whom can be as tough as any sparrow.

A small flock of purple finches came two weeks later, their feathers dull in the shadows, ruby-bright in the sun. It was warm that day, with dripping icicles and leaves starting to show on the willows, and Ade went to the carport to see if he could dig out some firewood. As I turned from the window where I was watching the gleams of purple-red on the finches' feathers, I caught a glimpse of my own winter-dull, stringy hair and decided to wash it.

Anyone seeing me dash from the cabin with soapsuds flying a bit later might have thought the house was burning, at least. But it was only that Ade, returning with the wood, had yelled, "Geese!"

We stood on the shore while the faint cries grew louder and the thin, shifting line of flyers passed high above the gray and rotten ice, whose surface was dotted with pools as blue as the sky they reflected. Then more geese came over, flying low, banking on a wind that preceded clouds—calling, calling in high clear voices of opening waters and the death of winter.

Three crows came to strut near the cabin and eat the corn spread there, so after I finished the interrupted shampoo, I decided to write a little piece on crows, as a sample for a juvenile nature series I hoped to sell in the future. I was well started when I got the feeling that someone was staring at my back. I turned my head. One of the crows was perched on a branch of a leafing elder bush, hunched forward, peering through the window, and seemingly trying to read over my shoulder. Crows have such a *knowing* look! I burst out laughing and the crow flew away, complaining raucously. While I was wondering what an editor would say in such factual days if I put this little tidbit into writing for five-year-olds, I heard the flutter and rush of air that accompanies the settling of a large flock of birds.

I ran to the kitchen window to see two hundred juncos, in the trees and on the ground, already arguing in their twittery voices about who would get to the grain first. While Ade was putting out corn in long lines to give room to all, I looked to see if one special junco might be there, a leading character in the bird story that needed an ending.

On that special April morning a year before, when the story began, the whirring of many wings had brought both of us to the window. Juncos bent the twigs of the cedar, hopped on the ground, darted in the air, clustered around the cracked corn.

They are such plump, lively little birds: the males with almost black hoods and backs, gray sides, and white bellies; the females lighter and grayish brown. They spent more time ducking and bobbing for position with spread wings and cries of *tchu-tchu-tchu* than they did eating. As they moved, their white outer-tail feathers flashed and were hidden again.

One seemed unable to find a feeding place among the rest. At last he flew to a windowsill and pecked at some crumbs left by the chickadees. "*Twit, twit-twit, twit,*" he said in an unhappy-sounding voice. He held his right leg awkwardly and did not put his weight on it. I opened the window a crack and spread some corn on the outer sill. The bird flew only a short way and returned to feed as though he were very hungry.

We named him Mr. Twit.

When the flock moved on to more northerly breeding grounds two weeks later, Mr. Twit was unable to go. He settled down to feed with our summer birds and spent his spare time singing hopeful and coaxing songs. Then one morning another crippled junco hopped into the yard, dragging a left wing that had stiffened in a spread position.

We marveled that she had made her way so far and that she had escaped death from predators, but although she could not fly, she made long, hopping glides with the help of her good wing. Also, she easily lifted herself twenty inches to the top of the feeding bench.

Mr. Twit courted her in his best manner and she became Mrs. Twit. The pair disappeared and we knew they were nesting, but where? Ade went out one day to clear away a pile of brush left by Carl Johnson. He was met by a wildly fluttering Mr. Twit, who was prepared to defend his brush pile against all comers. It had settled until it was as dense as a briar tangle and as safe for the Twits as any place nearby.

We avoided the nest because we thought the birds had problems enough without interference from curious humans. Soon both birds began to come more often to the feeders, and we hoped that this meant their eggs had hatched. Later, we saw Mrs. Twit feeding her two black-streaked fledglings.

When the aspen leaves were lying like gold coins on the brown duff, the fall migrants arrived. When they went, only Mrs. Twit was left, hopping forlornly on the first light snow.

We made friendly overtures, and she soon accepted us as readily as the resident birds. Although juncos sometimes winter in northern Minnesota, we worried about Mrs. Twit because of her handicap. We would supply plenty of food and be ready to help if we could.

She stayed in her nest in the brush pile. This was a happy selection, because the thick mat of twigs held the snow, an excellent insulator. When heavy snow came, Ade poked a tunnel in the direction of the nest and Mrs. Twit did nicely in her "igloo." All went well until the soggy snowfall of March first. Overhanging balsam-fir boughs dropped great clumps of snow directly onto the brush heap. Not only was the nest buried but the brush itself was crushed down.

Ade and I dug frantically, tearing out brush and snow together. When we found Mrs. Twit she seemed lifeless, but was warm. We hurried her inside. I could detect no heartbeat, but thought she was breathing faintly. We wrapped her in warmed bits of wool I had saved to patch Ade's underpants, and waited. Half an hour later her beak opened and closed, and I dropped water into it from a spoon. She swallowed some drops, opened her eyes, then seemed to drop off to sleep. Fearfully I felt inside her coverings. The heartbeat was strong and steady.

Ade suggested that we look at her injury before she regained consciousness. The wing was probably broken and badly healed but there was always a chance that something could be done. Very carefully I felt along the bones. On the underside of the main joint, I touched something foreign. I looked closely. A bit of twig had wedged so that it acted as a brace to hold the wing outspread. Ade held Mrs. Twit while I snipped the twig with a sharp wire-cutter and pulled the two pieces out with tweezers. Drops of blood showed how firmly the twig had grown into its unfortunate position.

Mrs. Twit was stirring now but seemed dazed. She jerked and twitted sharply when I tried to move the wing, which had been immobilized for so long that the joints had stiffened and the muscles wasted, but the wing was sound and whole. If birds' wings were anything like a human arm—I had once injured my own arm and for a time it was in much the same state as hers—Mrs. Twit might fly again.

At the moment, food was most important. The junco's normal diet is a quarter insects and the rest seeds and small fruits. Ade and I decided on some of the suet we had left, enriched cereal, assorted wildflower seeds, cracked corn, crumbs, and some of the mineral- and vitamin-rich feed we had for the chickens. We set this out in small heaps, with a water dish at hand. Mrs. Twit was very quiet for two days but ate and drank as she pleased without help. She took the familiar suet, corn, and seeds first; then settled to eat of everything with a good appetite. When she began to hop about she was very tame, sitting on our hands as though we had reared her from the egg.

We decided to keep her inside until she was stronger. She made no attempt to perch and liked to sit on the cloths we had used as coverings when she was ill, so we fixed her a temporary cloth-carpeted home in a hastily cleared bookshelf. It was high enough to protect her from the short-tailed shrews but not so high that it prevented her coming and going under her own power.

One day I noticed that the stiff wing was slightly folded. It was time to begin its exercise. Mrs. Twit did not mind my slow and gentle flexing of it, and it improved more rapidly than I would have thought possible, but, even after it had become perfectly flexible and the muscles had developed noticeably, she did not move the wing. We tried dropping her a short distance onto a cushion, but she used only her good wing to break her fall. Mrs. Twit was conditioned to being a bird with one wing.

A week later I put her in a favorite position on one shoulder and was slicing bread for lunch when the jays and squirrels set up a furious complaint. I opened the door to be greeted by a brown-and-white dog, whose visit indicated that someone was not far away in the forest. I let the dog in to quiet the uproar. There was a terrified chirp near my ear, and Mrs. Twit *flew* to the top of the corner cupboard. Instinct had done what training could not do and Mrs. Twit was whole again.

After some days of uncertain and wobbly trials, she began to sit on the sill and look out of the window. I opened the door. She flew out, lifted and dived, dropped down as though exhausted, ate from the food on the bench, then tried her wings again. Sometimes she rested, opening and closing them as though to strengthen the weak one. She often sat on the windowsill and when she wanted to rest inside, she perched on the feeding shelf beside the door and twitted until I let her in. Soon she rested less and flew more.

When the current spring's big cloud of juncos came down from the sky, Mrs. Twit stayed a little apart from them, as though uncertain of her course. Together, as we watched, Ade and I spotted a lone bird, flying above the scattered brush where the nest of the Twits had been, slightly favoring a crooked right leg and making coaxing sounds. Mr. Twit had come home.

There was a flash of gray and white, a swoop of wings, and Mrs. Twit was sitting on the brush, almost bursting her throat with song. Mr. Twit lit beside her. Then, singing and circling each other, they rose into the air.

They left with the flight, when the last patches of snow were melting and violet leaves were green. We were not to see them again, but we no longer cleared brush piles. Who can say how many travelers have sheltered in them since?

> *cut wood*
> *install wiring*
> **clear brush and paths**
> *clear trash*
> *running water*
> *make a living*

——— I was not very lively during the transition months from winter to spring. One day I was wiping logs and nicked my finger on a splinter. I bled something that looked like pink water. I was anemic, but that was no surprise, considering the lack of iron in our food. A few days later I noticed two round bruised spots on my chest, the sort of thing black-fly bites do to me. I had not thought they would be out so soon, but the evidence was there. I had headaches, but typing by lamplight is very hard on the eyes. My muscular cramps and pains were probably the result of being too casual about wearing wraps outside.

The pains finally got so bad that I thought it best to go to bed and keep warm for a few days. The next morning I crawled out to set things in order for breakfast and saw a dreadful bruise on the outside of one leg. It had not been there the day before, and I could not figure out how I could have bumped into something while lying in bed. But I must have. Then, as I brushed my teeth I saw blood on the brush and felt the looseness of my teeth. Shocked, I knew I had scurvy.

This was hard to believe, but then I remembered Great-Aunt Anne telling me of the "spring sickness" that was common among her forebears, and of her grandfather who had crossed the Atlantic with a sack of potatoes, which he ate raw—and rotten toward the end of the voyage—to protect himself from the disease. And we hadn't thought much of it when our potatoes froze! I had sneakily given Ade a big half of our vegetables and canned meat because he needed strength for all the hard labor he had to do, and malnutrition had caught up with me.

What I needed was vitamin C. Lemons. It was Wednesday, and the mail truck would come up the Trail because an experimental twice-a-week schedule was being tried. If Ade had a little money—*if* he had, because we had almost no use for cash where we were—he could mail enough along with an order to the grocery and we would have lemons in three days. The order and money went off two hours later.

On Saturday a parcel came from another grocery with a note saying that the first store, having no lemons, had passed the order on to them. And, since Ade had sent too much money, they had used the excess for a pound of ground beef, which was specially priced and which they felt sure we could use because we seldom came to town. They also enclosed a large chunk of suet, Jacques having once told them we fed birds.

"I've a feeling Jacques told them more than that," Ade said.

"Yes, which makes the note tactful in addition to being kind. If we get on our feet, I think this is our grocery."

"When, not if. And stay in bed. I'll make you some lemonade."

I still remember how completely delicious those lemons tasted. I even ate them in segments like oranges, without noticing the sourness.

It was a while before I was able to stir around much, and Ade learned to bake by means of instructions shouted to him from my bed. He made better bread than I did, by the way, because his hands were stronger and he could work it more thoroughly. A lot of people have asked me about our bread-making, and this is how we did it.

Put 2⅓ cups of warm water in a bowl and dissolve a package of dry yeast in it. Add 1 tablespoon of sugar and ½ teaspoon of salt. Work in about 6 cups of flour, first with a spoon, then with your hands. Set to rise in a warm but not hot place. (I will not even guess at temperature because ours varied greatly.) When the dough is puffed up twice-size—time shorter with warmer temperature—punch it down, work it on a floured counter, and shape into 1 huge or 2 sensible-size loaves. Grease pan with lard or bacon drippings, let dough rise in pan until it holds a finger dent, and bake for about an hour. I cannot guess at baking temperature, either, but we put it into a not-too-hot oven and, once it had risen some more, increased the temperature. We found out when it was done by taking the crusty loaf out of the pan and knocking on the bottom. If it sounded hollow, that was it. Otherwise it went back into the oven for a while. Any adventurous soul who wants to try this would do well to follow temperatures as given in a somewhat more conventional recipe.

———— While I was recuperating, I sat up in bed and tried to make a budget, but this was hopeless without a reliable income base. Then I tried to find something we might cut out of "necessary" expenses to allow more food money. We had canceled all subscriptions except to the local newspaper, which informed us of nearby doings that might affect us. Insurance had gone the same way except for coverage on our buildings and contents, which were our only tangible assets—and forest fire could always come. Then there were our real-estate taxes, which we had been paying as promptly as possible.

I went over our accounts for the calendar year of 1957. We had spent $1,464. Taxes and insurance $352; oil and gasoline (heat, light, and water transportation) $160; food $480; household supplies other than food $30; shipping for the last two items $90. These essentials had been held to our earnings of $1,112. The remainder came from our insurance money and paid for notepaper supplies, postage, six flashlight batteries, repairs to Ade's worn boots, a small box of aspirin, and the newspaper.

If our earnings had not increased by the time the insurance money was gone, we could drop the paper and taxes, trusting we might be able to pay delinquent taxes before we lost our property. And as a last resort, the fire insurance could lapse.

There was no way Ade could cut business expenses—he even gave me spoiled mimeographed pages so that I could rough my manuscripts on their backs, as I already used the backs of letters. But maybe I could find a few dollars.

I had already learned how to stretch a pound of hamburger into ten portions, and how to make a largish and fairly tasty omelet out of two eggs and water and salt and pepper. And that one can live for days on potato soup. And along with this I had learned to bear the ache of hunger and the discomfort that comes from stuffing with starchy food, only to feel hungry an hour later because of lack of essential food elements. To make white-sugar fudge to fill in the empty spots, and to be hungry again while still half-nauseated by the excess of sugar. To control the hair-trigger temper and unreasonable anxiety that comes with low blood sugar. There did not seem to be anything more I could do.

When I was able to be up part of the day, I discovered that our soap was almost gone. Postage from town would cost more than the soap so what we had must be stretched. We scrubbed with warm water and learned that one need not become lousy (literally), caked with dirt, ill, or billy-goat scented without numerous soapy baths. Water and elbow grease did wonders for our clothes, too. This left most of the fading soap supply for dish washing, because dirty dishes and cooking utensils can cause gastroenteritis, potentially fatal in our isolated situation.

It was about this time that the melting snow began to pour through the winter-cracked roof. There were so many leaks that we had to put all our pots and pans under them, and the water came in streams so that we had to put towels in the pans to stop the splashing. I managed to find a funny side to the endless dumping of the pans, but my sense of humor took a beating when the last drop of my hand lotion, brought from Chicago, was gone.

There had been a forty-below-zero night when I went outside at two A.M. to check the chickens' lantern-heater. A sudden gust of wind struck me with such cold that I gasped. The next thing I knew I was on my hands and knees with my dizzy head almost touching the snow. The shock of the wind chill, which for that temperature and the twenty-five-mile-an-hour wind, was equivalent to a temperature of about a hundred below zero, had stunned my heart to momentary stopping. I owed my life to falling forward, with my heart region protected by my curled-over position and my head down so that the increased circulation to the brain brought me out of my momentary blackout. I stumbled inside, conscious of my narrow escape, and for the briefest moment thought how easy it would have been if I had not come to. Then I heard Ade turn in his sleep and was horrified at the selfishness and cowardice of the thought that had touched me.

Ade and I had come to the forest believing that we would

have to work harder than we had ever worked and thinking the depression years had prepared us, but we discovered they had been relatively easy. We had been poor in the sense of having to cut corners during our first year and a half in the woods. Two years later we were poverty stricken—cold, hungry, ragged, sick, and touched by flashes of paralyzing terror. This was not the fear of death but the fear of living, of never having some small pleasure or physical comfort or a moment free of worry so long as life should last. But we asked for neither help nor pity. The mistake, if it should prove to be a mistake, was ours, and getting onto our feet again was our job. We would have felt the same no matter who or what was to blame.

As I thought over the many sides of our situation I knew that ever after, whenever I might hear someone who had once walked down a slum street, or had to skip a few meals, say something like "Poverty is dreadful, but ennobling," I would have an almost uncontrollable urge to use physical violence on him. But I would control the urge. The self-discipline of our woods life had given me control. Hardship was making Ade and me strong in mind and will, but it was not making us noble, we being neither saints nor ascetics.

And yet I warmed to the happy moments we were finding in this innocent forest. The wild creatures were our friends and companions, our teachers, our entertainers, the source of the material for our livelihood. In a sense they were our hosts, because they belonged to the forest and could not go elsewhere as we could if we chose to do so. That we should kill them for food was unthinkable. Instead, we helped them as we could and cherished the environment that was their home and ours. In return, the forest offered us such beautiful experiences that hope never vanished, not even in our darkest hours.

———— I was myself again near the end of May and was kneading bread when someone shouted outside. I opened the door to the oil man, who said, "Did your oil hold out? I knew you'd be okay on gas so I didn't stop when I came up in February . . ." He stopped at my blank expression.

Ade came from his workroom, saying, "I got the impression you didn't come up during the winter."

"Of course I do. Lots of places have too small tanks to carry through."

There was a silence. Then Ade pointed through the door to the living room at the oil stove and described our means of fueling it for the past nine months.

"What did you pay him?"

"Thirty cents."

The driver shook his head. "And no delivery. I'll sell you all the oil you want at 18.8 cents a gallon and pump it into a tank, if you want me to. As soon as I can bring it and you set it up. Why didn't you write me?"

"We don't know your name," I said.

"Henry Larson. And if you'd addressed it to 'the oil-truck driver' it'd've been delivered. You don't look it, but there's a little city not rubbed off you yet. Now . . ."

He and Ade conferred. Two weeks later the tank was set up and filled, and both of our forty-five-gallon drums held gasoline. We were set for summer and well into the coming winter.

We carried the chickens to their larger quarters and moved into the summer house as soon as it was warm enough for the sun to supply daytime heat through its big windows, and the fireplace to keep us comfortable on cool evenings. The once overgrown paths were reasonably open for walking now, and the ferns lifted with dignity and grace in the beds

I had cleared. My gamble in letting nature take care of the open area had paid off in white-starred carpets of bunchberries and tall stalks of yellowish flowers rising from the spreading patches of bluebead lilies. The grass was being crowded out so rapidly that the remaining clumps were negligible.

As we went back and forth between the houses we watched the destruction of the green on the short-needled conifers by worms, which the local paper identified as spruce budworms. The brown spots I had thought unimportant the previous spring were the early signs of an infestation. This year the worms had come in full force, and no one could have over-looked the attack.

On each balsam tip, protected by a thin web, was a smooth green-to-brown caterpillar, eating the pale young needles voraciously. When the new green was gone, some of the worms moved on to the spruces and some remained to attack the older balsam needles. In less than three weeks our sizable balsam and spruce trees were almost completely bare of needles, and were covered with a brown deposit left by the worms. Then they pupated. In a few days small gray moths emerged, to flutter around the barren trees and find the few remaining needles, on the undersides of which they laid their eggs before they died.

During the short season of the worms, birds flitted from twig to twig, cocking bright eyes in the search for caterpillars. There was the yellow flash of a goldfinch, the black and white of a warbler, the bright blue of a jay. The whiskey jacks dropped down to twitter at me before hastily returning to the feast. In the midst of the twittering and chirping were the voices of robins, more than usually came our way. And this continued through the time of the pupae, with the squir-rels joining the numbers that fed on them.

Since there was nothing we could do about the worms, we refused to worry about the trees, and went on with our work.

By contrast with the neat surroundings of the summer house, the log cabin looked neglected. On a morning when we arrived there, soaked to the knees after pushing our way through low growth dripping from the previous night's dew, we were sure of it. Ade wanted to plant the vegetables as soon as we could get the seeds by mail, and I wanted to try some flowers, just for fun. We could clear away some of the spreading raspberries and wild mint, improve the looks of the house, make some paths, and add color, all without disturbing rare or scarce native plants or removing the cover so much needed by the smaller wild creatures. I ordered onion sets, rhubarb roots, and carrot, radish, Swiss chard, and salsify seeds for Ade's garden; scarlet-runner beans, dahlia, and alyssum seeds for mine.

While he planted in the plots we had prepared the year before, I worked on the paths from the cabin to the road and west to the edge of the forest, which were already indicated by our walking from one place to another. I yanked out plantain, rough grasses, and incipient raspberries and collected white stones to outline our walks. They would be muddy, but perhaps later on we could get some of the vari-colored gravel washed up on the beaches. Together we set the outlining stones, then considered a barren spot under our one south window, which received almost no rain because of the wide eaves above. It offered clouds of dust and not even plants that spread by underground stems, like horsetail and mint, had taken hold there, although shallow-rooted sweet williams transplanted to each side of it were doing well.

Ade covered it with small flagstones and outlined it with stones to match the paths. It sloped away from the building so that water poured slowly at the top seeped under the stones, in between which I put alyssum seeds. To hide the bare strip along the foundation, I transplanted climbing false buckwheat, with a center break to let light reach the window. This plant has dark, arrow-shaped leaves, red stems, and clusters of small, bell-like white flowers, followed by equally attractive seed clusters. Ade ran wires from ground to eaves, using some of the wire that had once supported a wind-generator tower, destroyed by lightning shortly after we bought the place. Soon the vines were reaching toward the roof. As they shaded the bare earth behind them, wild straw-berries took hold in it. And while this was happening, a colony of brown ants were making a home under the flag-stones, adding their bit of cultivation and fertilizer.

Ade turned his attention to the outside fireplace footing that had been put in when the foundation was repaired. It looked as though we might never be able to complete the fireplace, so he built sides on the footing and filled them with dirt, where I planted my begonias for the summer and experimented with the dahlia seeds. The chipmunks hurried to nibble the dark-pink begonia buds—they are attracted by red as are humming birds—and the squirrels leaped merrily through the plants, breaking so many of the brittle stems that I was constantly putting sets into the soil beside the old plants.

"I'll have so many begonias there'll be no place for them at this rate," I said one day, "and it would be nice to have a few blooms."

Ade considered the situation, then built a cage over the flowers in the footing, using bits of hardware cloth he had found on the ground near the storage building. It could be opened from the front for watering and had a fan of wires leading to the eaves through the rear top mesh, "just in case," Ade said. I put the runner beans, which I had not planted because the chipmunks would have dug them up at once for food, inside the cage at the base of the wires.

It did not take long to do all this, the rain confining itself to brief showers with long periods of sun and shadow between, when cloud fluffs sailed across an azure sky and breezes blew warm enough to be pleasant and cool enough to make work easy.

Ade's birthday is late in June, and we decided to use that day and the week after to unkink our muscles, plan our work well ahead, and spend some time at whatever we might want to do. Leisure was so nearly unknown to us that this took on the glamor of a celebration. Ade chose to amuse himself by working on the radio from our damaged Chevy, which still sat forlornly in the carport. I settled on piano practice, which started off well in spite of a number of keys stuck by dampness.

At the end of the first day we were reading in bed when a series of bumps came from the chicken coop.

"Bear!" Ade yelped. He jumped up, grabbed the lantern, and ran out without his shoes.

I could see or hear nothing unusual from the window and went back to bed when I saw Ade's light turn toward the house. I was just opening my book when he called from the kitchen, "Come and light the lamp. Hurry!"

The lamplight showed me the Crown Prince, lying limp across Ade's arms, very pale of comb and wattles.

"Did the bear hurt him?" I asked, making room for Ade to lay him on the table.

"No bear. I think he fell off his perch," Ade said as he felt for injuries. "His wings must have flapped against the wall— that's what we heard."

The Prince's comb was bluish at its edges and I wondered if chickens ever had heart attacks. I slid my fingers under his breast feathers and felt his heart beat—weak, irregular, slowing, faltering. Then nothing.

Ade said, "He's not hurt . . . what's wrong?"

I turned away so that I would not cry. It seemed too cruel

that Ade, who had so little to cheer him, should lose his pet as a birthday gift.

We buried him in the morning and decided that the best way not to listen for his vanished crowing was to go back to work on the log cabin. I began to scrub the kitchen linoleum in strips, which I then brushed with clear plastic. The finished floor would be brighter and easy to clean. Ade once again climbed onto the roof to do what little he could about the many leaks that had opened in the rotten paper during the winter.

I stepped outside in the afternoon just in time to hear him swear and see his glasses slide off the eave to shatter on a stone.

He insisted that he could get along without them. I reminded him that reading was one of his most important diversions, to say nothing of his drawing, and that headaches from eyestrain would add no joy to his life. I did not say that things were already gloomy enough when Bedelia's attempt at crowing reminded us of the Prince, who had been our alarm clock and watchdog. I felt that the trip would cheer him, and I knew that taking care of all the chores myself for a day or two would be good for my mopy state of mind. I clinched the argument by locating a copy of the local paper, which contained the name and address of a Duluth oculist who had visited the Village to speak at a meeting. I wrote him for an appointment.

Two weeks later, appointment slip in pocket and wearing city clothes that looked very strange to me, Ade walked away to hop a ride to town with the mailman. There he would stay overnight and take a bus to Duluth, stay over there, get to his appointment in the morning, take a bus back late in the afternoon, stay over again, and finally get home via the mailman and his feet. The glasses could be mailed. It would have been simpler in the days when he would have ridden a horse!

I had long before lost any feeling that accidents, storms, and other disturbances of the peace were more likely to happen when I was alone than when Ade was there. Even being awakened the first night he was away by a scuffling sound and seeing a bear at the window by my bed, paws above his head and nose against the glass, did not disturb me. I was only glad that the bear was small and not heavy enough to crash through the glass he leaned on. The log building was better protection against bears, perhaps, but I stayed in the summer house to keep an eye on the hens. They were perfectly content without the Prince, but there could be danger from the woods.

I determined to make the best of my days alone by completing my samples for the possible nature series for children, which could mean income we could count on, small but a definite amount. I was very much aware that the cost of Ade's trip, prolonged by our lack of a car, would almost deal the death blow to our funds.

The second afternoon was brightened by a visit from the man who had been so kind when Ade had been laid low by neuralgia. He had heard that Ade was in the hospital for an eye operation and thought I might need assistance. I explained, wondering as I always did at the flourishing exaggeration of the simplest event, and thanked him, not only for his offer but also for a bag of grapes that he brought. We had tea, and after he left I put a bunch of the grapes on the kitchen table for a late snack.

Before I settled to read by the light of my Victorian wall lamp with its silvered reflector, I went for my grapes and was puzzled to find strips of skin in a pile on the edge of the plate. I got another bunch for myself, left a lamp turned low in the kitchen, and sat in the darkened living room where I could watch for the arrival of the grape peeler. A mouse appeared, seemingly from nowhere. He nipped one grape from the stem, peeled it carefully, adding the strips to the pile on the plate, then ate all the flesh and departed with the seeds, presumably to be stored.

The next night I left out some grapes that were softening. The mouse arrived and went through his performance as before. Then he returned and discovered a pottery planter in the form of a burro drawing a cart. The cart was full of dirt, which the mouse found interesting. I moved nearer the door the better to see what he was doing, and he heard me. Instantly he snatched another grape in his mouth, put it in the cart, then jumped in and stood over it so that he seemed ready to drive home with his find. I stifled my sudden laughter and slipped away, not wanting to frighten him.

A little later I heard rattling from the kitchen and got up to see what was what. The mouse was standing on his hind legs beside a tallish soup bowl, in which I had had some cornmeal mush for dinner. There was some left and I had covered the bowl with a small plastic plate in case I might be hungry later. The mouse braced his front paws under the edge of the plate and began to push and release rhythmically. After many tries, he gave a mighty heave and the plate slid off; the mouse rushed into hiding for what must have been a most anxious moment. When nothing happened, he returned to flip over the edge into the bowl, and feast.

To protect the chickens' corn, we kept it in a garbage can with a lid, which fit loosely. I had once watched two squirrels, working in unison, push and release the lid as the mouse did the plate, until the lid slid off and they could pop into the great plain of corn below. I have had people who should know insist that both animals are rodents and that this is an action instinctive to rodents. They never cited another incident, however, nor even a related one. I find it much easier to believe that, faced with food to be had by solving a problem, these little fellows solved theirs as people often must, by trial, error, and effort.

Ade returned in time to watch· the kitchen mouse go through his routine, and a few days later he saw another mouse investigating the inside of the baby grand. This was much too lavish a home for even the most discriminating mouse, so after making sure no felt had been chewed and no nest started, I closed the piano. The next night we watched through a window from the porch when she came back, moving back and forth on the polished mahogany, stopping now and then with an air of saying to herself: "I just *know* there is a way in." She gave up at last, and it was well into August, on a night cool enough for us to sit in front of a small fire, before she appeared again. She climbed up a window curtain, then crept along the top of the sofa where I was sitting, getting closer and closer to my face. She stopped only fifteen inches away, and she and I sat very still, examining each other.

She was a pretty mouse with huge ears, cream-white feet and underparts, and a dark coat of reddish brown. Her tail was well-furred and the division between its light underside and dark top was sharp. She was nervous: her frail hands, pink through their thin covering of white hair, quivered, and her sparkling black eyes shifted constantly. Once she was satisfied that I was not going to stir, she turned away and went down the curtain and toward the side of the fireplace. Standing in the corner made by the wall and hearth was one of those TV antennas with a spiral from top to bottom that we had used in Chicago and brought along with us, although we had no use for it in our Minnesota fringe area. She climbed the antenna as if it were a spiral stair, hopped from its top to a small table, and vanished behind the inoperative TV set. She reappeared, carrying a bumblebee-size baby in her mouth. Carefully she negotiated her staircase, scampered across the hearth in front of Ade's feet, and went into the bedroom. She returned to move another gray-furred child, and another and another. As she was moving across the hearth with the fifth, Ade moved one of his feet. She stopped, watched his feet, looked up at his great bulk, waited a few seconds, moved forward an inch or two, watched again, and when she was safely past him, hurried away as before. She moved two more babies, and when she stopped in front of Ade to make sure her way was safe, we had wonderful views of tiny tails wagging feebly and bright dots of eyes that did not seem concerned or aware of what was going on. She made one more trip and stayed a long time, scattering bits of cotton and shreds of pink and green (from an old chair cushion and a discarded potholder) as she searched her nest in the TV set for any youngster she might have left behind. We do not often think of it, but animal mothers cannot count.

In spite of producing one litter almost on the adolescence of another, mouse mothers are very devoted and watch carefully over their children. Even so, one may crawl from the nest too soon and perish, although young mice can get along pretty well on their own. We once had one still wearing her gray baby fur come to the step at the kitchen door of the summer house for food, easily the youngest self-supporting mammal we had ever seen. She survived, too, because she still nibbled graham crackers there when she was dressed in her adult coat of light fawn color. Later she made a round winter nest of cotton (probably from the same old chair cushion that Little Brown Mouse had used) in a sheltered corner of the porch and buried it warmly in strips of cedar inner bark. Ade and I put corn and graham crackers inside the porch for her when we came during the winter to feed the red squirrels on the steps outside.

Occasionally we saw young jumping mice on the flagstones, hopping so briskly that at first we thought them young frogs of brownish color. One night Ade went to put out water for the hens and discovered a mother jumper with three young ones in the corn pan, so concentrating on eating that he came and went without disturbing them. Two of them may have been a pair who later came to grief through a mistaken location for a hibernating place. I found them years after their tragedy, two incredibly frail skeletons and fluffs of gossamer-fine brown hair, in nests made deep in a folded shag rug we had not taken from the summer house shelf since we unpacked it. Unfortunately, the cold had penetrated, turning their winter sleep into the permanent one.

The log house had its mouse quota, too, and it was in 1954 during our first summer there that crippled Mrs. Mouse had come into our lives, and we had found and restored to her the four pink babies she could not reach because of her disability. Her change from bedraggled misery to bright-eyed and well-groomed alertness was deeply moving, as was the care with which she reared her youngsters, as though she did not have a broken back and paralyzed hind legs. After their time with us, we pampered the cabin mice.

They rarely appeared during the day, and I left corn in a plate on the kitchen floor at night and tied a few short lengths of cotton rug yarn to the handles of the lower kitchen-cabinet drawers. The mice came, carried off these supplies, and had no need to run all over the house.

One evening when a pouring rain made it best for us not to get half-drowned returning to the summer house after work, we heard a crunching in a cupboard, supposedly mouse-proof. I looked and saw only a nibbled chocolate cookie, one of a package Ade had brought as a treat when he returned from Duluth. Before we retired, Ade opened the cupboard door, put a finger to his lips, and beckoned. On top of the cellophane package, curled up on his half-eaten cookie, the mouse was sound asleep, a forest portrait of any youngster dreaming of that Rock Candy Mountain.

Meadow voles lived near the log cabin, those small-eared, short-tailed, fat gray creatures often known as meadow mice. They nested in the grass under ferns by the cabin doorstep and later, when we grew peas in the garden, harvested stem lengths and pieces of pod. Luckily for us, we had eaten most of the peas before they found this food source. Their young, about three-quarters grown, did not imitate their parents' harvesting, but one of them discovered and ate a small pea I had dropped on the path. At once he climbed a vine, laboriously chewed open a pod, and loosened a pea, which fell to the ground. He tried vainly to carry it, pushed it a little way with his forepaws, and finally rolled it with his nose some twenty-five feet along the irregular surface of the path. From there he tugged his prize through the dense jungle of grass that hid his home nest.

We had boreal voles, too, much like the meadow mice, but brown. They looked larger than the others but were still very small, as I found out when I discovered a relatively large one dead. I took him inside to examine him and learned that he weighed a whole ounce.

They lived under the house, the woodshed, tree roots, and the heaps of stone we had piled up the year before when we cleared the garden plots. The first pair we saw came trotting out from their home under the stones to get corn. Sometimes the parents came with twins, all feeding together and the mother stopping often to nuzzle the little ones. During the winter they made snow tunnels to the feed, and in the spring we saw the young, peeping out of the tunnel entrances in late mid-May snow.

We had seen no weasels for two years, and missed their

lively antics. Perhaps the fishers who had hunted near the
cabin during our first forest winter, when our pet, Walter
Weasel, was with us, had frightened them away. Whatever
the reason, we needed them because mice were increasing and
there was such an upsurge of voles that it looked as though
serious damage to both our garden and the wild plants might
occur. But a fox came down the path one day, a saw-whet
owl appeared on a branch in the night, and a barred owl settled on a stump, to hunt when hungry, day or night not mat-
tering. We soon saw fewer mice, and the voles' numbers decreased sharply, most of them going to the fox, I should
say, his favorite food being voles and not, as some people
insist, game birds. There were enough mice and voles left to
survive the winter and start another crop in the spring. I was
glad. These little creatures were so timid and gentle, and
watching them was as interesting as watching any other animal. I wonder that so many people are afraid of them or feel
that they have no right to their small lives.

———— I had fallen into a pattern of making up the grocery
order early in August, then revising as circumstances indicated before I mailed it at the end of the month. This time,
although my list was austere, there seemed no way to pay for
it, and we always waited to buy until we could pay cash,
because we believed that running up bills when income is uncertain and sometimes almost nonexistent is unfair to the supplier and oneself. I looked at the quotation from Dickens's
Mr. Micawber, lettered by Ade in 1954 and still tacked to the
wall: "Something will turn up." This time it had better—
and in the next mail it did, in the form of an IRS refund we
had applied for so long before that we had both forgotten
about it. It was $547.90, almost twice what we had expected
and a small fortune to us. If my $600 a year average from

writing held up and Ade's fall notepaper business was good, we could eat better and relax a little during the winter.

A week later I opened an envelope and took out my returned story about the wolf at Christmas time, which I had held a year until I found what I thought was a suitable place for its submission. I was so disappointed that I almost let the accompanying letter go unread. Fortunately I did not, because it asked me to change the story a little, into the form of a fairy tale, and return it as soon as I could because the magazine wanted it for their forthcoming December issue. They also liked the nonfiction nature pieces I had sent, and would start the series next summer if I would write one on the weasel, which they thought would be unusual enough to make a good opener. Shouting with glee, I dashed out to read the letter to Ade, who was still working patiently—and probably uselessly—on the leaky roof.

It was hours before I even looked at the rest of the mail and found a letter from the Metal Treating Institute, to whom I had sent an article based on a metallurgical project I had done in Chicago. The editor of the institute's magazine was enthusiastic and enclosed a check several times larger than I had received for any previous piece of writing.

My crowing with delight was over, and I stared at the check and thought. If I could write and sell such diverse pieces as a fable for children and an article for heat treaters, something more than luck was operating. I had best dig in and make the most of it, whatever it was. I did celebrate mildly, though, by ordering a packsack for Ade to carry parcels from the mail—so much easier than shifting them from hand to hand as the string around a box cut into his fingers. And for myself, yards and yards of red denim, on sale at a mail-order house, to replace the old drapes, which were now shredding as a result of rough washing and exposure to dampness and sun.

————— The garden had produced erratic crops. The radishes went to leaves, enjoyed by the snowshoe hares. Ade saved the other plants from the hares, and the hares from being poisoned on rhubarb leaves, by improvising ramshackle fences from ends of chick wire, old window shutters and boards, anything he could find. The lettuce flourished and was promptly attacked by slugs. Awbutch's sister-in-law recommended saucers of stale beer. The slugs crawled in, drank themselves sottish, and died happier, I presume, than those eaten by toads.

The onions went to tops, but we found these flavorful and good. The chard did fairly well, and we left some plants to supply seed, which we could gather later. A few potatoes that Ade planted in a leftover spot produced a few potatoes, so small I boiled them whole and we ate them all in two meals. The salsify and carrots loved the forest soil and we could count on a good crop for winter.

The scarlet runners had produced large racemes of red flowers. And these brought hawk moths, like enormous bees, and ruby-throated hummingbirds, hovering and darting on wings that whipped so rapidly they were a blur in the sunlight. Later, these flowers gave way to fuzzy pods, very good when cooked, containing spotted beans with a mealy texture and delicious flavor.

The wild buckwheat vines crawled to the roof and hung down. When their clustered flowers gave way to green-covered, pyramidal black seeds, the chipmunks rushed to the harvest. They scurried up the stems and hung on with a hand and a foot while they waved the other hand out and out until it captured and pulled in one of the clusters. One reached too far and found himself hanging one-handed, in mid-air. He grabbed on with the other hand, and not until he had chewed off enough seeds to fill his cheek pouches did he look down, let go with one hand, then the other, and drop.

Along about this time I crossed "Clear brush and paths" from Ade's list. I had not done it in the spring because the paths were only started, but I could see by fall that they were going to grow more flowers than their edges and so would not be finished. And since almost everything growing here was new to us, and interesting, or produced berries or flowers, or provided cover for our small neighbors, by the time we could get around to considering what brush might be removed, the small growth would be large, there would be a new growth of small plants, and we would be too used to it to remove any of it.

———— The business mailer and the grocery order had gone out together after Labor Day. Consequently we dug the carrots in spurts between filling notepaper orders and storing groceries, the potato sack blocked up on boards this time to prevent freezing. The carrots were big, sweet, well formed, and so numerous that we wondered what to do with them. Then Ade recalled that he had knocked down some apple boxes, the old-fashioned kind made of wood, and moved them from his workroom in Chicago. He nailed some of these together, got sand from a pile left by John Anderson when he repaired the foundation, and we packed the carrots in dampened sand. We had stored more than a bushel, and were hoping we would not run out of boxes before we harvested the remaining carrots and the salsify, when we had a rain followed by an unexpected hard freeze. Ade tried the spade, then a pickax, on the frozen ground but could not even break the surface. Well, we had more carrots than we could eat, anyway.

Ade hurried to clean the chicken house and get the lantern-heater ready with fresh wick and water-free oil so that he could transfer the suppliers of our precious eggs before a deep cold snap might freeze their combs and wattles.

Until November our time was devoured by the details of the business, which had been so good in the first weeks of the fall season that we had ordered enameled covering for the floors in time to catch the last freight delivery. Having no place to put the big rolls but on the living room floor, we were still hopping back and forth over them, hoping that soon we might both be free at the same time to lay the foot-trapping stuff.

Every day, regardless of the changeable weather of fall, I took a walk and looked and watched and sorted impressions which I would some day use in my work. One day I stopped to listen to the distant whine of chain saws. As far as I knew, we were the only people still on the shore. When I came in and mentioned it to Ade, he shook his head.

"What do we get the newspaper for? They're cutting the right-of-way for the power line."

"Where?"

"Along the Trail and up this road." I thought of how our little road would look with one side cleared and lined with poles, and must have shown something of my dismay because Ade said, "Not along the road. A quarter-mile south of it, I think. The thing is, do we want power?"

"I'm so used to doing without that I don't much care. It'd be a tight squeeze, even with what we'd save on fuel we use for light now. But we've a little more cash coming in."

"I think we can afford it, but I'm not sure whether it'd be worth it."

"Let's wait and find out what they'd want to do to run it in, in case—and I do mean 'in case.' "

A week later we sat with a representative of the power company, who looked curiously at our rolls of floor cover-

ing while I was reading the easement we would have to sign
if we took the power. ". . . and to cut down from time to
time all dead, weak, leaning, or dangerous trees that are tall
enough to strike the wires in falling . . ."

"How do you determine 'dangerous trees'?" I asked.

"Any tree that's within its own height of the line," the
man said casually. "Could start a fire if one fell on the line."

I knew this, and I also knew that many of our trees in
the area where they would have *carte blanche* to cut were
more than a hundred feet tall. Signing this would mean that
they could, if they chose, clear all the virgin timber on a
swath two hundred feet wide, which would be a third of
our property. I gave Ade the paper and pointed out the
line.

He read it, smiled slightly, and said, "We don't want it."

The man stared and then began to talk—and talk. "Everyone but you will have it," he said, and I was mildly shocked
to realize that we were being classed as nonconformists. And
I had thought we left conformity in Chicago! "Of course,
there may be a few people too poor to take the power . . ."
We both let this ride. "And think of the thousands of dollars
it will add to your property value."

I picked that one up with, "Have you ever thought there
are some things more valuable than money?"

He deprecated this. "That's an old-fashioned idea. I don't
mean the affection of your husband, or anything like that."

"Kind of you to make the exception," Ade murmured as I
looked out of the window at the great pines and the young
maples deer might browse on in passing, our bit of land untouched within the memory of man—and knew that we were
happier as we were.

A sudden gust of wind shook the house, and the light
faded as though louvers were being closed in the sky. I turned
to Ade, whose eyes were also on the forest.

"We don't want it, do we?"

Still looking outside, he said, "No. Sorry you've had your trip for nothing, but we'll live without commercial power." It was now almost dark, and snow rattled against the window-panes. "Something big's coming out of the northwest. If you don't want to be stranded, you'd better get on the road quick."

If the power salesman thought he was being ordered out, he changed his mind before he had driven the three miles to the Trail.

The snow came slanting on a high wind, so thick that the west wall of the cabin soon would have been drifted eave-high if we had followed the local custom of cutting brush and trees near a house in the woods "for ventilation." When storms like the current one came, we reaped our reward, be-cause many trees together not only brace each other but pro-vide a windbreak and snow fence for humans as a side effect.

It was not very cold, and the wind died quickly. The big, damp flakes clung to the balsam needles and twigs until the trees bore many white-gloved fingers, which blended into mittens, and finally became part of the mantle that covered each branch. They packed into the thickly needled tops of the spruces until they lifted above the shorter trees like huge, misplaced, white beehives. They balled on the needle sprays of the white pines, piled up on their shelf-like branches, grew heavier and heavier until the silence was broken by a slow cracking and a sudden snap, as one more branch tore away from the tall trunk. In the morning the chain saws were stilled and the land was white and soft and very clean.

Then the jays came, and the chickadees, and the nuthatches and the squirrels—and Ade and I swept and shoveled to un-cover their buried feed while snow thumped down from the branches and now and then a tree fell under its burden with a long, tired, splintering sound. Already steam rose in sunny spots and the snow was packing and settling. We withheld extra feed because it might be urgently needed later if a sudden freeze after this slight thaw should lock in the food on the ground. The winter had come, and we, along with the hens and the guests at our canteen and all the rest of the forest, began to adjust to its whims.

We had ceased to wonder how long it would be before the snowplow came. We were not concerned that visitors were as rare in the clearing as moose. We did not mind when old acquaintances lost interest and stopped writing, because the mail was bringing new friends like Winnie Hopkins, whom I "met" in connection with a notepaper order and whose letters are as entertaining and inspiring to me now as they were then. Her old-fashioned Christmas in a carton, with fun gifts and home-made delicacies, pressed flowers and greens from her yard, brought the warmth of home and people to our set-apart cabin in the snow. Once her fun gift was a back-scratcher, almost hidden by a big plastic rose and its leaves. A squirrel slipped in when the door was open and found it on the sofa. She looked at the flower, patted it, sniffed it, and altogether seemed completely charmed. With such contacts —I include the squirrel—personal isolation was an empty term.

And we had done without news for so long it now meant little to us. Anyway, the mailman passed on items of importance. Not learning of disasters about which we could do nothing and that we might never have heard of, even in a city, in days of less far-reaching communications, left our minds free to plan our work, and to think our way to a better understanding of both earth and man.

——— The snow's cutting us off from the mail gave us an opportunity to lay the floor covering. It went directly on the floor without padding, so getting it down should have been a simple matter. However, the room width proved to be a few inches less than that of the roll, and none of the room's corners was a right angle. Also, some of the floor boards had cupped upward and had to be planed down.so that the covering would not break or wear off quickly at the high points. We piled the living room furniture side-wall high in the workroom, where there was not enough floor space to set the pieces singly, slept on the floor for two nights, and had the room livable after three long days of hard labor.

In December a check came from my aunt for our Christmas dinner, and we hastily sent an invitation to Jacques. I wrote an order for a feast with all the trimmings and mailed it to the grocer who had sent the ground beef along with the lemons in the spring. I said that if they would send the bill with the groceries, Ade would take a check when he went to meet the mailman and would fill it in so that it could go back to town with the mail.

Next Saturday he dragged the big carton back on the toboggan and said he couldn't find the bill. It was there, on the bottom, along with more suet and a scribbled "Merry Christmas" attached to a bag of old-fashioned hard candies. It took both of us back through the long years to times when the grocer always had a licorice whip or a chocolate cream for a youngster who came to get the groceries for mother. And we knew we had found, in the wilderness of modern times, people who still had understanding and a reasonable trust in their fellow men.

Jacques came and the feast was a success, from the turkey to the chocolate-coconut pie, and, while Ade and Jacques leaned back and looked as stuffed as the turkey had been, I went to the window and gazed across what had been a garden plot into the forest and up at the great white pine at our clearing's edge.

And a deer stepped out of the forest.

He headed straight for the Swiss-chard seed stalks that still protruded above the snow and began to eat. He did not seem aware of the house. His coat was ruffled and he was so thin that every rib stood out and I could see the bones of his flanks. His legs trembled as he stood and his head shook as he pulled the stalks loose. When I beckoned and Ade and Jacques came to stand, one on each side of me, the buck looked up at us. His face was gaunt and his fur pitted. His right ear was raggedly notched and his eyes were dull. The left one was bluish, half-closed—blind. He jerked as though to run away, then dropped his head again to the seeds.

Jacques named him Peter Whitetail and told us how to feed him, and that night we saw him come stumbling down the path over rose-quartz snow under a red aurora, to bury his nose in the cedar Ade had cut fresh for him. And later when I went out to get wood for a helper fire we would need in the airtight because of the bitter cold, I saw him curled to sleep in the snow under the cedar tree, in the place that was to be his own for the rest of his life—and beyond, as long as Ade and I may be alive and remembering.

In the morning he staggered through a savagely cold wind to our doorstep and ate most of what would have been our next meal from the Christmas-dinner leftovers. Then he begged for more, with head bobbing and hoof tapping on the step, and I gave him ground carrots that he liked so well they brought a twitch to his ears and a sparkle to his eye.

From that day we felt that his coming was part of some plan we could not yet know. It was an oversight that we had not gathered the Swiss-chard seeds that attracted him. It was fortuitous that our soil had produced a bumper crop of carrots. It seemed that he might have been guided to us, in all that unpeopled land, and so we felt that our most important task was to see him strong and sleek as he once had been.

Our own hardships were as nothing beside his, so we did not notice the difference when I took the cornmeal from the morning pancakes and cut the oatmeal portions in half so that Peter might have the cereals. It was enough to see him shaking less and holding his head higher day by day. When the oil man, who had learned about Peter from Jacques, arrived in January to refill our tank, he brought two sacks of cracked corn and one of scratch feed, "for the chickens," as he thought we would not want the word about our buck passed around for his safety. And Peter's bones became less prominent and he began to bound into the brush when he heard cars on the road, instead of walking as fast as his weak legs would carry him.

We laughed at the tales that had contributed to our isolation because seclusion was important to our job of saving Peter, and to his gaining confidence again. We did not talk about it, but we both felt that the sincerity of our feeling for the forest was being tested.

Except for helping Peter to learn to look to the left with his good right eye, we did nothing to train him. Instead, we let him show us what *he* wanted, and where and when and how. And so we learned truly to live *with* the forest, not just in it; to understand the animals instead of trying to make them understand us; to leave them wholly free and independent in the use of their all-important protective instincts; to be accepted by them as harmless suppliers of food, not as intruders from the world of men who expected them to pay for their suppers with undignified tricks.

When the snow melted enough to show patches of bare ground, Peter began to roam, looking for his own new green. And when he left with another buck on an April morning, he was fat and strong and handsome, and we did not expect to see him again. We did not know that his coming had been one of the most important events in our lives. We felt only a deep thankfulness for having had him as our teacher and for being able to bring him back from the edge of death— and some regret at losing a good companion.

cut wood
install wiring
clear brush and paths
clear trash
running water
make a living

1959

——— Although the winter's snow was almost gone when Peter left, the spring was late. There were waves of cold from the Arctic, which brought more snow instead of the expected rain and which prevented our getting at the outside work. I felt restless, so I invested two dollars by mail in a paperback volume of H. Rider Haggard, containing *She, King Solomon's Mines,* and *Allan Quatermain.* These great imaginative tales were fantasy on the verge of the possible when they were written in the late nineteenth century, and they still have that quality. The stories roll out like richly patterned carpets, and in no time my fidgets were gone. No amount of fact and opinion on how to build a good life—in the woods or elsewhere—could have left me as ready to slay any dragons that came my way.

I had paid little attention to the crunching and grinding of the lake ice, so it was almost a surprise when the still thick sheet heaved and buckled and rumbled and went out with a roar one afternoon. While the loons and gulls voiced their ancient calls above the freed blue water, the thick slabs of

ice piled like a wall on the shore and began to melt by day
and by night. From plaited leaves that had been green under
the snow, the buds of calypsos were showing, and soon their
yellow-touched, tiger-striped cups and lavender crowns
would be bright against the duff. I saw a bat darting through
evening air speckled with insects. And somewhere the black
bears were yawning and stepping from their dens to loll in
the sun and give new cubs a first look at the edge of their
world.

In May we received notice of a proposal to build a road
from the middle of the Trail to the east end of our lake,
where only a narrow flow of water separates the United
States from Canada. The ostensible reason was to open certain lakes to fishing, but since their waters were largely
Canadian, using them would require an extra fishing license.
Besides, there was already a rough road through the American
forest that could be improved and extended a short way to
these lakes. Something lay behind the obvious, and many
speculations were made to no purpose. It was clear, though,
that such a road would route traffic through American wild
land already accessible, and that a Canadian road that ended
not far from the border would be extended to meet the pro-
posed road at some future date. This would mean customs
stations, which would destroy the wild character and as yet
untouched beauty of parts of our lake's east end. Also, lake
property owners could, whenever the east wind blew, enjoy
the floating beer cans and other trash donated by the heavy
flow of tourists through the check point.

A wave of outrage swept along our shore. A local newspaper column called for expressions of opinion from summer
home owners and visitors to the area and received many re-
plies, all against the road. I worked on petitions. Ade drew
and mimeographed a detailed map for circulation. Letters
were written to lawyers, senators, the governor, the state

highway commissioner, and anyone else who might be concerned with the preservation of the wilderness. An exchange
of pro and con letters to the local paper became personal,
and passed the stage of polite invective to approach the libel-
ous. At that point the editor wisely—and to the disappoint-
ment of certain fascinated readers, including us—cut them
off, saying that both sides of the question had been adequately
covered. By the end of July everything had been done that
could be done and only pops and bangs of indignation remained. Then the Highway Commission informed us that no
funds had been appropriated for the road in their 1959 budget, nor in the corresponding federal budget. We could
breathe naturally again, but we had had a warning of things
that might come.

———— In spite of the hubbub we started our gardening
early by watching the movements of the shadows cast by the
big trees. In this way we located two more plots that were
not waterlogged and had several hours of direct sun daily.
We worked two hours a day at the stone-removing job and
had the new beds ready before the weather warmed.

When the snow was melting off the previously planted
beds we saw green shoots—carrots. Ade dug as soon as the
ground thawed and found those we had not been able to get
the previous fall in perfect condition. The salsify had also
survived the winter, but the roots were much shrunken. We
left the plants and were rewarded with a tall green row,
topped by purple flowers like huge daisies, that opened and
closed as the sun came and went.

When we bought our seeds, we included some ActivO, a
biological composting material, and worked it, and some
chicken manure and dead leaves and moss, into the garden soil
as soon as we had it clear. Our garden tools, by the way, con-

sisted of a bent shovel, a nicked hoe, and a partly tineless rake, the corroded heads mounted on little poles cut from the trunks of dead cedar saplings. They had been passed on to us by a very old and kind man, who had been caretaker for the Larimers until his health failed, and who must have used the tools for thirty years.

By the time it was warm enough to plant, the mixture of clay and sand that lies under the thin topsoil of the forest had darkened considerably from our treatment, and there was no danger of burning the roots with the manure. The rows of sprouts showed green about a week before the weeds, which came up everywhere and would have made a miniature jungle if I had not weeded—and weeded and weeded. I did find starts of columbine, wild geranium, and black-eyed susan, which I transplanted and which still greet us with flowers every year. We finally discouraged the weeds a little by mulching with cedar leaves and pine spills.

The weather was warm with light showers, good for both the garden and the budworms, who denuded the spruce and balsam trees and went through their life cycle even more quickly than the previous summer. The infestation was spreading, too, and the hills across the lake showed the same depressing and ominous brown as did our shore. Then heavy rains came, rumored disastrous to budworms, but too late because the moths' eggs were already laid.

The continual drenching brought us a problem, in that it arrived when the zucchini blooms were ready for fertilization, and washed the needed flying insects into the ground. I had to go from male bloom to female bloom, transferring pollen with one of Ade's camel-hair brushes. Then I spotted cutworms in the cabbage, the kind that eat leaves instead of cutting off plants, but still ruinous. I crawled around gathering a handful of the fat, gray worms. When I creaked upright two whiskey jacks dived out of the trees to grab as many worms as they could cram into their beaks. From then on, there was nearly always at least one of them standing on a stone at the edge of the bed, holding some worms in his beak and eyeing the plants for more.

Ade smelled of green onions until a young deer came into the yard and ate those that remained. Two weeks later the onion space was green with wild shoots, and long after the surrounding plants were brown and dry, we ate dandelion and plantain leaves. Even after the first snow these hardy plants were green, and ruffed grouse came to nip off the out-of-season leaves.

There was also Gregory.

One morning I noticed that the pea vines were disappearing, and Ade pointed out some blue-pod pole beans stripped of their leaves to a height of four feet. Both plantings were inside the fence. Chipmunks could get through the openings and climb, but they would not eat leaves. As we wrinkled our brows, a rounded hump of fur sat up outside the fence and contemplated us with the gravest suspicion. A groundhog—and he had come unerringly to the only garden within miles!

Just before sunset I saw carrot tops waving where no breeze blew. As we approached, Gregory sat up in the carrots, chewing his last-plucked mouthful, and studied us with the calculating squint of a bettor figuring track odds. Deciding they were not in his favor, he tried to dive through the wire mesh.

He stuck at the hips. He clawed frantically as he tried to pull himself through, while his fat rump waved and his stubby black paddle of a tail almost twitched off. At last he attacked the wire with his teeth. I am convinced he thought he had cut it, because at once he gave a complicated wriggle and was through, lying flat and panting while he kept a bright and wary eye on us. Slowly, as though he hoped we might not notice, he crawled an inch, another inch—then bolted into the ferny ditch at a lumbering gallop.

We considered Gregory's discerning taste, huge appetite, and compressibility in relation to our garden. The peas were through bearing. If the carrots were as rugged as those we had planted the year before, they would survive a lot of leaf-nibbling. The blue-pod beans were ready to eat and could be picked and stored for a short time, but the Kentucky wonders needed protection. Ade decided to use old window screening, with posts inside, where Gregory could not get his arms around them to climb, and to make the bottom ground-hog-proof by edging inside and out with heavy stones. It worked, Gregory not learning that he could dig underneath.

When he discovered corn, he spent much time relaxing outside the door, lying down to eat brunch and dinner. He was young and almost full-grown. His coat was thick, glossy, and well groomed; only a light frosting broke the sleek black of his melanistic head and back fur. His vest and sleeve-guards were a strong rust-red, and contrasted sharply and effectively with his dark back and black-satin gloves. His bright, black eyes and bushy, frosted side-whiskers gave him a jolly, Dick-ensian pomposity. The birds ignored him. The red squirrels moved in to retake the corn pile, but retreated when he lifted his head. The chipmunks stared at him with dumbfounded eyes, hopped near in little jerks, almost touched him, and leaped away. He considered them too small to merit his at-tention.

He selected wild greens within a hundred-foot radius of the cabin. He climbed the fence awkwardly to finish the pea vines. He shinnied up the posts to reach the damaged bean plants that we had not bothered to protect, and clung pre-cariously with hind feet and one arm, while he waved the other until he captured a distant leaf—a caricature of a chip-munk harvesting the false buckwheat seeds. He eyed the

Kentucky wonders longingly from outside their new fence. Seeming to think the carrot bed too dangerous for daylight feeding any more, he demolished the leaves in midnight snacks. He waited until my violas had a nice crop of blooms before he ate them. He found graham crackers on the step, held them daintily to his mouth between the fingers and stub thumb of one hand, then gobbled so fast that crumbs dribbled down his vest.

He grew fatter and fatter. In early September he tried to climb a post after a last bean leaf, but gave up and slid breathlessly to the ground. His belly dragged as he spraddled to the corn pile, and he lay down every few feet to rest on the return journey to his burrow. He settled to sleep on September eleventh, when the days were still warm, maybe because he was so fat that he could no longer pull himself to the food—or maybe because he had reached a stage of fatness that triggered the need to hibernate.

———— Then Jacques came whistling down the hill with the good news that he was going to spend the winter within walking distance. The cutting of timber for the power line had left many good logs lying where they fell on the ridge south of the cabin, and he was going to set up a permanent camp and salvage the wood, such waste being abhorrent to him, because he knew from experience how much of this country's timber had been burned to clear land or left to rot where it was felled. He said he was camping temporarily at his future location and was going to town the next day, and would we like to go along? We accepted with enthusiasm.

After Jacques left I made a list of perishable groceries, then turned to the wholesale catalog. In spite of the distractions, we had kept our profitable work going and there were gratifying signs that we might end the year in the black for the first time since our move. This meant more and better winter staples, and I could make the storing less of a task if I ordered the canned vegetables now and got the rest later. I ended up with ten cases, a can a day from the end of September through May.

Next afternoon Jacques dropped us at the post office and went off to buy supplies for his winter camp. Glancing through the mail, we walked up a steep street past neatly gardened houses to the grocery from which our Christmas dinner had come.

It was a fine supermarket, grown from a small store bought twenty-seven years earlier by a gentleman who had come as a boy to this country from Norway, in the 1890s. We met him that day, white-haired, soft-voiced, nearing eighty years, but still almost as active in the store as his three amiable blond sons. They had bought the store in 1947, when, as one of the brothers told us, "Dad said he thought he'd retire." Meeting them all was a rich experience, especially for city-bred Ade, who had not previously encountered their kind of small-town hospitality. We were treated as friends because they had known about us for some time and had seen Ade in town before. Then one of the clerks wondered why she had never seen me, and I was surprised until I realized that this was only my second trip out of the woods in five years! I had been too busy to think about the passing of time.

We asked if we could order perishables in suitable weather and pay by return mail. That we could rarely afford the postage earlier we kept to ourselves, but I doubt that we fooled anyone. They were agreeable, and we sealed the bargain over coffee and rolls in the back room.

Then we walked to the harbor and sat on a dock by Lake Superior, watching hundreds of gulls, gray-and-white adults and brown young, floating on the blue moiré water and soaring against the fading blue of the late-afternoon sky, slipping on tilted wings, crying softly as they circled above a fish house, waiting, as did a patient brown tomcat, for their portion of the day's catch.

This reminded us of food, so we went to the bus station, where Jacques was to pick us up and which had an excellent lunch counter. We had eaten there on our first trip to the Village and the proprietor and his wife were as good friends as Hilda and Sven had been. We were still catching up on our doings and theirs when Jacques came for us.

———— We had planned a lot of outdoor work for the remaining days of August, but teeming rains came, and the few clear days were enlivened by blasting on the road, which tossed pieces of broken rock into the clearing at odd moments and jarred the cabin. We grew pretty tired of grabbing lamps and dodging missiles near the door, especially since inquiries brought us no satisfactory reason for the heavy charges. This was over in a week, but the rains kept on until Ade's gauge had measured ten inches. The wild growth was lush and very green; the few leaves that had yellowed early fell; fungi sprang up in quantity and variety I have not seen since.

There were mushrooms with white concave tops large enough to hold a quart of water, others with smaller but still large caps—pale green and deep violet, bright orange and dark red, white and gray and brown and almost black. Brackets, fluted and delicate, smooth and hard, sprang from logs and dying trees. Under the pines were ranks of short, slender, dull-yellow clubs, and lifting from the duff were fragile red and yellow and white parasols, spreading no wider than a thimble. The earth was dotted with small white puffballs, and clusters of honey mushrooms grew from the cedar roots. Both of these were edible and unmistakable, and consequently were greatly enjoyed by the Hoovers.

Near the end of the month, when the cedar flowers had turned from green to yellow and the squirrels were cutting them down and eating the young seeds, various people came to see us about getting a telephone when Northwestern Bell ran their lines in with the power. The idea seemed to be that we would surely want a phone and that would mean taking power also, because the power poles would carry the phone lines. We knew by this time that explanations about our trees would be met either with lectures or blank stares, so I said that neither power nor phone was any novelty to us, since we had lived with them most of our lives—and so we would continue to live without. This probably sounded flippant, but was easier than bringing up the idea of conservation, which was still an extremist's dream to many in those days.

We knew even then that conservation is not just something you talk about, but something you do. The idea came indirectly from a friend of twenty years' standing who lives in Cincinnati. Off and on we had kidded each other about being born integrated, and once he said, in his softly blurred Southern voice, "You don't talk about integration. You just do it." I hang onto that thought whenever I hear long and often inconclusive comments on either of these very important matters.

I mailed my final grocery order on the day when Mr. and Mrs. Conrad, who had built a new lodge to the east of us, came to call for the first time. They were also from Chicago, and thought we might like them to bring us something when they returned in the spring. I thought of *yellow* margarine. Colored margarine could not be sold in Minnesota, and even the white was heavily taxed, so that we bought the cheapest brand, which not only contained no coloring for me to add but came in pound blocks, so that it looked like lard. Oscar said he would be glad to pick it up for us, and Martha looked at the folded red denim, which was waiting on the table in case I could get at it. She askéd how I was going to make it up and I said by hand. And—miracles do happen—she said she had a treadle sewing machine, if I would like to use it for the winter? With visions of curtains, patching, sheets, and such going through my head, I accepted.

On their way out, just after Labor Day, they brought the machine, an end-of-the-century model, its cabinet elaborately inlaid with different woods, and the machine itself having bright-colored floral designs with gold trim baked into its black enamel. It would even be a pleasure to look at it. As we watched them walk up the path, she tiny and fair, he tall and graying, I decided that, although they looked very different from Hilda and Sven, they were closely related in other ways.

With the abrupt stoppage of summer activities, I remembered the order for canned goods I had mailed weeks before in town. Had it been lost, or what? I was writing an inquiry when the freight truck arrived.

When I asked what had happened the driver said, "Poor business. So much of the road is good now, a lot of people think it's cheaper to drive their own truck. Considering the initial cost and the wear and tear and loss of time, I don't get it, but the way things are going we can't promise regular delivery any more. Just come up when we have a full load. This is our last run this year."

Horrified, I explained about our big order, still to come from Duluth, and ended, "We can't live without food. What'll we do?"

He thought it over, then said: "Henry is my father-in-law."

I said "What?" and Ade said "Who?" and the driver said

"He drives the oil truck. I'll tell 'em in the office to have the truck from Duluth leave your stuff at the gas station. Then when Henry comes up to fill your tank, he can bring the groceries."

———— The weather was perfect, and Ade went to work on the trash heaps. There were several of these, the worst of them the former owner's dump, filled with old clothes, bottles, cans, and assorted junk that Ade got in order to haul— on some distant day—to the public dump maintained by the forest service. He salvaged an undamaged three-pound can of coffee, which came in handy because we ran out while waiting for our groceries. Things happen to coffee that has been frozen and thawed for a few years, but the brew was brown and hot even though it tasted like stewed wood chips.

Ade was late with the notepaper mailers, and before I began to address them as they were ready, I crossed "Clear trash" from the list in the desk drawer and added "5" for the years passed. Getting anything done except keep alive and earn the means to do so seemed a very slow process indeed.

The extra outside work and the rush to get the mailers out on time put too much pressure on Ade, and the neuralgia struck again. It was not so bad this time, but the oil truck and the groceries arrived before the pain had subsided.

Henry carried the hundred-pound sack of potatoes down the hill to the house, but had no time to help with the rest of the 1,174-pound shipment because he was running late. I got the home-built wheelbarrow, which came with the cabin and is so heavy it feels loaded when you push it empty on the flat, and began the job of bringing in the food. Ice on the path was no help in braking the loads on the steep hill, either. It took me half the day and more energy than I thought I had, and when it was done I pushed everything into a heap in the middle of the kitchen and left it there until I was limber enough to move without suppressing moans.

Jacques dropped in the next day and scolded me politely for not coming up to his camp and getting him to move the groceries.

"It would have made more sense," I said, "but we've been alone so much I didn't think of it."

Ade was fine when it was time to harvest winter vegetables. The garden, helped by the plentiful rain, had repaid all our efforts. We had eaten tender rhubarb very early and fresh peas almost as soon as lettuce. The Kentucky wonder beans had climbed fifteen feet into the trees, and we gathered, off and on, thirty-five pounds of them. The matured pods were a foot long and sixteen to the pound, yet tender when cooked. We had pulled small carrots all summer and still had a bushel of big ones for winter, and our zucchinis weighed in at from two to eight pounds.

We had just finished tucking away the carrots when the mail brought me the announcement that I had won a national metallurgical award with the technical article I had sold the year before. The writer said that the plaque would be presented at the annual dinner of the American Society for Metals in Chicago, and that he hoped I would attend. A sizable check was enclosed.

It would be fun to go, I thought—to meet old friends, to talk shop again. Then I admitted to myself that this desire for travel was based mainly on less altruistic reasons.

There are always some in business who suffer from professional jealousy, and this was aggravated in my case because I had solved a fifty-year-old problem that had been pronounced unsolvable by some of my immediate supervisors, as well as many others in the industry. Then, too, I was a woman in a man's field and had much less experience than many of my male co-workers, and women working in the metallurgy of steel were very few. This was understandable because the shop part of the work was hard, rough, often very dirty, and sometimes required considerable strength. However, because my close business associates, many of whom were good friends, were all men, I grew used to masculine company and would have felt perfectly at home at technical meetings where I was alone among two or three hundred men, except that one man resented my presence loudly because he felt it put a damper on the kind of dirty story he might tell from the speaker's platform. It would be a great satisfaction to my less noble feelings to sit on that platform and receive the award while my critics watched from the crowd below.

I looked at the check, then at Ade's frayed shirts and my pants, past mending and so full of holes I should have risked arrest for indecent exposure had I worn them to town without a long coat, and mailed an order for clothes. And when Jacques went to town later, he picked up not only our groceries but hand lotion for me and after-shave for Ade. We went around sniffing delightedly for some days. All this was much more satisfying than figuratively thumbing my nose at a few people I would never meet again.

———— It was late on the night of December first. I was writing at the kitchen table, but stopped short, chilled by the sound of a knock at the door. An accident? Someone lost? I pulled aside the curtain and looked through the glass panel —straight into Peter Whitetail's face.

He did not move when I opened the door but stood, his antlers almost as wide as the doorway, tapping on the step with his hoof, bobbing his head as he asked for supper. Everything was brighter because he was with us again, and his coming was the beginning of a time of wonder and purity, as near the Garden lost to man as is possible in these later days.

A time when deer lived naturally in our clearing and paid us little more heed than they gave to others of their kind.

That winter we saw only four people. First, a poacher, the only intrusion of ugliness, who slipped down the path on the afternoon of Christmas Eve when Ade was gone for mail. He threatened me with a rifle, and if I had not had a gun of my own, would have shot Peter while I stood helplessly by. Next, George and Esther Barnes, long-time friends from fifteen miles away, who arrived with one of Esther's wonderful cakes for us, a sack of corn for Peter, of whom they had learned from Jacques, and a cabinful of good cheer. And Jacques, who dropped in on the rare occasions when he left his work to go to town for supplies.

But Peter was a good companion, and when Mama came, he, in some way of his own, taught her that we were safe for her and for her twin half-year-old bucks, whom we later named Pig, for his appetite, and Brother, for his gentleness. If I had not finished my work at the sewing machine earlier, I would have let it go, because this was the time when we watched Peter and Mama training the fawns: teaching them good deer manners, and the things they must know and do if they were to survive in their dangerous world; disciplining them immediately and firmly if they disobeyed or forgot. A deer rarely has a second chance if he makes a mistake.

So that there would be enough of the cedar they enjoyed so much, Ade walked miles every other day, cutting high branches from well-separated big trees, so that he would not harm any single tree or grove, bringing the stripped leaves home in a carton so that he could carry enough. I did not go out when the deer were near unless it was necessary, because I did not want them to get too used to any human, even me. Once I broke my own rule and walked almost within touching distance of Pig. Mama first came at me, blowing and ready to rear and strike. After I fled, she turned to whack

Pig's rump. Evidently she agreed with me on the dangers of too close association between deer and humans.

If it seems that I am not saying all I should about these very special animal friends and the days they were with us, it is because I have already told their story in *The Gift of the Deer*. Here they must pass through the days as only one of the marvels that the forest spread around our little log cabin as generously as it spread its snow.

Near the end of the winter a storm passed at sunset time, and I went down the marble-white of our path, regretting that my feet should mar its flawlessness, and walked out on the lake ice. The hills of the opposite shore were black and white against an opal sky. Between the hills and me, as far as I could see to right and left, the snow lay in small waves, rounded and rippled by the wind into a likeness of shifted sand, touched with a color that was not quite blue or rose or violet or gray. Mauve comes nearest, if a color that is ever-changing with the light can have a name. The hills near the setting sun briefly seemed to be covered with pink frosting, and the opposite end of the lake faded away in a violet mist that might have been hiding the very gates of eternity. Then the sun was gone and dull red overpowered the softer shades in the sky as night began to fall.

For a while I did not think at all, just took in the clean scent of the snow, caught a faint wisp of something acrid and animal, probably a fox who was passing nearby and watching me. There was no sound. Nothing moved but light, and that slowly in this expanse of earth without man. I saw myself as a sojourner, not only in the forest but against the vast stretches of time. I would have this view to remember, but only for a little while, even by my own standard, which was man's; for a moment so short by the standard of creation that I could not grasp it. And I thought that this was good, for I was too small, too weak, too full of human faults, to be worthy of a longer stay. I felt humble and content and some-how cleansed when I turned away from the growing dark to the yellow-lighted cabin windows.

———— When spring was near and the warming winds stirred the trees and set their turquoise shadows moving on the snow, Mama was growing heavy with her fawns to come. She was at the corn one day when a snowshoe hare, almost invisible in his whiteness against the greater white, startled her and she bolted into one of the garden fences, pulling down posts and falling in a general entanglement. She was not hurt, but Ade yanked out what remained of the chicken-wire fence and rolled it up to prevent further mishaps. I remem-bered the demise of the other part of it in the fall when a bull moose in rut had tangled his antlers in the wire and bellowed and twisted until he yanked the posts from the ground and shook his head free. I can do without annoyed bulls around the cabin. Even when in good humor and at a time of the year when they are less irritable, their size makes them formidable.

As the snow settled and melted, the deer browsed sepa-rately more and more, and when the ground was bare, Peter went away to his special summering place. Mama and the twins stayed on while the pussies opened on the willows and the ice rotted and the hurrying showers of wet spring snow gave way to rain. Then there were the tracks of only one deer, and finally the corn we put out for Mama was un-touched. She had gone to the place where her fawns would be born.

cut wood
install wiring
clear brush and paths
clear trash
running water
make a living

———— I crawled out of bed and into pants and shirt, socks and moccasins, and flipped the top sheet on my desk calendar. "May Day," it said, in fancy type encircled by curlicues and spring flowers. I pulled the red denim curtain that kept the rays of dawn from waking me and looked out—at a foot of new snow. Spring flowers, indeed! The nearest thing to spring flowers were my begonias, so weakened by the long, dim-lighted winter that their stems drooped to the window sill and the few remaining leaves clung feebly to the stem tips.

I touched a match to the fire Ade had laid in the cookstove before we went to bed, put on the coffeepot as the wood began to pop and purr, and looked in the bread box. Apparently Ade, now stirring around in the other room, had been hungry during the night because the last of the cinnamon rolls I had baked two days before was gone. As I reached for a loaf of bread, the cabin shook under a blast of wind and the downdraft forced smoke out of every possible crevice in the stove. I flung the door open and finished my coughing and sneezing outside.

Then I saw that water was running off the roof and splashing in brand-new puddles. The sun was warm, the thermometer read fifty degrees—above, not below. The snow was
only a farewell gift of water from the winter, and the spring
that had been creeping nearer and nearer was really here.

I brushed snow off a stump and set the gasping begonias out
for a sun treatment. When I went back in, Ade was putting
bacon into a skillet. I reached again into the breadbox and
touched a lively piece of fur. Mrs. Crackers, a matronly red
squirrel, had slipped through the open door and was trying to
consume a loaf of bread before she might be evicted. I
poked, and she ricocheted off my stomach onto the counter
top, where she sat, looking innocent and hungry. I cut off
the damaged loaf end and gave it to her.

I stepped outside to watch her scamper up a cedar, carrying her breakfast in her mouth, and turned to see a snowshoe
hare eating the begonias. At my outraged squawk, the hare
fled and Ade came out as to a fire. As we carried the plants
into the kitchen, I wondered aloud if he could make some
kind of transparent cover for them. Sure he could, but he
had a better idea. He would build a screened box outside the
south window so that I could haul the invalid plants in and
out without traipsing through the slush, and inside which
they definitely would not be eaten.

While we were evolving plans for this, a smell of scorch-
ing spread from the stove. Again I opened the door to clear
the air, this time making sure that the bread box was closed.
The bacon was burnt, but not much. The bread was good and
the coffee delicious. The sunlight slanted through the trees,
melting the snow from the branches on its way, and reached
past the windows to touch the spice boxes, the snowshoes,
the oil lamps, the books. The day in the north country when
you know it is spring is always good, no matter how much
confusion may cover its start.

———— A few days later the "conservatory" was done—an enclosure on a small platform supported against the house wall by three short, slanted lengths of birch. The wood was painted light green, the screening dark green. The cabin window formed the back, and in warm weather when this could be left open, the box of flowers made the room look spacious. On such days, I moved my typewriter in front of the window box and enjoyed a vicarious feeling of typing under the trees, which was deepened when a cabin mouse dared to creep past me while I was working and nibble the stem of a begonia leaf.

Then the forest presented us with a perfect day to do our first outdoor washing. The idea had come to Ade during the winter when he watched the deer shying away from their food, frightened by a line of clothes, half-frozen so that the arms and legs of long johns flapped and wriggled as if the whole thing were alive. And what an improvement this was over doing the job inside.

Our washer was powered by a gasoline engine that belched fumes and left the cabin smelling of oil and gasoline. The exhaust hose burned the linoleum on its way out through a hole drilled in the door. The wringer drenched my feet as often as it drained back into the machine. The door had to be open a crack to let the drain hose through, and this let in clouds of mosquitoes in summer and blasts of cold in winter.

Under the new system the space in front of the woodshed (which held the washer when not in use) became the Sylvan Glade Laundry. Ade hauled out the machine, filled it with water, and coaxed and threatened and prodded the ancient engine until it started with an outsize roar. I popped in the soap and the first load, set the machine to work, and settled

on the step under a delphinium-blue sky, where Ade, puffing
from hauling more water from the lake, joined me.

A breeze from the south dissipated the fumes and the greening vegetation waited to destroy them. Blue jays gathered
to complain and whiskey jacks to investigate. The crows told
the forest dwellers in no uncertain terms to have nothing to
do with this uproar, while the squirrels grew so nosy that
Ade had to keep shooing them away from the exhaust pipe
lest they burn their feet. One refused to be discouraged until
he was drenched with dirty water from the unpredictable
wringer.

The one disadvantage was hauling endless buckets of
water from the lake. However, a summer resident who took
power put in a pressure water system and we bought his old
one cheap—a pump, a small gasoline engine, and an oval
stock tank. Ade set the tank near the "laundry," fitted it with
a cover to keep plant debris and wild life from falling in,
and bought some plastic hose, which could be used to fill the
tank, water the garden, and fight fire. Perhaps I cheated a
little when I crossed "Running water" off Ade's list and
wrote "6" for the years it had taken, but I knew this was
as near as we would come to a city water system.

——————— Around the first of June it turned hot, so hot that
the plants drooped their leaves to conserve moisture and
Bedel a and Tulip, behind their screen door, sat panting on
the floor of their little house. We would not have time to
move them and ourselves to the summer house, and Tulip
had changed her spring molt to fall and was laying. To move
her would surely interfere.

Bedelia shed a few feathers at a time during most of the
year, so that she hardly ever stopped laying. I kept a record
and during 1957, '58, and '59 she produced 309, 289, and 315

eggs—all of them very large. Incidentally, she laid until she was past eight years old and gave us her last egg on a Christmas morning. A real champion, although one would never have guessed from her appearance.

Sometimes she was bald-headed, or had so few wing and body feathers that she looked shrunken. Once her new tail feathers came out as bare quills and her comb was pale and small all summer. Then she developed a featherless neck that was permanent. For the current year, both head and neck were bare, so that she looked like a small, malformed turkey vulture. But she was our Bedelia, and neither she nor her beautiful "sister" was going to suffer from the heat if we could prevent it.

Ade and I considered their problem. Then he said, "I'll just build them a run here out of the chicken wire from the fence."

He found some old posts in our stack of miscellaneous wood and fell to, while I looked at the weedy garden plots.

"What do you think about a garden?" I asked. "If Gregory shows up, and he probably will, we'll really have to fence it in."

Ade put down the post he was sharpening to drive into the ground. "We ought to use hardware cloth, and that would cost more than anything we could grow. We haven't any more old screening. We might buy some . . ."

After more useless speculation we decided to wait and see, and he went on to finish the chicken run, around the front and one side of the little house, well shaded, and topped with fencing for protection. The hens were delighted. They explored their grounds, ate all the greenery in it, and settled blissfully to have a nice dirt bath. They rolled and scratched, dug and wiggled, fluffed and looked as ecstatic as hens can. They rewarded Ade by laying two huge eggs, then settled to bathe again. It was wonderful to me that they could cover themselves with dust and emerge looking so smooth and clean that their black feathers shone blue and green. This is a secret known only to birds.

The hot weather favored the budworms. Again they ravished their favorite trees, and the local newspaper printed a release from some authoritative source that stated that, on the affected 96,000 acres, trees completely defoliated for three years would die. Ade and I were not happy about this, but we knew that if we lost every balsam and spruce on our land we would still have plenty of trees left. I also knew that the damaged species would not be lost because I had looked around carefully and found seedlings protected by ground growth and little trees up to two feet tall that were untouched. But cries rose from people who had burned the birch in the fireplace, cut the aspen because it might fall on the house, used the cedar for posts, and sawed the pine into boards. The sounds of chain saw and ax rose as these people cut down their "dead" spruce and balsam trees, all they had of the original mixed stand.

Ade and I, from our years so close to the earth, knew that in a forest like ours, where the oldest trees had lived two centuries, it is always harvest time for some. They grow less vigorous, beetles bore into the wood, fungus adds its weakening process, and wind finishes the felling, to make room for young growth. It takes many years after that for the trunks to again become part of the soil. We also knew that budworm attacks had come many times during the life of the big trees, the last severe one, on the best authority we could get, having been in 1912. It was perfectly clear that if all the spruces had died at that time, there would be no two-hundred-year-old spruces in 1960. We had counted rings on some of these that had fallen after we came and were sure of their age. Again we decided to wait and see.

About this time the local paper carried a late story on my

metallurgical award, and my magazine articles with Ade's illustrations began to appear in the area. This established us, both in the past and the present, and opened the way for us to know more people.

One Saturday Ade returned with the mail looking dazed. "We'll have a refrigerator in about a week," he said, and it was my turn to look dazed.

While he was waiting by the mailboxes, a man who, with his wife, had been summering on the lake for many years, drove up. He and Ade discussed, of course, the prolonged hot weather. Ade said something about the problems of keeping food without refrigeration, and the man said, sounding surprised, "Don't you have a refrigerator?" And when Ade said "No" the man said, "We've one we don't use. It was too small when we had guests so we got another. Do you have power?" Ade said "No" again and the man grinned. "That's fine. This one's gas."

"How much?" I asked.

"Nothing."

I was silent. What can one say about such a miracle of friendliness?

On the first of July the refrigerator was installed, supplied with gas, and working. It even had a plug-in light inside. Ade went up to Conrad's Lodge to make arrangements for returning Martha's sewing machine, now that she and Oscar were well settled for the summer season, and brought back two bottles of Coke, a pound of ground beef, and a half-gallon of strawberry ice cream. With ritualistic care we made the meat into patties, wrapped them in wax paper, and stored them to freeze. Then we put as much of the ice cream as we could into ice trays and ate the rest of it. Believe me, it tasted like a cone when I was ten years old.

I had never before known how much fun a refrigerator could be. Five years, eleven months, and thirteen days without one had taught me to properly appreciate the wonders of automatic cooling I had once taken for granted. Ade came in one day from tending the electric plant, which he had started to heat a soldering iron, just as I opened the fridge door and squealed. He cackled like a demented parrot when I said, "The light went on!" We were thrilled with meat that did not have to be gobbled the day it arrived so that it would not spoil. We made a ceremony out of dipping an ice tray in the water bucket to loosen the cubes. We discussed the wonders of a glass of chilled tomato juice. I thought I had lost the feeling I had had as a child when Santa Claus brought me my very own sled, but I had it again every time I took a Coke out of that fridge.

———— Two days later Gregory Groundhog, still slim and handsome from his winter fast although he must have emerged several weeks earlier, came into the yard at a nonchalant amble. He settled first to systematically demolish the dandelions. Well, no more greens from them until next year. Then he found the new leaves of some painted daisies I had planted late the previous summer. These are ideal flowers for our rough climate because they maintain themselves, and I had not even seen what color the blooms were yet! I chased Gregory, who went straight to "his" garden plot of the year before and looked at the weeds and unplanted earth with disgust. Ade and I looked at Gregory and gave up the garden. Ade tried to appear reluctant, but I think I detected a sigh of relief, which turned to a gasp when I pointed out the daisies. With resignation, he ordered enough hardware cloth to enclose the daisies—to be temporarily surrounded by an odds-and-ends fence, to protect a triangle rich with wild flowers, and to make a new cage on the fireplace footing, because the begonias were now too tall for the one he had made earlier. Once these things were out of the way we settled to a fine summer of groundhog watching.

That year there were two reasons why we had not been leaving graham crackers on the step for the squirrels: we had seen a number of large bears we did not wish to attract to our door, and the squirrels were feasting on budworm pupae. Gregory, whose attitude the previous summer had indicated that he considered grahams, though odd, eminently tasty, came to the step after some days of eating his supply of wild greens. He examined it closely, poked his nose into cracks along the sides, and went away with puzzled over-the-shoulder glances. When he returned the next day I tried to slide a graham through the partly open door, but this sent him off at full speed. I watched him hump away at his stubby-legged, slow run and thought how helpless he was when only a short distance from his burrow entrance. He had strong claws and formidable teeth, but he was at the mercy of any fast-moving animal with more than his fighting power.

Our kitchen door has panels, the top glassed and the bottom solid, which can be removed to let air come through screening attached to the outside of the door—an arrangement that beats a screen door because it allows you to let in as much air as you need for ventilation without chilling the house on a cold day. The next afternoon Gregory arrived when the panels were out. He looked through the screen, saw something frightening, and bolted. Then he returned and looked in again, sniffing. Something must have smelled interesting because he tried to push past the screen, then stood up, arms above his head and claws caught in the mesh. Abruptly he grew tense, his claws slid down the screen with a rumble, he moved off the step, sat as though trying to identify something, then dashed across the few separating feet to dive under the hen house. A few seconds later Ade came around the corner of the cabin.

We puzzled over this for a while. Ade was downwind from Gregory, who thus could not have smelled him. The tossing branches were noisy and it was unlikely that Gregory could have heard the slight sound made by rubber-soled boots on soft pine needles against the wind. We decided that he must be very sensitive to vibrations in the earth. As a protective device for an animal that lived underground, this seemed to make sense. We could not be sure, but not wanting to frighten him or any other underground animal, we stepped softly thereafter. Since then we have watched groundhogs head for shelter when we saw no reason, and some time after, a piece of heavy road equipment or the like would pass our property.

I saw Gregory peeking from under the coop, and moving slowly, I put out a cracker. As soon as the door closed he came over and sat on the step to eat it. This done, and while he was still sucking crumbs from between his teeth, he stood up and scratched vigorously on the screen. Then he settled, folding in the middle of his back so that his nose almost touched his "knees," to wait for the next course.

Within a week he was coming regularly, scratching on the screen for service and keeping up the scratching until he got it. This was disconcerting when he happened to want a treat in the middle of the night, especially since Ade slept so soundly I was always the one to hear and stagger to the door with food.

When the door was open on a breezy, bug-free day, Gregory decided to come in. He humped over the sill, took a few cautious steps, and stretched tall to look for danger. I stood by the stove; Ade sat at the table eating his lunch. Gregory chose Ade as a suitable food source and walked confidently to him, stood up, and clawed his pants leg. Ade offered a carrot strip. Gregory tasted, gobbled, and clawed for more. I went around through the other room and handed

Ade more carrots from our still large store. Gregory ate six carrots, two double graham crackers, and a large cabbage leaf. He was eating a round oatmeal cookie, going back and forth on it like some kind of furry mower, when he had enough. He dropped his cookie on the floor and went out, to immediately begin on a large course of greens!

From then on he came in once a day. If Ade was there, he sat down by the table at the sound of scratching and Gregory settled to eat by his knee. He even permitted Ade to break our no-touch rule and smooth his fur, although his expression was more one of tolerating a familiarity than enjoying a caress. He demolished quantities of sweet apples, canned peaches, and chocolate cookies, but had a bad time with cinnamon apple sauce, which he tried to hold in his hands. After he half-froze his fingers on ice cream, he learned to eat treacherous foods from a dish, with much spattering of the contents on the floor. Then he formed a habit of stopping when he was full, but waiting to be given a carrot to take with him.

All this was fun, but had a drawback in that Gregory frequently broke off his meal to hurry to the door, look out, and check carefully to right and left. This meant that the door must always be open during his visits, flying things or no, because safety to him was having his line of retreat clear.

One evening, when the days were shortening and his time of retirement was near, he came in after dark. I stood by the door between the bedroom and the kitchen, looking from Gregory at Ade's knee to our door, open to the humming black velvet night, from which mosquitoes were drifting in, as fragile as gossamer but with annoying potentialities. A cecropia moth entered and spiraled toward destruction at a glowing lamp. As I moved to rescue the small-bird-size moth, a hoary bat, larger and of a frosted-mahogany color, flapped past me and captured the insect with a snick of teeth. The bat swooped low over Ade's head on the way out. Startled, he jumped up and Gregory fled under the table with a squeal. There was a noise outside and Ade picked up a lantern and went out to see if we had a bear.

Gregory, low to the floor and looking in all directions, crept from under the table and took up his place by Ade's chair. When food was not forthcoming he went in turn to the cook-stove, the counter, and the fridge, standing up with his hands against each, and waiting hopefully. Anything *tall* might have food. Only when Ade came in and sat down, saying "No bear," did Gregory discover his error and go to his knee. This was deflating for Ade, who had convinced himself that Gregory had a special preference for him, instead of for food. He now joins me in the opinion that groundhogs are not among the geniuses of the animal kingdom, but have only as much intelligence as a groundhog needs. And that this, be-cause it makes them the bumbly, laugh-making animals they are, only adds to their attractiveness.

——— In September, when the first yellow leaves were showing and Gregory was sleeping soundly, Ade and I stood outside the cabin, looking at the high tops of the surrounding trees. The pine and cedar were green and full of promise, but the spruce and balsam were brown and barren. We stepped onto a little bridge Ade had built over the drainage ditch during the summer and looked at the thick stand of shoulder-high balsams that had sprung up from seed along the ditch. Their branches, feathery and fragrant with new green in the spring, were twisted, thinning, and bare. We went on into the forest dimness to see unexpected patches of light and color, where the sun shone as through stained glass, and spreading rays left green trails as they touched pine twigs in passing and spattered like golden rain on the forest floor. In the newly brightened places, maple and honeysuckle had sprouted. Above, the bare tops of balsam and spruce made the new openings for light. At least three hundred of these trees were completely defoliated and looked dead. Spruce budworms in this, the fourth year of their infestation, had wrought the change. It depressed me, even though we knew that, given enough time, the worms would be overcome by the same natural forces that would work together to build another balanced forest.

Not long after that I received confirmation of my belief that human affairs, too, will balance out if one works and waits with patience. Within a month, I received inquiries about possible books from three publishers who had read my articles. I could not believe it even though this was the thing I had unconsciously been striving for. After I had replied as best I knew how to all three, I was restless and often walked in the dark hours to let the drowsing forest quiet me.

One night I had just stepped out and closed the door when I heard a moose bellow nearby. I paused on the step and was startled by laughter and lights from the cabin nearest us on the east. The people who owned it were up for an overnight stay while the leaves were at their richest coloring. The moose sounded again—a sort of combination of a flat note on a cornet and a diesel horn—and lights moved in the woods as our neighbors trailed back and forth to what is euphemistically called the biffy up here. Then I heard a faint scuffling, very near to me. The moose? I froze.

In the dim glow from the stars I made out the great-granddaddy of all black bears, ambling along. I had a notion he had gone next door to investigate the lights and sounds, and then decided to come over and see what we were up to. He sat down in the path fifteen feet from the door and sniffled and snuffled in my direction. I also sniffled and snuffled; a bear does not smell of roses, but I daresay he thought I needed a

deodorant, too. A little breeze drifted from the lake past me
and the bear and on up the hill, where there was a sudden
crash in the brush and the fading thud of hoofs. With an in-
ward shout of joy I knew that some of the deer were back.
I went in and left the bear contemplating whatever bears
contemplate. How thrilled the people in the nearby cabin
would be if they knew of the moose, the bear, or the deer.
But, hurrying to get inside their little lighted space, they
would not see or hear or smell the life that was outside in the
big dark.

The forest wrapped us in the languor of Indian summer,
and while the days were still warm and full of the smoky
scent of decaying leaves, the wild geese streamed overhead,
telling us that the tundra was freezing and the white silence
of winter was near.

Mama brought her new little does in October—Pretty,
long-legged and lithe, pearl gray of coat, graceful of body,
and serene of face; Fuzzy, short and chunky, with an extra-
thick coat and a face so hairy that from some angles she
looked a little like a buffalo calf. Then Peter came out of the
forest's shelter to tap on the step and bob his antlered head
before he courted Mama and followed her into the quiet
places to mate.

I moved the plants in the window box to safety behind the
closed window, and took away the box's front screen because
the open platform would make a good feeder.

In November, when the leaves were down and crackling
under foot, Pig and Brother, now a year and a half old, returned. Alike as they were, they were still individual—Pig
with his calculating look and six-point antlers, Brother with
his gentle expression, a little black mane, and a seven-point
rack whose left antler beam, apparently injured in its forma-
tive stages, turned forward over his nose so that he looked
like a caribou. For the first time I was nervous about hunters

and Ade posted our land, but no one disturbed our quiet and I was grateful for the consideration of those who lived nearby but hunted so far away that we did not hear a shot.

The snow fell, soft as down, on Thanksgiving Day, heralding the silent months when we would share the forest's shelter with its wild children. Corn and suet in the open window box brought chickadees, woodpeckers, squirrels, and now and then an ermine to feed almost at my elbow, and often they looked in a questioning way at the out-of-season greenery beyond the glass. The begonias were too many for the window sill and I had to keep some of them on my desk, which was not large enough for me to work on conveniently in the first place. So Ade made a note to enclose the screened box, when it was warm again, with windows from the storage building, which, in turn, he would replace with heavy plastic. Incidentally, this worked out well. The begonias had more light and a year-round home, and although the glassed-in box did not let in more light, it seemed to.

Deer watching and mail took up my time through December and Ade, when he was not putting out feed, shoveling snow, or watching the family life that centered around Peter and Mama, was putting together something that he kept a dark secret. We planned to relax on New Year's Day with Jacques, who had invited us to dinner in his new trailer-house.

On the last day of the year, a letter came from one of the book publishers, asking me to write a sample along the lines of certain paragraphs in my last letter, and not to wait lest I lose the feeling I had when I wrote it. I knew I must not go to Jacques's and break up the long days of mental preparation.

This worried me, because I did not want to neglect our friend, and Ade told me not to be silly. "Just show him the letter when he comes tomorrow. Of all the people we know he understands best why we came here and what we want to do."

I agreed and muttered, "I wonder why."

"Don't be stupid. Because he's as independent as we are, of course."

We ate late that evening, and afterward Ade brought out his surprise—a wind-up record player. It was made of old phonograph parts and a wooden case left in the cabin, with pick-up and needles bought by mail, and it played all speeds with only an occasional wail when it needed rewinding in the middle of a long-play.

We got out our records, and while Ade selected and cleaned, I made sandwiches and got the coffeepot ready for later. Then we settled to enjoy ourselves.

It was a sentimental night, a night of looking back as one should on New Year's Eve, before turning to look ahead once more. Ade found a 78 record of a tune called "'Geechee Stomp," an organ solo by one Thomas Waller before he became the famous "Fats." Glen Miller's theme song smoothed the wrinkles out of the day. Eddie Duchin's singing fingers performed for us, and Bing Crosby was young again with "Good Night, Sweetheart." Then we went still further back to hear Henry Burr sing "I Wonder What's Become of Sally?" and to listen to forgotten orchestras playing the dance music of the early twenties, where Krupa's drums, Wayne King's saxophone, Rocco's boogie piano were foretold by the ragtime beat of even earlier years. Then we went to the classics. The thunderous chords of Beethoven were too much for our small speaker, but Enrico Caruso filled our little house with "Celeste Aïda," and Alma Gluck sank "Aloha Oe" to the passing year, since Ade had played "Auld Lang Syne" to open the concert.

On the stroke of twelve we went out into the night, dim-lit by stars and the faint green glow of the aurora. Ade let the lantern beam swing through the blackness under the trees, and glowing eyes told us that Mama and her fawns were getting up from their beds in the snow and walking toward us for some feed. After Ade took it out, we stood in the window, watching them eat, while Peter and Pig and Brother came to join them. When we finally turned away, Peter was lying under his tree as he had lain on the night when he had first come stumbling down the hill to the cedar that was waiting there for him. The merrymaking of past New Year's Eves seemed empty beside this one with our deer and our music and our forest.

———— It was in January that the cats arrived, a lynx and a bobcat traveling together. I wrote about these animals in *The Gift of the Deer*, emphasizing the nervous truce set up between them and the deer, but it seems that more should be told about such little-known animals in such an unusual— according to theory and general knowledge—companionship.

We first saw them moving across the path to the road and identified them the next morning. Ten feet from the kitchen window the lynx, clawing and spitting, was trying, with teeth too long for the task, to chew browned grease from a drip pan put out for the chickadees. His haunches were almost skin and bone, and his emaciated ribs showed through the long hairs of his coat. He had come into the dangerous day-light, and the even more dangerous presence of man, because he was starving. At last he moved aside, slowly, with hind legs stiff and head hanging, and sat up to lick his paws. The sun broke through clouds and as the warmth touched him, he lay down wearily in front of our feeding bench and dozed.

His fur was thick and gray, like ruffled, deep-piled plush, with faint spotting on his lower sides and legs and a darker shading down his spine. He had a reddish snub nose, eyes like disks from a harvest moon, faint black face stripings, and luxuriant whiskers. His ears bore upright black tufts

almost as long as my thumbs. The whiteness of his thick ruff
was broken by two black splotches, one on each side of his
jaw, and hairs met in a point below his chin like a white
Vandyke beard.

He turned his head and we saw the bobcat stepping from
behind Peter's tree. He was thin but showed his still good
physical condition by supple, graceful movements and a
sleek, glossy coat, rust-colored and richly spotted and marked
on the body, shading from white to pearl gray on his legs,
which were lavishly cross-striped with black. He had a tiger-
cat face, yellow eyes marked round with white, and a reddish
snub nose like the lynx's, but more strongly outlined with
black. His black-and-white-striped whiskers spread from the
sides of the face and curled forward in two little tufts under
a receding chin. The ears, smaller than the lynx's, also had
shorter black ear tufts. The stubby tails clinched the identifi-
cation, the lynx's being black all around on the tip as if dipped
in ink, the bobcat's splotched with black on top only. The
backs of their ears were similar, white across the middle and
black at top and bottom.

This companionship between two species that are usually
thought of as competitive was even more surprising to the
game manager I sent snapshots of the cats to than it was to
Ade and me. Though I call both animals "he" because I find
it hard to think of any living creature as "it," the bobcat
moved so swiftly and was so much in the shadows that we
could not discover the sex. The lynx was male. Sometimes
wildcats are found who seem to have both lynx and bobcat
characteristics and are uncertain of identity. We do not put
aside the possibility that our cats were a mated pair. They
were amiable when together, and if one may say so, treated
each other with the greatest consideration.

The lynx—named Big Cat because he was one—stood up
when the bobcat—Tiger from his movements and markings—

came into view, and returned to the drip pan, while the late arrival waited until Big Cat walked away after pausing for a moment by the feeding bench. We estimated his size by comparison with it: some nineteen inches tall and thirty-eight inches long, without his four-inch tail. When fattened up he should weigh around forty pounds. Tiger was about four-fifths his size.

While Tiger licked and chewed ineffectively at the pan, Big Cat vanished. Then we noticed that there seemed to be two cedar stumps where there should be one. The lynx had stopped to investigate something in the snow, and his rump, the reddish color of the cedar wood, camouflaged him perfectly. He straightened at last and moved away, almost dragging himself but showing vestiges of a dignified gait. When he reached the brush he simply became part of his surroundings.

Ade and I, remembering our own times of hunger, were filled with pity. We also knew that these animals would not be safe at any human habitation within miles because they were feared and hated, and moved under the shadow of bounty money. When Tiger had also gone, with considerably more spring in his movements than Big Cat, we put out suet, bones, and a little ground beef in locations about ten feet apart, not only to appease their obvious misery but also to encourage them to stay within reach of what protection we could offer. As soon as we were inside the cabin, the two animals walked down the packed snow of a deer trail and ate quietly, one at each pile of food. After a short rest for whisker-licking, during which their relief at being given even so small a meal showed in their relaxation and somehow brightened attitude, they went away again, this time to go between the logs that supported the storage building. Underneath there they were sheltered, and this was their den while they were with us, although Big Cat's trail often circled

widely from his feeding place through the woods and back
to a tarpaulin that hung tentwise from the end of our woodpile—something special in lynx dens. Later we found many
of the bones we had given him under the tarpaulin. There
must be a much larger heap under the storage building.

Tiger was more of a climber than Big Cat, leaping up tree
boles and clinging to the bark, little tail twitching and curling
while he looked hungrily at the fleeing birds. One afternoon
Big Cat climbed far enough to pull a suet cage from its nail
with his teeth. Ade found the empty cage by the storage
building and rehung it on a propped-up clothesline. The
lynx tried to get it the next day by creeping out on an overhanging branch, which snapped off and dropped him to land
on his four feet. He looked covetously at the suet but did not
attempt to jump for it, nor did the bobcat ever try.

It thus seems doubtful that these animals will attack deer
from the ground, and this is borne out by our deer's learning
to feed when the cats were in the clearing as long as a careful
watch told them where the carnivores were. The cats were
wary of the deer, too, and made no attempt to move near
them and their sharp, slashing hoofs. That wildcats, especially
bobcats, do kill deer is known, but it seems that they do this
by dropping from branches, hunger driving them to risk
being brained against a tree while riding a terrified deer
through a forest.

We had a great many chickadees that winter, some of them
the brown-capped variety, all done up in muted shades of
what looked like velvet—white and gray, brown and black—
and their soft, blurry *zhee-zhee-zhee* was a joy to hear. One
day Big Cat walked into the yard accompanied by loud complaints from the jays and squirrels and tried to catch a
chickadee. He approached the bird with stealth, unaware
that what was an effective hunting technique in the dark was
completely conspicuous by day. The watchful chickadee

flitted to safety as the lynx sprang. He batted his forepaws together well under the bird, stared after it with the air of a commuter missing his train, then turned away with a great show of indifference as if to say he really had not been interested in it at all. He moused at night from behind a tree, his face appearing and reappearing. I doubt that he had any luck, because the mice stayed close to the woodshed where grain, fallen from the flying squirrels' rations, was always to be found on the shed floor and adjoining ground.

As I watched him night after night, I wondered how the wild hunters manage to get enough to eat. Hares, for instance, are the favorite food of the lynx, but there were very few in our area, most of those that had been present having passed through our clearing some time before, going east and paying no attention to us. Perhaps some movement like this in their home area had brought our two cats to their state of hunger.

Both of them improved rapidly with our help, Tiger looking livelier and fatter, Big Cat filling out before our eyes. As he gained weight his haunches showed graceful curves and his stiff, languid movements gave way to lithe crouches and glides. The ripple of muscles on his back as he walked was leonine. Sometimes he hurried at a fast trot; occasionally he leaped three or four feet. As his confidence and strength increased he fed undisturbed while I watched by flashlight from a window. Often he crouched with his back to me, so that I saw the long, slim taper from his shoulders to his tucked-in tail. With his special night vision and keen hearing, he followed the slightest movement inside the window. If I opened the door or even threw a light on its glass panel, he walked away.

We were running low on scraps for the cats and had decided to order something from town when Ade returned with the mail to say that the driver had told him we had better watch out for ourselves because some ice fishermen had seen a couple of bobcats cross the ice from Canada a while before, and "they were as big as dogs!" (The size of dog was not mentioned.) This meant that almost everyone who came to our area would be looking for the cats to collect the bounty. If we ordered a large quantity of meat scraps word might leak out and give away their location. As for watching out for ourselves, we were so accustomed to the cats' acting like their domestic cousins that we had forgotten about their size.

A few days earlier Ade had gone outside, his eyes on Tiger who was crossing the yard a short distance away. He did not see Big Cat, who had crawled from under the woodpile tarpaulin, until he was only a few feet from the lynx. Ade stopped, and the animal looked up at him for a full minute before departing in his leisurely way, with occasional glances back. He could have attacked if he had wanted to.

And I once stood in moonlight outside the cabin, enjoying the cleanness of the air, the faint whispers of the trees, the grumbling of ice freezing a little deeper. I leaned against a cedar by the woodshed and heard rustling in the branches above me. Snow fell on me, and as I turned my head the better to listen, Big Cat stretched down to crunch into the drift beside me, longer than I was tall between outstretched fore and hind feet. He turned his golden eyes up to me, then blended into the shadows. He could have dropped onto my back and killed me with one snap at the base of my skull—but he did not. At that moment I wondered greatly about the many tales of lynxes, as those of wolves, who *almost* kill people.

When the suet ran out we gave the cats hot dogs, which they ate after considerable sniffing and consultation. I put out some leftover gravy, which Big Cat lapped up with gusto, so I made gravy for him out of flour, beef cubes, lard, and water. At last I took the remaining two cans of boned chicken from the quarter-case I had bought at a special low price and

put one in each feeding place. The big cats sniffed, ate, licked whiskers, licked the cans, purred like boilers, and rolled kittenlike in the snow. I thought of Walter Weasel, our first-winter friend, neck arched and head high to keep his chicken can out of the way of his pattering front feet as he carried his treasure home, of Peter's delight in ground carrots. Even though Walter was gone and Peter snorted at the cats from the edge of the woods and had to do without his carrots for a while, the cats had found us as the others had and we knew we must feed them some way.

There was a light snow that night, and in the morning the tracks of both cats were on our doorstep and around the woodshed, perhaps hunting mice. They had to be very hungry to come so near to the house. Bedelia gave her morning attempt at crowing, and then I remembered the cats' enjoyment of boned chicken. Up to now, they and the hens seemed to know nothing about each other, but if Bedelia decided to be afraid of them and attracted their attention by one of her squawking sessions, if in any way the cats learned that birds lived in that little house . . . We had to get some meat for them without giving away their presence, and soon, if we were to keep our hens.

The next local newspaper carried an ad for short ribs, very cheap, as well as a notice asking for information about a Siamese cat lost in the woods. Ade made an extra trip to the midweek mail and ordered twenty-five pounds of ribs, six cans of boned chicken, some canned cat food, which would be thought bait for the Siamese, and our usual supply of suet and scraps. Everything was well-received but the cat food, which neither Tiger nor Big Cat would touch. Even the whiskey jacks passed it up, and it was eventually eaten by some ravens. When we heard some months later that it was the newest thing to bait bobcat traps with cat food, we were pleased no end.

As soon as we supplied food, the cats went back to their earlier way of waiting at night for us to bring out their meal. When the door opened our lantern beam picked up the two pairs of fiery green eyes as the animals appeared in their "den entrance" below the storage building wall. After they ate, the lynx, often leaving a little of his portion for later, went back under the shed, and the bobcat took up a place on the path from where the deer, feeding to the west, could be watched. The cat sat quietly; the deer blew and stomped; nothing further occurred between them.

Then came a night when I woke at three o'clock and heard faint growling. I slipped outside without making a light, in time to hear a man quiet his dog. I raised a great noise for Ade, and was rewarded by the cracking of twigs as the pair retreated.

In the morning we found the tracks of man and dog, behind our storage building, on the hill above the house, very thick around some snow hollows like small deer beds, where one or both of the cats had been lying. This made us doubly glad that we had not tried to persuade the cats to stay in the yard when we were outside, so that they might keep the natural caution that is their protection against hostile or greedy men. From then on I kept a night watch, sleeping late the next day, not only to protect Tiger and Big Cat but also because it is unpleasant to know that someone is snooping around your buildings in the dark.

Tiger developed a way of coming from their "den" alone to select something from their meat supply. He was met by Big Cat when about halfway back, and the two examined the food, like people discussing the merits of something in a market. Then they went together to eat under the building. We never knew why they changed their feeding habits.

It was March and the days were warming. As the snow softened and melted in the sun and packed a bit, the deer fed even when the cats were near, as though determined to keep their home. That they could move more easily and faster on the shallow snow layer probably had much to do with this.

The cats were roaming now, and hunting together and singly, and they were back to the beauty and weight and strength that had been theirs before some disaster brought them near starvation. Big Cat made three trips across the ice to Canada and back in ten days, as though he might be checking on conditions there.

Then came a snow like tapioca, lying white in the crevices of earlier snow and ice grayed by thawing, and the particles moved in the air in thin waves like cold ghosts riding the wind. And then it grew warmer, and the white snow was gone. The cats had not appeared for five days and the deer were frisky, as if in high glee.

We saw the tracks of our cats occasionally, and sometimes food was gone from their supply, probably when their hunting had been unsuccessful. Bare ground began to show, and the deer went away on a spring jaunt and then came back to eat the cedar that had fallen during the winter and was now waiting as the snow released it.

On the morning of April 11, when there had been no sign of the cats for eight days, I heard gulls along the shore and went down to scatter coarsely chopped suet on the ice for them. There were twenty, swooping and sailing, and while I watched two ravens and four crows lit on the ice to get their share of suet and complete a starkly beautiful picture in black and white.

The ice had cracked near the rocks that held the lake back from us, and slanting sunlight brought into shadowed relief some marks out from the shore. I waded through slush deepening around the crack and looked at a double line of tracks, melting but still clear—the neat, four-toed marks of a bobcat's feet and the big snowshoe tracks of a lynx. My eyes followed them across the ice until I saw heat waves in the air along the far shore. I remembered a crash in the night and knew that the unstable ice had broken to make a channel over there. Perhaps the cats had not intended to return. Perhaps they did not care for an icy bath. In any case, Tiger and Big Cat, fat and rested and strong, had gone home.

cut wood
install wiring
clear brush and paths
clear trash
running water
make a living

———— At the beginning of May the lake ice was still thirty inches thick. It had air holes in it, though, and the wind had started the water moving underneath and on top of it. At night the ice roared and boomed as it refroze, and Ade said it sounded like big guns he had heard off the China Coast. The rhubarb popped up, yellow and red and golden-green, and Ade looked at the cabin's ceiling panels, shown by the increasing daylight as a depressing smoke color, and announced that he would paint them. This last was more spring-like than anything else, to my way of thinking.

Then the nights as well as the days were above freezing, and on a morning when the wind was soughing through the pines and spruces, there came a heavy undercurrent of sound —the grinding of a giant's teeth. The ice was moving eastward in a pack, giving way resentfully before the warm breath of spring. The soft gold of morning tried vainly to brighten the dying gray layer, while the whole western half of the lake sparkled and danced before the breeze. Little ice islands, honeycombed and almost gone, clinked and ground together near the shore. By noon there was only a tinkling mass of melting crystals in the wavelets lapping over the stones. And in the evening the lake was blue and clear, ready to reflect the sunset.

Three days later the spring fishermen arrived. In the past there had been runs of small boats. This year, due to the widening of much of the Trail, the men towed-in cartop boats and cruisers fit for inter-island service in Hawaii. When they rushed in schools toward the east end of the lake, waves rose as in a storm, and smaller boats put-putted hastily for the safety of the shore.

Then the days turned very warm and very clear and very dry, and I was glad that the first rush of outsiders was over, because spring, when the sap of trees and brush is still in the roots, is dangerous—although to a stranger it does not seem to be a time when a campfire might start a disaster.

———— The weather brought the budworms earlier than before, and a sort of hysteria seized on people, both local and visiting, and there were calls for spraying with DDT in high concentrations. Rachel Carson's *Silent Spring* was a year away, but there was already plenty of evidence of DDT's dangerous potentials. In an attempt to bring some reason to the scene, I wrote to the local paper. I got a number of letters saying, in effect, "Get out of the county, you crackpot, or you'll regret it," and a few from summer visitors. I quote from a representative one: "The accusation that DDT is killing off birds and fish is scare tactics. I am not ready to accept the loss of *all* the trees in the forest. We should weigh the certainties of the worm against the uncertainties of the spray and ask the Forest Service to spray."

This was getting me nowhere, so I wrote to the Forest Service. From Washington came a "There, now. You just let us look after the fish for you." From a forest insect laboratory came two entomologists, who looked at our affected trees, said most of them were still in good shape in spite of the worms, asked me to take observations on certain trees they marked and Ade to send weather data. They also suggested that we pray for cold, wet weather.

We had the "bad" weather at the end of May and on into June. When the worms' attack was over the tops of the big trees were still green and many of the smaller ones showed green branches. Ade and I rejoiced, and the forest burgeoned as though exulting in its own way. In spite of a cold, soggy, sunless atmosphere, the wild chives shot up a foot, last year's fallen grasses disappeared under green, violets bloomed in every open space, and Gregory arrived to eat the leaves of my potted dahlias. Since the dahlias were on the step where he was accustomed to come for treats, I could blame only myself.

I thought the sudden greening had gone to Ade's head when he decided that we *must* have a garden. He walked to Conrad's Lodge and phoned an order for forty feet of window screening to a store in the Village. He painted the screening before he set up the fence so that it might last two or three years. Then he enclosed our largest garden plot, with inside posts and stones along the fence bottom, as he had done to keep Gregory from our Kentucky wonder beans earlier. It seemed a lot of work for such a little garden, but when the sprouts came up I understood. Outside of lettuce for me, the whole plot was in carrots for Peter and Gregory.

One after another Pretty, Fuzzy, and Mama appeared, and we were thrilled that they seemed prepared to spend the summer near us, but it was not until mid-June that the forest offered us a share in one of its most beautiful happenings. Ade was on the roof, calculating its area, and I was looking up, visualizing roofing-paper colors, when he motioned me to silence and made inconspicuous gestures toward the forest.

Mama stood at the edge of the trees, head thrust forward, forefoot lifted and ready to stomp. Between the fronds of the interrupted ferns I saw the tips of two pairs of little ears. I held my breath.

Slowly Mama backed away and the ears moved toward her through a clump of balsam seedlings. Then she came to a grassy spot where her favorite bluebead lilies bloomed. She stopped to nip off a plant and her new fawns moved shyly to her on wobbly legs.

They were not much taller than the lilies and their white-spotted coats made them almost a part of the sun-dappled duff. Their eyes were wide and dark and full of wonder. Either of them could have found room and to spare for all four hoofs on the palm of my hand. One of them, with a white star on his forehead, took shelter in the safest place he knew—under Mama's belly. He lost interest in us soon and nudged Mama's udder, but she drew aside and led her twin miracles into seclusion.

At the time I did not question why she brought them to summer with us; I only felt thankful for her trust. Now I think she may have been influenced by a drouth, which had settled in after the early rain, and by the scent of smoke from forest fires eating away square miles of Canada. We had a brook where one might drink, underground springs that kept the surface growth green while it shriveled and died else-where, and our land bordered the lake where one might, if it came to that, plunge in and survive.

The Fourth of July holiday came and went with hardly any increase in the numbers of visitors. The word was spread-ing—as were the fires—that the woods were dangerous. I think the whole area would have been closed if the resorters had not needed what business they could get. All open fires were forbidden in the forest, though, and the few tourists

were cautioned. To us, it was a time of fear for the forest that
sheltered us and for all its creatures, and of thankfulness for
every hour and day that they were spared.

Day and night we smelled smoke and the sun set red behind the murk of fires. One afternoon after hearing on the
radio that 157 were burning north of us in Ontario, I sat on
the lake shore and watched the smoke of one of them rise just
behind the hills of the far shore, straight up in the blessed
absence of wind, to reach a higher moving air layer and
spread to the south above a line as straight as if it were ruled.
It was a little fire—yet. Then great white puffs came up from
behind the hills. Steam. Special planes were scooping water
from a nearby lake and dumping it on the blaze. This one, at
least, would not spread.

As I watched the diminishing smoke and steam, my mind
turned back to a time when Ade and I were still looking for
our place in the woods. We followed a rough road into another forest on a day made dusty by a hot wind, and after
miles of bouncing over stones and chuckholes, we rounded
a curve and came out of the trees at the top of a cliff.

A mass of thick, yellowish smoke, its lower bulges touched
with flickers of red, lifted like an inflamed swelling against
the blue-white sky of late afternoon. Its source was only a
short distance away, in the forested land at the foot of the
rocky height where we stood.

A building was afire from wall to wall. Some small trees
nearby were only glowing stumps, while others were blazing,
and falling as fast as ax and saw could bring them down.

While we watched, the towering smoke column wavered,
scattered. A lance of fire shot upward, and riding on the up-
draft, glowing fragments rose high and slowly spread out to
fall into the nearby trees. The acrid fumes began to choke
our nostrils and sting our throats, and a terrible glare showed

through the haze. We heard faintly the snarl of chain saws and chock of axes mingling with the crackle and roar of the flames.

Without warning a dead birch a hundred feet away flared into a torch. Heavy smoke mushroomed and sputtering flames licked along its ragged bark toward the surrounding evergreens. I watched their deadly progress, sickened because we could do nothing to help.

The roof went in with a roar and flame rose like a devil's steeple, flicking sparks into the forest. The evergreens around the tall birch caught from its trunk. Fire shot up a balsam, and brassy death sprayed from its top. There was a puff of wind, another. The snake of fire above the burning building reached avidly toward the trees beyond the wreckage and the vanguard of the woods became a blazing wall. There was a rustling, then a roaring as wind rushed past us to move the mass of flame on to engulf the forest. As the wind dispersed the smoke I saw that the clearing around the ruined building was full of people, now running from the out-of-control fire.

I heard thunder behind us and realized, as a blue flash lit the scene, that it was almost night. I stared down and out at the fiery orange that was leaping across the forest from crown to crown. It could not possibly go like this, all in a flash and a crackling. But it was going—all its beauty, all its life. Because someone had dropped a hot match into a wastebasket?

Weary and defeated men neared a lower road at the edge of the clearing. The last one stopped and faced into the wind from the thundering clouds. Slowly and with infinite dignity he lifted his arms toward the sky, and I knew that he was an Indian, calling to the forest's ancient gods.

And it rained.

Water pounded on the earth and hissed into the blaze. The fire fighters ran back to work. As the flames lessened and shone dull-red through steam, which almost obliterated the scene, the son of the forest lowered his arms, bowed his head, turned back to work.

It was near sunset when my thoughts returned from the past and I stood up on our shore and stretched. Nothing remained of the blaze in Canada but a line of dirty mist high above. But tomorrow's sun might have risen as a crimson ball, to look down through sulfurous air at a blackened earth, where smoke still rose and coals still glowed. The waters, bearing the debris of death, could have steamed from the hot rocks of the shore. Nothing would have moved on the land, no leaf would have remained. The only life would have been in the deep water, as it was in the beginning.

———— In spite of our uneasiness as the drouth stretched on and on, we had a lovely summer. I had never seen things so green, although a few maples hurried to make their seeds and were already turning red in July. We were glad that we had not cleared near the log cabin because the deep-rooted plants protected the frogs and toads and held enough moisture to keep their supply of insects alive. We had to watch our steps after dark, when the toads came to sit like stone carvings in front of the cabin, their eyes reflecting light as pure gold while they waited for night-flying creatures. One young brown frog, only an inch and a half from the back of his folded legs to the top of his bug eyes, sat every night on the doorstep, a fine place for catching insects and with a thick growth of oak ferns at the side for a quick retreat.

Our struggles with the garden were less satisfying, although it, like the forest, went wild with sprouts. It also went wild with chipmunks, who like nothing better than budding leaves. So poor Ade hunted up a couple of hundred bottles and jars, accumulating until we might have a way to haul them to the dump, and covered the sprouts with them until they should be big enough no longer to attract the chippies. Both of us were constantly checking temperature and sun, because the impromptu hothouses had to be removed when it was too hot or they would cause the tender plants to burn up. Of course, Ade had to replace them when it cooled before the chipmunks, who dozed away the hot hours in their burrows, discovered that the feast was again available.

Clouds often drifted across the sky and gathered threateningly in the west at sundown, but, since only a few spatters of rain fell, we decided to water the garden. The old pump chose this critical time to break and the replacement part had to be ordered from Milwaukee. We exhausted the water in the storage tank and learned that there is a limit to the number of buckets of water one can haul uphill at the end of a hard day's work. At first, they weighed no more than a portable typewriter; an hour later they were as heavy as the office safe.

Eventually we had some small and rather brittle leaves of lettuce. The carrots reached farther into the ground and did better, but they were small. Even the dandelions we tried to pick for greens crumbled apart, although they looked normal. There were a few showers, which summer people called "good rains," but Ade's rain gauge showed only a few hundredths of an inch and the puddles that formed did so because the ground was dried too hard to absorb the water. A man digging for a foundation said there was plenty of water—three feet down the earth was wet, but he did not notice that the leaves atop the seventy-five foot birches were wilting, withering, then falling. He was about to build over an underground spring.

———— It could have been depressing without the animals. Their need of assistance in the days of almost nonexistent seeds and moist greens, and their confident gathering around the cabin, kept us busy and diverted our thoughts from the fire danger.

In July I was sitting at the typewriter when I heard a strange sound outside, something like the *blub-blub-blub* of an outboard motor exhaust when a boat is being used for trolling. I looked out but saw nothing. Ade came in, saying he had heard it and gone down to the shore, but there was no boat in sight and the sound seemed to come from the woods. We listened when it came again, and this time it might have been just outside. We were still puzzling over its recurrences when I happened to open the door in time to catch a glimpse of a grayish nose disappearing under the woodshed. I went back in and squinted sideways through the glass door panel. The nose reappeared, a snub pad with a little fur visible beyond it. A red squirrel hopped over to investigate and the nose withdrew. In the morning a mound of dirt showed that a groundhog was burrowing under the shed. We saw the nose occasionally during the following week, then a normally colored groundhog, about the age of young Gregory when we first saw him, with grayish-brown head, frosted brown back, red vest and sleeves, ventured into the daylight. Her name—naturally—Nose.

Gregory trotted down the path to the newcomer. He was making the mysterious burbling sound. Once I knew its source, it sounded like an oversize, widely spaced purr, and it was, from all appearances, an expression of groundhog delight.

Nose and Gregory seemed to be well acquainted, and pressed their snub noses together affectionately when they met, then went scampering around the yard, bowed front legs pattering and fat rumps rolling. After a good romp, they rested, panting, on top of a log pile high enough to be a lookout point. They foraged separately for greens after they recovered their breath, and Nose proved to be a good climber, sometimes going fifteen feet up the bole of a small tree to teeter on a branch, snatch a mouthful of leaves, then back down slowly and with caution.

Gregory forgot the dignity he had attained with maturity and played as though he, too, was a youngster. They romped and touched noses, chased each other through the grass and round and round trees, their burbling filling the air like laughter. Often they came to the bank whose lip overhung the entrance to Gregory's burrow. There they wrestled and squealed and made mighty efforts until one or the other, usually Nose, was vanquished and rolled down the bank into the ditch.

One day Nose hid in her burrow until Gregory had given up searching for her and lain down to doze at the base of a small cedar stump on the bank near his doorway. Creeping without sound and with much care, Nose slipped around to the far side of the stump and nipped Gregory's tail. When he woke with a squeak, she scurried to the top of the stump and looked smug. Then Gregory half stood, leaning his hands against the bark, and stretched his nose up to touch hers in something that might have been a groundhog kiss.

Gregory came regularly to the step for his treats, but Nose was disdainful of such recklessness. Finally she came, but backed under the woodshed floor to have her cookies thrown to her. When she at last mustered the nerve to wait on the step beside Gregory while the door opened, his burbling stopped short when she clawed his nose and snatched his cookie—a special one, too, a chocolate-wafer sandwich with mint filling.

After this, if I handed a cookie to one, its possessor ducked under the shed, the other followed, and squeals, grunts, and yips announced a battle. I solved this problem by simultaneously handing one to each, but there came the day when

Nose was alone and I handed her an oatmeal cookie just as Gregory arrived. He bit her tail so sharply that she fled, wailing. I yelled at him, and for three days after he withdrew from the yard if I appeared in the doorway, although he accepted Ade as before. I think my harsh tone of voice had frightened him, and most unworthy of me it was to have made such a sound to any animal, especially since he was only following his instinct. To get back into his good graces, I sat outside and tempted him with a molasses drop. He looked at it, walked off, looked back, approached slowly, and then, with a movement hilariously like a shrug, accepted my peace offering.

As summer advanced and the birds and squirrels brought their young to the yard, Ade put out separated heaps of cracked corn. He had withheld it earlier in case a failure of the berry crop because of the drouth should bring bears, many of whom will eat corn; but the bears were absent—we did not see one that summer.

Gregory and Nose both loved corn. On this concentrated fattener they expanded like balloons. When they sat up they looked like squat milk bottles, swathed in thick cascades of glossy fur, with small flat heads perched on top. Early in September, Gregory started to drag himself from his burrow to the corn, lay down to rest, turned around, and went home for the winter. Nose made her last appearance on the now sizable mound by the woodshed a week later, accepting a chocolate cookie, eating half of it, yawning, and backing out of sight.

We had deer with us off and on all summer. Pretty grew nervous at the sound of strange voices and went away, but Fuzzy, in spite of my efforts to persuade her that caution was the thing with strange humans, stayed on. Mama, after she had brought her newborn fawns to the yard, had appeared a few times to stomp for grain at the edge of the forest, but always alone. In August she returned with her twins, now sure of step, eighteen inches high at the rump, and fidgety with the desire to explore.

While Mama and Fuzzy browsed and ate their grain and rested on the edge of the bank, the twins took over our clearing. They rolled in the tall grass, drank together from a tiny spring, reared on their slim legs to box, rushed up to Fuzzy as she lay resting and pattered their front hoofs on her paunch, then were gone before she could more than lift a hoof to wave them away. They chased each other across the clearing and through the forest, raced on the path, sampled leaves and berries and flowers—two white-dotted, red-gold sprites; quick, dainty, lovely beyond dreams; exuberant and joyful in their quiet, safe world.

No rain had fallen for weeks. The ground plants dried up and leaves fell from the trees without their color change. Unconcerned, the fawns lost their spots and turned to more adult games, like mock fighting. Mama watched complacently, as though nothing could please her more than to have her sons growing up with the correct competitive instincts.

Late in September I saw the deer quietly fade away and heard voices. I went out to goggle at two grouse hunters, lurching onto the little bridge while waving a shotgun, a .22 rifle, and a quarter-full fifth of whiskey. Ade was in the woods cutting cedar for the deer, so getting rid of this pair was my job. Keeping a wary eye on their weapons, which they mishandled as if they had just bought them, I told them there were no grouse on our land and it would be a good idea for them to take their bottle elsewhere.

Both straightened as well as they could, which gave them the appearance of bookkeepers who had overestimated their capacity at the office party. The one with the bottle tipped it up, emptied it, and flipped it casually over the bridge rail. Then his face turned scarlet, his eyes bulged, he quivered from boot to cap, and leaned slowly sideways, his body perfectly stiff, to come to rest against his companion's shoulder. The still functioning one of the pair made some unintelligible sounds, turned his companion around, kicked him behind one ankle—to start his legs moving, I suppose—and they reeled off along the way they had come. It was a truly memorable performance.

It was funny until I thought of the danger such irresponsible men could be in a time of such drouth as we were experiencing. The result was that when Ade took the boat to get the mail a couple of days later and I heard footsteps outside, I burst out of the cabin to confront a smiling, sandy-haired young man in the green uniform of a forest ranger. He quite literally shied back. Feeling silly, I explained and invited him in.

While I put the coffeepot on, he introduced himself as Chuck Martin and said he had been around our area warning people about the fire danger. However, he had passed us up because he thought that, if we could live without transportation for years, he did not need to warn us. I thanked him and Ade came in, to make a third at a pleasant kaffeeklatsch. Then Chuck said that he brought bad news. Hurricane Carla, after devastating the Texas Gulf Coast, had veered to the north and was due to pass over us within a few days. I could feel myself turning pale. He watched my face and nodded.

"With this virgin stand beside you, you'd be fools not to get out, but I came to tell you that I'll be back in plenty of time to take you to town, along with some others. In fact, I'll come in now and then in the future—for some more good talk and coffee. Or you can drop me a line if you need something."

As he walked out of sight, the little knot of fear that I had tried to ignore since we lost our car untied itself and was gone. Although we had not mentioned it, we had always

known that a time might come when, without help, we would
be lost—or one of us, which would be much the same thing.
This man, like Jacques, was going to be not just a sometime
friendly acquaintance but someone we could depend on in a
crisis we could not handle ourselves. And he was stationed
where he could be reached, as Jacques, with his work deep in
the timber, might not be.

"You noticed," Ade remarked, "he said he'd be up here in
the future."

I nodded. Chuck Martin of the USFS had sized us up well
enough to know that it would take more than a hurricane to
defeat us.

The radio was at its rasping worst for the next two days.
Then a voice slipped through from Duluth, reporting that
the storm would pass north over Lake Superior and that its
winds were largely spent. The lake was a safe number of
miles to the east of us, and we were so relieved for our trees
that we stopped work and settled to play records.

That afternoon the sky turned black and it began to rain.
There were five and a half inches in an hour, followed by
eight inches during the night and the next day, and all that
time we heard the deep rumbling of continuous thunder and
could see the blue and purple of lightning far away to the
south and then the east, as the great storm moved by. There
were, we learned later, enormous seas on the big lake, but
our only damage was road washouts, a small price to pay for
the end of the drouth.

———— Late in October Pretty brought her beautiful self
to join her family and the mail brought a letter from the
publisher I had sent sample chapters to. He liked them, and
commenting on Ade's mimeographed wild geese on my
stationery, asked if he would do the illustrations for the book.

A contract to be signed and returned was enclosed. Two weeks later Pig and Brother returned and I received the first installment of the advance on the book. With the yard full of deer, our purse full of money, and my head full of ideas, I was overwhelmed to the point of dithering by our good fortune. I tried to start the book but was too excited. A good walk usually set me straight, so I went out on the road.

I walked a long way, stopping to watch the brook weave frills and lace over its stones, hearing the last calls of the crows, breathing in the rich scent of autumn earth. A friend drove along and stopped to talk a bit. I turned homeward with the sun in my face and joy in my heart.

The long, hard pull was over. I had no doubt that I could write a reasonably successful book that would lead to others. Ade could get back to his drawing board. With these things, and the articles and notepaper, we could earn a living. It would not be lavish, but it would be all we needed for the homely life that had brought us fulfillment. In letting the power and the phone pass us by, we had retained the peace and serenity that gave us time to think, and we had also kept our little bit of the forest wild for our birds and animals. Soon Peter would be back to make everything complete. There would be difficulties yet, but we were now very experienced in the art of coping. All in all, the view from the rim after the years of climbing was good.

Content, deeply happy, I came down the path to the edge of our clearing. Pretty and Fuzzy were lying side by side on the bank, chewing rhythmically and enjoying the warm, quiet afternoon. Pig and Brother stood in the open; first one, then the other, lay down in the dry grass for a snooze. Mama and her youngest twins stood near the big bucks, Little Buck nuzzling her neck and Starface squinting away from having his face washed. Bedelia was taking the last dust bath of the season, while Tulip watched from the henhouse doorway

and Ade stood beside their run, an empty feed pan in his
hand, watching the deer.

As I slowly came on to become part of this scene of peace,
I thought of the words of an ancient king:

> *He maketh me to lie down in green pastures:*
> *he leadeth me beside the still waters.*

part two

THE
YEARS OF
CHANGE

1961

FROM NOVEMBER 18

> *get another car*
> *clear small cabin*
> *finish inside*
> *inside toilet*
> *fix roof*
> *take a vacation*

———— Something woke me the next morning in the gray light before sunrise. I sat up, trying to locate any unusual sound, but there was nothing but the chittering of two squirrels arguing for possession of the woodshed. I was wide awake, in spite of having been in bed only a short time, so I might as well get up. I still felt the glow from my walk of the day before, so I decided to start this day in the same heartening way. I stepped into the woods between the cabins just as the first rays of the sun touched the treetops.

I followed an animal trail deep in the brush and saw tracks with the edges still crumbling that told me Pig and Brother had come this way just before me. I was idling along when the crash of a heavy rifle racketed through the woods, then another, not a hundred feet from me. I realized with a shock that the deer season had begun, and started toward this hunter who was shooting within sight of the summer house. Then I heard a man's voice: "Listen! There's another one!" I stopped, suddenly cold. I was in dark clothes, on a deer trail, and one might expect a sound shot from a man like this one. I dropped behind a ledge of rock, then slithered across the twenty yards to the road, just in time to glimpse a car with an out-of-state license disappearing around a curve.

I was shaking and felt sick, so I sat down on a rock and closed my eyes. But I could still see the antlers of a deer, slung across the trunk of the car. Then I felt very calm and in control, and I walked toward the gate of the summer house. I did not go through because I did not want to see the blood sinking into our green pastures, but I looked carefully at the tire tracks in the road. Then I walked half a mile or so to the east of the gate and then to the west of it, examining the road and its verges before I went back to the cabin.

Ade sat me down at the kitchen table and poured me some coffee, saying, "You're white as death. What happened?"

After I got over an attack of delayed jitters, I gave him a rough summary. ". . . and they got Pig and Brother—both of them."

"You can't be sure."

"Yes," I said, "and this didn't happen by chance. A car and a truck drove in and parked, one on each side of the road at the summer house gate. The tire tracks were plain. I checked the road and they didn't go down the road and come back or stop anywhere else within half a mile. They knew where to come and they came early because I'm sure now what woke me was the shot that got one of the deer. It was before the sunrise opening time. And the truck was gone when I got there. It carried the first deer. There's something else I ought to remember, but I can't figure it out."

The rest of the nine-day hunting season was a horror that I do not like to think about even now. I either could not sleep or woke from brief naps filled with nightmares. I heard shots, not as near as the first ones, but that brought on fits of muscular cramps and vomiting. I could not eat or even read, and working on the book was out of the question. And all the time I kept trying to recall the thing connected with the shooting, and could not.

The only hopeful circumstance was that the other deer were gone and that Mama, being old and surely wise to the ways of men, would have done her best to get her family safely away when she heard the first shot. If she had time. We kept corn out for them, but a light, new snow showed no tracks but those of a snowshoe hare and some mice. We waited.

On the day after the season closed, a man knocked at the door. He was a friend of years' standing from Minneapolis, who hunted but would spit on anyone who would kill a half-tame deer or shoot on posted land. He did not smile as he usually did, and after a good look at me, said, "So you know about it."

"My two young bucks? Yes. And I know it wasn't acci-dental." I told him about the tire tracks. Then: "I don't understand how they knew they were here. Bucks aren't usually hanging around houses in the rutting season."

"There are people who ride up and down the roads look-ing for places where deer cross so they can tell hunters where to go."

"That wasn't it. I checked in both directions and there wasn't a deer track on the road or the banks beside it for half a mile each way. Our deer don't cross near here except when there's deep snow. If there'd been tracks nearer the Trail the hunters would've stopped there. If there weren't, they'd have gone on past us, still looking. They wouldn't have stopped here if they hadn't been directed here. And they had to know we had bucks. I can't see the type of man who did this going to so much risk just to get an old doe and some fawns. They'd want antlers—to prove something."

"Likely. But you're right. They *were* tipped off."

"Who?"

He mentioned a name, but neither Ade nor I had ever heard it.

Then the missing link began to come back to me. I half stood, wobbling, and both men started toward me. I waved them away. I remembered meeting the "friend" as I walked along the road on the afternoon of Friday before the season opened, and I heard part of the conversation as I hear it now.

"Any deer down your way?"

"Just our old doe and her kids. Two baby bucks and two does from last year and the young bucks she brought with her when she came. They're really beauties."

"I thought you had a big buck with a fine head."

"Peter? He doesn't come in this early."

I felt a kind of relief as the memory cleared, but wanted to cry. Instead I sat back in the chair.

"I did it," I said. "Stupid, trusting, big-mouthed me. I told somebody."

"You could be wrong," our friend said, looking almost as sick as I felt. "Couldn't someone else have seen them?"

"No. Pig and Brother came into the clearing at two-thirty on Thursday night—I mean Friday morning. I'm a night owl, you know, and was up the rest of the night enjoying them. They didn't leave here during Friday because one or both of us had them in sight all day—and you can't see in here from the woods or the road or the shore. And I was writing and deer-watching, so that I didn't go to bed until around four on Saturday morning and they were both outside all that time, lying under the big pine. Nobody came snooping either night or all the deer would have taken off. The first shot woke me around six, and the deer were certainly shot inside our gate. There wasn't any time left."

He sighed. "It figures. The word was passed along. I'm sorry."

Ade got up, went to the window and looked out, came back. "I don't get it. We've had too few contacts with people to have personal enemies, and some of these deer've been here since 1958. Surely people knew they were here. Anybody could see the tracks after the snow was down. And we've had no deer hunters before."

Our friend got himself some more coffee. "It's just that there are more hunters. And a lot of 'em won't come back to spend their money if they don't get their buck." We must have looked puzzled because he went on almost impatiently. "The road, the power, the phone. They bring these guys who are too green or too lazy to find a deer in the woods and who'd be uneasy unless civilization was at hand." He looked from Ade to me and back again. "You've kept it out of here—and I'm with you a hundred percent. But it won't stay away from you any longer."

———— The next night Starface returned, a terrified five-month-old baby, bleating most pitifully for his mother. We were heartsick at the thought that Mama might be dead and even more dispirited by our inability to help Starface. He ran from us and would not eat, and we feared for his life until Pretty, limping from a bullet in her right hind quarter, moved cautiously through the brush and came back to her old feeding place. She adopted Starface, who took heart and began to eat again. Then Mama came in during a snowstorm and Starface ran to her. She licked him on whatever part he displayed near her face as he bounced and leaped and cur-vetted around her. He pounded her with his front hoofs and ran in wild circles, while she turned this way and that, trying to keep him in view. He bounded to meet Pretty, who was making her beautiful, quiet entrance, jumped up and bumped her face with his head, whirled to sidle against Mama with

such force that she had to sidestep to balance herself. Then
he stood quietly, rubbing his chin on the back of her neck,
while she curved her head around to lick his side. And, at
last, our beloved Peter stepped out of the forest, antlered and
unharmed.

Mama took her two remaining children away for a while
and came for food only at night, and I was always awake
until I heard her *stomp-stomp* and went out with their grain.
When they ventured to come to the yard by day again and
settled into their old ways with Peter, all four of them
vanished at the sound of a car or a strange voice. Ade and I
were touched that they felt we were safe humans, but this
did not take away my painful thoughts of Pig and Brother,
whom I had inadvertently sent to their deaths, of Fuzzy who
loved people, and of Little Buck not six months old, all of
whom had met the bloody hand of man. Then in January
Peter went to meet his destiny, and I knew that something
rare and irreplaceable was gone from us. But he had left us
the other deer, and as I saw Starface growing more like him
every day, I knew that I was part of the endless cycle of life,
from which nothing is ever lost, because nothing exists alone.

Only a short time after, I went out for a night check of the
hens and found Tulip dead on the floor of the little house. She
had shown no signs of illness, had been eating normally, and
had not been injured. Bedelia was sound asleep on the perch,
so there had been no fatal but temporary failure of heat or
ventilation. Tulip, like the Crown Prince, had simply died.
Sadly and regretfully, Ade found an animal-proof container
for her and left her outside to be frozen until spring softened
the earth and he could bury her.

This intensified the lingering effect of the shock from losing
Peter on top of that caused by the shooting in the yard, and
worst of all was my growing feeling of uncertainty about the
people we knew. In spite of what had happened, I wanted to

believe that those who lived in the morally clean atmosphere of the forest had more consideration for others than those who lived in contact with civilization's corrupting influences.

In Chicago I had been as wary as the next person in what I said and did, but during the years isolated in and surrounded by the innocence of the forest I had not needed this protection and had forgotten the duplicity that can dwell in man. And I was paying highly for forgetting. Because the realization of fulfillment and the seed of its spoilage had come from my walk, I could not remember the one without the other, and so could not hope to forget that a few words spoken in misplaced trust had brought man's violence to scar the Eden Ade and I had labored for years to attain. And attempting to wipe out the good memory to forget the other was unthinkable, even if it were possible. I had been perfectly content when I came from the road to our green pastures—and I would never know such contentment again. For perfect contentment rises from perfect trust, which cannot exist after childhood in the world of men.

I caught myself watching and listening for things not of the forest, and became sharply aware of cars on the snowy road at a time when we had learned to think of a passing car as a rarity. Ade told me that the Lodge was staying open all winter and had both fishermen and tourists who wanted to see what the forest was like in its supposedly ominous season.

We reached back through the years to the time when we were considering the purchase of the log cabin, and remembered the talk of plans for the road, the power, the telephone, and how Ade had said that if we bought Carl Johnson's place we would go back a hundred years and have some privacy—for a while, at least. And how our Minneapolis friend had said recently that civilization would no longer stay away from us.

During our first year and a half away from man's world

we had learned how to live within the rules set down by the forest. During the following years we had found a way to make a living from the forest's bounty. Now the whole thing was threatened by something from outside. We could still try to keep our place in the woods as a sanctuary for the animals and for ourselves. But we were uncertain, because civilization and the ways of men are uncertain, as the ways of the forest and its creatures are not. We could no longer plan for the future; we must play our cards as they were dealt to us.

> *get another car*
> *clear small cabin*
> *finish inside*
> *inside toilet*
> *fix roof*
> *take a vacation*

——— As winter dwindled, a bulldozer worked in the near distance, human shouts stopped the squirrel chatter now and then, and I listened with increasing edginess to every man-made sound. This apprehension spread until I worried about falling trees every time there was a breeze. At this point, I looked around for a way to combat such nonsense.

Piano practice was impossible because the piano was in the summer house, where it was colder than outside. The deer had left early, the jays and chickadees were nesting, the squirrels did nothing but quarrel over territories, and the groundhogs were still asleep. Moving around outside was a series of spills into crusted, wet snow.

Then I recalled that the man who had been so kind when Ade was ill spoke Polish. I dropped him a note that led to a hilarious once-a-week language session. Polish is richly in-flected, with exceptions to its exceptions to its exceptions, and I cannot imagine any student of it learning to pronounce it even as well as I did without help. The animals must have sat up in their holes and nests and wondered what the noise was about, for I am sure you could have heard us laugh across the lake if the wind was right. At any rate, I stopped jumping at every sound and had a start on a fascinating language.

Between winter and spring there was a sort of extra season, when the willow pussies opened and waited, shivering in their fur coats. In 1962 this chilly, damp weather lasted through May and gave way to heavy rains that washed the budworms out of their webs to die, leaving only the normal small population. Of the hundreds of large trees affected, we lost only five, two balsam and three spruce, all of which were in poor condition before the infestation. We also lost a certain amount of the newly developed friendliness of people who had cut their trees. Whether this was because we still had ours or because we had been right in letting the forest manage its own affairs I have not discovered.

After the rains squirrels came in large numbers to the cabin—thin, patchy-coated, clawing—desperate with hunger and weakened by malnutrition. I cooked up some "squirrel cakes" of flour, dry milk, and water, adding vitamin- and mineral-rich materials, and flavoring half the mixture with cheese, half with sweet chocolate. This helped greatly. Meanwhile, Ade cleaned Bedelia's house, scraping from its floor a thin layer of grain embedded in droppings. The squirrels snatched pieces of this and ate them eagerly, their noses or instinct or something else sending them straight to this unusual supply of minerals. Soon they were in normal high spirits and their coats were smoothing up, but their matings were sterile. In other parts of the forest many of the squirrels died.

Their poor condition resulted from the budworm infestation, and was only a small part of the disruption that it had caused. It was not merely a battle between worms and trees but was linked to everything—animal, vegetable, and mineral—in the forest; and it started and ended with weather changes.

There had been five rather dry springs, not dry enough to desiccate new growth, but with fewer rains than usual and these spaced well apart. The periods between rains allowed the forest's population of the worms to explode and go through their short life cycle. The following chilly, damp spring began to decrease the number of the worms, and the current year's rains, which fell when the worms were young and weak, ended the infestation until the next time.

During the six years when the worms were prominent in the trees, the insect-eating birds had a feast, and although there were larger numbers of them than in other years, there were no such flocks as had followed tent caterpillars to my home town between 1915 and 1925. The 1950s were the time when heavy spraying with DDT had failed to save the elms from Dutch elm disease but had killed thousands of birds who ate poisoned insects. And it so happened that, two years preceding the severe budworm infestation in 1912, late freezes in Wisconsin, Iowa, and southern Minnesota had caused a disaster of migrating birds, and so greatly decreased the insect eaters in the northern forests. It seems probable that the reduced numbers of such birds contributed to the severity of both budworm infestations. This hypothesis is strengthened by reports that uprisings of budworms during the 1920s and 1930s, when birds arrived in the large numbers usual in those days, were quickly over and did not reach the proportions of the one we saw.

The red squirrels enjoyed the budworm pupae as something special to eat, but their staples for winter are the seed-laden cones of balsam, spruce, pine, and white cedar, along with dried mushrooms. The weakened balsam and spruce produced no cones for four years, beginning with 1958, and drouth inhibited the crop of mushrooms and pine and cedar cones in the last of those years.

This led to the pitiable condition of the squirrels in the affected parts of the forest. The reduced squirrel population would affect deer during the coming season, because cedar cuttings brought down by the squirrels as they harvest cones for themselves are an important help to the deer, especially in overbrowsed land like ours, where the deer have eaten the cedar branches so high that they can no longer reach them.

The wandering grosbeaks and crossbills, who eat evergreen seeds, did not appear, because there were almost no seeds to attract them. Few evergreen seedlings lifted through the grass of summer. The absence of green balsam affected the moose, who use it as one of their staples. Deciduous ground growth increased with increasing light in areas where dead trees fell, and this brought snowshoe hares to thin the growth as they ate. Since most of these windthrows were already damaged and punky, they had woodpecker holes in them. These birds not only lost eggs and young but had to find new homes, and their reduced numbers allowed the population of insects in the immediate area to increase. Even the material that fell from the trees to fertilize the ground was different during the infestation, as was that carried into the lake by rain.

The details of such interlinked changes are endless, and there is no change that does not affect everything else. If I but lift a stone, the creatures under it must die if they cannot immediately find other protection from heat and drying, and their passing brings about changes in the immediate area.

It is normal for natural balances to swing back and forth, like the pans of an old-time scale, one dipping and then the other, with changes in the weights they bear. Overpopulations starve or die of disease or are otherwise limited, as when lemmings move in large numbers and fall into the sea. Such damage as their feeding has done to the earth is repaired in their absence, or gives way to some other form of food and life. The earth and its life are not static, and man is only one among its many life forms, none of which is valueless to the whole.

The forest, through such examples as the time of the bud-worms, made this clear to Ade and me. We, as representatives of a species of forest dweller, *lived* ecology, which deals with the mutual relations of living beings, and of the relations be-tween them and their environment. To us, the efforts of man to "conquer nature" and so prove himself greater than the unity of which he is a part or superior to the forces that created him, seem not only dangerous and presumptuous, but stupid and silly.

———— In March, when the snow was just starting to melt, Gregory had emerged from his burrow almost at Starface's feet. The young buck flipped his ears forward, lowered his head, and stared. Gregory backed off, looking at this great beast much as he had looked at Ade and me when we first caught him in the carrots. Then Starface stomped and Gregory fled, thereafter to study the terrain gingerly from his doorway before he emerged.

Somewhat later Gregory scratched at the screen and de-voured four oatmeal cookies and two large carrots. That evening Ade reported that his tracks had entered Nose's retreat and we might look forward to young groundhogs. When Gregory came to the door some days later, he ate hugely as usual, then sniffed at the dry stalks of last year's plants. These he found uninteresting, so he trundled back to his burrow, there, I suppose, to drowse until a fellow could again eat properly, but I was wrong.

As soon as the ground was bare he reappeared and went to

work on his burrow, making two secret entrances—one beside a boulder, the other under a stump. When he came in the afternoons to the kitchen for strengthening delicacies he was powdered with earth. Although we never saw him groom his fur or even lick his peach-juice-stickied paws, he was always shining clean a short time after.

Nose came out in May and set about cleaning her den and gathering grass, leaves, and bits of paper for a fresh bed. She dug a new chamber under a place Ade had filled with trash, pushing out flattened cans, rocks, and bits of root nipped off by her strong front teeth. These discards lay beside our path, and when the accumulation began to spill onto it, Ade removed the excess, but only bit by bit, because if he but touched a can Nose poked her head out and gave him a dirty look.

In the midst of this remodeling Gregory came to play with Nose, but she growled and chased him. He watched her awhile from the bank, then accepted his dismissal and wandered away. In the evenings he watched until she had had her dinner and gone in, and only then came to the door for his share.

After Nose had her babies she cleaned out their bedding daily and replaced it with fresh, dry material, swatting impatiently at mosquitoes that buzzed around her plump, hairless, pink breasts. Then she ate a large meal of wild leaves, topped off with grain and graham crackers, before she went back to her underground nursery.

One day I decided to gather dandelion greens, but could find only tiny leaves, struggling to grow from the roots. The field daisies were in similar condition. Apparently Nose liked these best, and as long as we had her, our clearing would have no flood of golden blooms, no polka-dotting of white. We had plenty of flowers, though, because she did not care for sweet williams, wild asters, yarrow, or begonias.

When her favorite ground plants were depleted, she climbed the stems of the red-berried elder to feed on the leaves, sometimes slipping on the small branches and hanging upside-down by her four feet like a sloth. She pulled down raspberry canes with her forepaws to get the berries and gobbled every wild strawberry she could find. The chipmunks searched in vain for dandelion seeds and had to feed at dawn if they were to get any berries.

In July Nose brought out her roly-poly twins, who galloped and climbed and poked their snub noses everywhere. Ade and I tried to make friends, but Nose herded her precious charges into the burrow the instant we opened the door. By August they were well grown, both partially melanistic and looking much as Gregory had when we first saw him. One day he was standing tall on the bank, watching mother and twins with interest, but he kept his distance and Nose, after a sidelong glance, ignored him.

Before the end of the month the young groundhogs went away to find burrow locations of their own, and when one of them returned, Nose sent him packing with squeals that might be thought to mean he was big enough to be on his own. My personal opinion is that Nose wanted no new competition on her excellent home grounds.

———— I was spending many hours at the typewriter, and when I felt mentally stale or physically stiff from the close concentration in one position, I groundhog-watched or took walks or fed Bedelia.

She seemed to like her independence. She ate heartily, laid two or three eggs a week, scratched and bathed in the dust, and grew so confident that she paid little attention to events outside her domain.

One afternoon I stood up to stretch and looked out a

window. A fox was standing just outside Bedelia's run, staring at her. Safe behind the wire, she was picking gravel, completely unaware of him. Then I saw that the run gate was not hooked and was hanging slightly open. Once the fox saw that opening . . .

Ade came in view with two buckets of water. The fox sat down, perhaps determined not to lose his meal. Bedelia saw the movement and looked up, to rear back at an improbable angle and let out an appalled screech. Ade dropped the buckets and ran to the rescue. The fox stood up, was lifted under the belly by the top of Ade's boot toe, and sent flying through the air. Bedelia, her comb almost white from fear, pushed through the gate and sat down, quivering, on Ade's feet.

The fox picked himself up and loped away as Ade lifted our terrified hen and brought her into the house. She wailed when he tried to put her down, and he held her for an hour until she stopped shaking and her comb resumed its bright coloring. When Ade started out the door with her, she flapped free and hid under my bed. Plainly, she was refusing to go back to that fox-ridden run.

If we were to get any more eggs, she had to be coddled until the fox was a dimming memory. Anyway, we did not want our last pet chicken to be unhappy. We fixed her a wire-fronted box in the kitchen, as a temporary coop.

All went well until I decided to make a casserole for dinner, and having my hands full, called to Ade: "Hand me a can of boned chicken, will you?"

Bedelia squawked and then began to cackle an alarm. Probably my loud voice had startled her, but her explosion sounded so much like a protest at what I had said that I found myself saying, "I beg your pardon. I meant boned C." Ade will never let me forget this, and "chicken" has been "C" to Ade and me ever since.

———— When the book was roughed out, I roamed the forest, burdened with field guides that I carried around my neck in a two-pouch clothespin bag, checking my reported observations for accuracy.

On clear days I looked at the earth under my feet, the small things that crawled there, the low plants that grew in shadow, and the tall weeds that sheltered them, the brush that had to be pushed aside, the old trees and their seedlings, the birds that perched in them, the clouds and the sky and the changing light. When it rained I watched the frogs that sang in wet grasses, the rise and splash of our little brook, or stood on a twisted cedar root by the lake, feeling the freshness of the air and following the interlocking rings of the drop patterns on the quiet water.

When I grew tired I sat at the base of a big pine or spruce, leaned back, and closed my eyes. My skin grew sensitive to the touch of the special air of spring, the drier air of summer. Faint creakings told me of branches rubbing together. One day my nose crinkled to an acrid scent, something like rancid oil, and I opened my eyes to see a black bear strolling toward me. I sat without moving while he came almost to my resting place, observed me with shifting eyes as I was observing him, sniffed and wandered away, presumably no longer curious.

I learned to walk so softly that I could hear the little rustlings of the forest, and could tell the movement of a mouse in dry leaves from the sound of a breeze's stirring them. And I separated the common sounds from the uncommon, like the thin cry of a broad-winged hawk in a tree where there was no hawk, which turned out to be a blue jay mimicking the enemy so that he might have our bird food to himself.

I had already learned how to tell temperature by the feel

of snow under my boots—soft and compressible around twenty degrees, crunching at zero, squeaking at ten to twenty below, crackling like small firecrackers at thirty below and colder. And I learned that humidity can make these effects vary. I could sense rain coming by the faint scent of the earth on the wind, and be ready for frost when there was a certain tightening in my nostrils.

I found that air can have taste, as when the "showers of sulfur" from the pines give it a different savor from that brought by pollen falling from the deciduous trees and covering the lake with golden glitter. And the lake water, clear and pure as it was, tasted like cucumbers in late winter when heavy snow blocked sunlight from the water plants, which were said to be "frozen out" when they died.

In my night wanderings I discovered a sixth sense that told me mysteriously when the ground was about to rise sharply or there was something large in front of me. And once in a rare while I had the feeling of being watched by day, and turned to see a deer, tensed at the edge of the brush, nostrils wide and ears turned toward this stranger in her world.

The field guides were invaluable in clearing up local misinformation. For instance, I had it on allegedly good authority that there were no ravens in our forest, only crows. Subsequent checking assured me that crows have fan tails and upslanted wings when they soar and a sleek silhouette when perched, ravens have wedge-shaped tails and flat wings when soaring and a shaggy throat and chest when perched. We have crows and ravens around the cabin in summer, ravens only in winter.

A headful of facts, gleaned from courses in biology I took to pass the evenings when Ade was in the World War II Navy and that I never thought would be of the slightest use to me, kept me from jumping to conclusions, as did a man who showed me a hole in a door, which he said was gnawed by a weasel. He knew this because he saw the weasel coming out of the hole. Actually, weasels have no gnawing teeth, and the supposedly guilty weasel was using an opening made by mice or squirrels, both supplied with gnawing teeth, as are all rodents.

My observations helped me find meaning in the mingling of many kinds of lives and sometimes a story in the simplest things. One late-winter day a whiskey jack dropped onto my hand for a bit of bread, and rising, left a molted feather— a soft-gray, white-tipped feather—hanging from my little finger by a hair that was tangled into it, along with bits of dried vegetation and a fragment of another feather, tinged with violet-blue. I had never seen a whiskey jack's nest because they are high and well-concealed in the thickest evergreens, but I felt pretty sure that one such nest was made at least partly of grass, leaves, blue jay feathers, and hair, and was probably being refurbished for its third year. Why? Whiskey jacks nest before the snow is gone, and it was at that time two winters before that I had decided short hair would be less bother under our rugged living conditions. I put my shorn locks outside in case some wild neighbor might have a use for them, and they were gone shortly after. Nothing goes to waste in the wilderness.

———— The day after Labor Day, when the rush of boats was over and the forest could again relax, was still summer, a summer of days bright with butterflies and nights when great moths bumped and fluttered against our lighted windows. Wild blue flags bloomed from clumps of leaves that had not shown a bud to us before, and the sunset was like a fire that sent rose and bronze and violet smoke up to vanish overhead. It ushered in a time of wild plenty.

The balsam-fir tops were purpled by cones so frosted with resin that they glistened in the sun. The spruces were crowned with what looked like golden buds from far below on the ground. The white cedars were so laden with clusters of little wooden flowers that their blue-green branches bent, low enough for our deer to munch the leaves, although I hoped they would stay away until after the hunting season. The white pines had produced few cones during the dryness of the previous summer, but these had opened, shed their seeds, and fallen, and a new crop of green cones hung thickly from the high, wide-spreading branches.

The red squirrels cut down the seed-filled green pine cones and buried them, to be opened and eaten at leisure. They stacked the balsam's lovely flowers in middens against stumps and boulders. To walk under a cedar was to be hit by a falling cone cluster and to be the target of the harvesting squirrel's frantic protest against one's probably thievish intentions. The Wealthy Squirrel, whose territory included our two largest pines, four cedars, and two balsams, chattered herself almost voiceless in trying to prevent Ade and me from crossing our little bridge into her domain. The chipmunks carried pouch loads of seeds to their burrows. The deer mice rushed back and forth, so small and frail to have to work so hard, carrying seeds one by one to their winter nests.

And the squirrels had been collecting mushrooms everywhere. The neighbor who gave us the refrigerator said that one had "canned" five quarts in jars that he kept in his workshop for odds and ends, and Ade showed me a battered hat in our storage building, brimful of honey agarics. I was glad that I had forgotten to dispose of it in the airtight.

The days were warm and the nights frosty, the air as sharp and clear as on a mountain. Slowly the ground plants faded, darkened, dried, and lay down. The leaves on the mountain ash turned bit by bit, from green to chartreuse to gold; those on the maple and sumac, to the clear, deep shades of zinfandel and burgundy.

Ade put up additional *No Hunting* signs and I stored in my mind the crying of gulls and the laughter of loons that I might hear them through the winter, waited for the day when there would be no crow calls, for as Jacques told me, "The crows know when to go."

There was shooting in our yard from the opening of the grouse season, though. This so disturbed my concentration that I started to work at night, from ten until dawn. I finished the revision and typed steadily on the draft to be mailed in spite of a shortage of sleep, a dull awareness of the approach of the deer season, and a worry that gradually became a fear that the deer might return any day. They were later than any year before and I tried to make myself believe that Mama knew something about hunting and was being more cautious than usual.

Then, on the afternoon before the season opened it began to snow, and Pretty, tall and graceful and looking modest and proud at the same time, brought her firstborn fawns to the feeding bench. They were little does as beautiful as their mother, nervous and eager, curious about this strange place, twitching snowflakes off their noses, leaning against their mother when she bent her head to lick an ear or touch a nose.

Ade and I stood at the window, and I could feel myself quivering.

"She trusts us," I said. "She knows we won't hurt her children. But she doesn't know that we can't protect them from others of our species."

"We'll have to get them out of here," Ade said, "and soon, so the snow can cover their tracks. But if the fawns see that we're threatening or anything like that, they may never be at ease here. And Pretty won't understand it either." He sighed. "It's been such a safe and happy place in the past."

I stopped shaking and began to think. "I know how. I'll take grain out and put it under one of the big pines. You get the automatic I used to chase that poacher that was after Peter. When they move toward the feed, slip out and stay behind the cabin. I'll tap on the window when they're through eating."

I watched Pretty's approach to the grain, her gentle encouragement until the timid fawns came, too. When they were satisfied and had moved some distance away, I stood for a moment, bitter at the thought of destroying the peaceful scene, then signaled to Ade. Through the roar of the big gun, echoing back and forth from hill to hill, I heard the thud of hoofs receding, dying away. Pretty's confidence had been damaged, but if she did not connect the noise with us, she would bring her family back. *If* she did not.

I flopped into a chair as Ade emptied the pistol and began to clean it.

"If Mama and Starface are anywhere near, they heard that," he said. "I don't think we'll have to worry about any of them. They know where to hide." He paused and stared at me. "My God, what a racket! In this stillness—" He looked at the heavy metal in his hand. "Well, we don't have much use for it, but when the time comes, it's handy."

The next morning the snow lay thick and white and there were no hoof prints. Ade took the boat to get the mail and I settled to check my amateur typing for errors, using the monotony of the task as a buffer against too much thinking during the hunting, when night work and daytime sleep would be impossible for me. I had finished only two pages when I heard a car stop on the road, and voices. I went out and glimpsed red through the wall of bare brush stems. Hunters.

I went in, picked up the automatic, slid in the clip, and started toward the road. Then it struck me that, although I had no intention of shooting anyone, it might be impressive if I appeared to have. I jacked a shell into the chamber, snapped the safety catch on and made sure it was tight, because a loaded gun with the hammer up not only looks formidable but offers splendid potentialities for shooting oneself if not properly handled. Holding the gun behind me, I proceeded to where a pair of hunters were just about to climb over a fallen tree and into our woods.

"What are you doing?" I asked.

They looked surprised. "There's deer down there," the tall one said. "Nobody lives there."

I pointed to our posting and down the hill. "If you look through the brush you'll see a house."

"Yeah—some old shack," he said indifferently.

"There're no deer around. You'd see the tracks if there were. And my husband and I live there."

"But we were sent here. Where all the signs are, he told me."

"Who told you?"

He was opening his mouth when the other man, who suddenly seemed to sense something wrong, pulled at his arm. "Let's get out of here."

"Yes," I said. "Let's."

The first speaker decided to get truculent. "You can't keep us out."

Smiling, I flipped the big handgun from behind me, thumbed the safety down, and said, "You think I can't?"

They went, with great speed. Feeling like someone dreamed up by Zane Grey, I eased down the hammer of the automatic and started back along the road. Then I got mad and made a few choice comments to myself. I was all over this before I reached the clearing and thought, as I looked at the snow-covered bank, of Gregory and Nose, curled into fur balls in sleeping chambers softly bedded and high enough to be safe from ground water in the spring. Bodies chilled, heartbeat and breathing slowed, bypassing the cold in the deep sleep of hibernation, living on their layers of converted corn and cookies. They, at least, were safe from the violence of man.

That evening our ranger friend dropped in and asked abruptly, "Did you have some trouble down here today?"

"Not exactly," I said, and explained, while Ade grumbled that these things always had to happen when he was gone.

"That may not be accidental," said Chuck, and looked very amused, which seemed incongruous. He went on: "Do you know Jack Wickersham? No? Did a car pass you on the road?"

I thought. "Yes. I seem to remember one, while I was coming back here. But I was in no mood to pay attention to the passing throng."

Chuck leaned back and snickered. "Well, I was up at the Wickershams' place on Shinjak Lake this afternoon and he told me there was a crazy woman down here, running around with a gun and mumbling to herself."

"My God! My husband grows a beard and I'm a kook. I protest DDT spraying and I'm a crackpot. Now I run some outlaw hunters and I'm a maniac. What did you tell him?"

"Nothing." He grinned happily. "He described you pretty well, and I just said, 'Oh, that's Mrs. Hoover.'"

Slowly the laughter grew. Finally Chuck wiped his eyes and said, "I figured something like that going might keep some of these heroes out of here. Just in case, I'll drive down the road and back when I come up the Trail. There's nothing like an official car to put a damper on things, and most of these guys won't know whether the Forest Service has jurisdiction or not."

One ploy or the other must have worked, because we passed the following eight days without hearing a shot or even much traffic.

———— The days slipped quietly into December, with a little more cold but nothing to cause heating problems, a little more snow but not enough to set Ade shoveling. The road was plowed once and I stuck doggedly with my manuscript correcting, although I was uneasy until the deer came back. First Mama, with Starface following in a couple of hours; then Pretty with her now very timid twins. Ade fell into the routine of feeding them, but we both stayed inside as much as possible until the skittish fawns gained confidence and began to eat their share.

On the strength of the portion of the advance to come after the manuscript was mailed, we had gas-mantle lamps put in at my desk, and in the kitchen and living room. For the first time since our move I could work at night without aching, watering eyes. And cooking almost in the dark had been an experience anyone should want to miss. I had to look into pots with a flashlight and later on a newspaper photographer used this antic as an illustration for a feature on us.

We invited Jacques for Christmas dinner and spent a happy day, touched with sadness as we remembered Peter, who had come to us on Christmas but would come no more. Then the other deer arrived to remind us of his legacy, and we found ourselves looking ahead instead of back, as we should.

Jacques's truck was giving him trouble, so he came back three days later and took Ade down to his place to see what he could do about its innards. I ran through the last pages of my typescript while he was gone, and it was ready to mail when I heard Jacques drop him off at the top of the hill. I rushed to start dinner, but paused in the act of opening a

can of wax beans when Ade came in, looking blank and
rather dazed.

"What's the matter?"

"Nothing—only Jacques has given me his car."

I almost dropped the can, not being used to people who
gave away cars as they might "a nice trout for supper."

"But what'll he do— Oh. Use the truck, of course."

"It's a good car," Ade said in a distant voice. "And it's
another Chevy. Not new but not too old. It needs repairs,
but I can handle most of them. And there's a good mechanic
in town who can do the rest and he doesn't rob you. But
there's insurance and the cost of gas and oil . . ."

"Don't give it a thought. We've plenty of money for supplies, and I can't think of a better way to use the rest of the
second book payment."

"Oh yes," he said. "I'd forgotten the book."

I threw a wet sponge at him and finished opening the can.

———— During the next days, when Jacques regularly
picked Ade up and brought him back from repair sessions,
I felt a growing excitement about being on wheels again.
After more than eight years this would be an adventure. The
snow was light and the lake ice only six inches thick, and if
the winter continued to be so open we would have pleasant
exploring and driving, our favorite recreation from the time
when we met in 1930. The thin ice kept cars from running
back and forth on the lake, and even snowmobiles, a noisy
novelty in those days, moved cautiously. Ice fishermen also
were few, and all this meant light traffic on the Trail, a bonus
toward safe backwoods driving.

I pulled Ade's list from the drawer, and a little ahead of
time, marked off "Get another car," adding "8" for years to
accomplish. Nine of the fifteen items were done. No, ten. I

crossed out "Make a living." We had managed to do that the year before but I had been too disturbed about losing our deer to think of the list. Anyway, only five items remained.

On January 8, Jacques towed the car to the mechanic in town, and Ade went along to take his written driver's test. There was also a field test two weeks later, and this would be a breeze for him, in spite of the strange car and his long time away from the steering wheel.

On the night before Ade was to get the car we were both so excited we could not sleep. It was after midnight when the cabin logs began to snap and bang and from the lake came the rumbling and zinging of ice, freezing fast and cracking under the pressure of its expansion. I felt the wall. The logs were chilly and I turned up the oil stove, to keep the unconquerable winter outside. Ade checked the thermometer, which showed a drop of twenty degrees in two hours.

In the morning it was forty-nine below, and we knew it would be even colder on the higher land where Jacques lived. "No car," Ade said. "Jacques isn't a fool to make an unnecessary trip in weather like this." There was nothing to do but wait two weeks for the next test date, so we settled down to indoor tasks, but first I tossed a pan of wash water out into the air, to have the fun of seeing it go away in frost as fine as fog, dropping only a few glassy beads to the snow.

The ice sounded like a bull alligator bellowing along the shore and its cracking shook the cabin. Through this noise, I heard the clamoring of birds and squirrels. There was a weasel, small, with completely bare pink paws and fur like whipped cream; two ruffed grouse, their feathers fluffed against the cold; a dozen blue jays, some of them acting almost tame, which is not the usual way with blue jays; as many whiskey jacks, all warbling from the woodshed roof and the cedar nearest the door; chickadees, I do not know how many because they darted about too quickly for me to count them; two nuthatches; two each of hairy and downy woodpeckers; a brown-and-white mouse, shivering under the edge of the shed floor; sixteen red squirrels, so busy trying to attract attention and food from the house that they were not quarreling with each other; and five strange deer, standing at the edge of the clearing with Mama, Starface, Pretty, and her twins.

Since we would soon be able to replenish our supplies when needed, we were lavish with feed. Ade went out with ten pounds of cracked corn, to have chickadees light on his shoulders, his cap, the flaps of his pockets, even his arms and hands, where they clung while he measured out the feed in a number of places. I got hamburger for the weasel, and he snatched it from my fingers as soon as I offered it. Ade refilled and hung the suet feeders, but the fat froze so quickly and so hard that even the woodpeckers had difficulty in breaking off the smallest pieces. He brought the feeders in and we chopped the suet fine enough for the birds to pick it up from the bench.

The mouse was still shivering in his place, with head bent very low. I picked him up and held him between my bare hands in the kitchen until he was warmer and began to move a little. I offered a small piece of graham cracker, which he took and ate, then washed his face and hands and began to look around for a way to get out of this unprecedented situation. I held him as firmly as was safe for him, put a handful of grain under the shed floor, and let him go. He ate some of the grain and came back every day for three weeks to be fed. He was too small to compete with the birds and squirrels for grahams, so I fed these to him by hand. Fortunately for him, the weasel was too busy eating and storing his bits of hamburger and suet to bother with hunting.

A wind blasted out of the north on the second day of the bitter cold. One of the chickadees was flying into it and lost his forward motion, to tumble around in the air. Once he had righted himself and perched, he had the strangest look about him—almost nonplussed. Then I saw one of the nut-hatches, sitting on the cold surface of a bare stone, his head tucked under his wing. I got him inside at once and Ade supplied a box near the stove, covered lightly and with suet inside. Birds do not freeze except when they have not man-aged to get enough food to keep body temperature up, but this one was very near the sleep without end. He was peck-ing at the suet within an hour, though, and showed no in-clination to want to go back outside.

"Very smart," Ade said. "Why freeze your tail feathers when you can rest by a nice warm stove?"

We let him stay until the next day and thoroughly enjoyed watching him, perched on the edge of his box, sharp little beak tilted upward, black-and-white striped head cocked to one side, back and wings the exact shade of gray-blue to set off the feathers of his breast, which to me are not rose but a soft shade of salmon pink.

It was during this day that a snowy owl drifted into the yard like a little lost cloud. The birds flew away in a group before the owl lighted on a cedar branch just above one of the bird feeders, refilled with chopped suet but now almost empty. The second nuthatch was perched on the wire mesh. The owl lifted from the branch and banked downward. The nuthatch squeezed into the feeder through its partly open top and clung to the back of the cage. The owl tried very hard to get at him, pushing his beak as far as he could through the mesh, but finally soared upward and out of sight. The nuthatch was out and away like something shot from a bow.

One squirrel learned to jump up a foot and field pieces of

tossed graham cracker between his hands. It was the more interesting because he taught himself this trick. It snowed a little, too, and I went padding around in the drifts, digging out corn and other food for the mixed clientele, who watched anxiously from convenient vantage points.

When the two weeks were up and Ade waited for Jacques to take him for the driver's test, the bitter cold and most of our visitors had gone. The dark part of the winter had started its gradual retreat. The sky was a deeper blue than earlier, and the sun was high enough to look between the tree tops at midday and make bright spots in the snow, like pieces of sunshine that had frozen and broken off and fallen into the yard.

It was a fine day for going to town, but Jacques did not show up. We imagined all kinds of calamities and it was mid-afternoon before we discovered that it was February 12. Abraham Lincoln had had the temerity to be born on that day and so close all the State offices a hundred and fifty-four years later. Ade muttered that the weather would probably be impossible again on the next test day, but he was too pessimistic. Jacques came for him a day early so that he could stay in town for the test, scheduled for early morning, instead of tiring himself by starting before dawn on the actual day. The test over, Ade would run our errands and drive home.

An hour or so after they left, a woman I had met once or twice at Conrad's Lodge, and who lived ten miles nearer town than we did, came down the path. After brief prelimi-naries, she said, "I just saw Jacques Plessis and your husband going to town. I thought the driver's tests were tomorrow."

That see-all, know-all moccasin-telegraph, I thought, as I replied, "Yes. But Ade's is scheduled very early. It'll be easier for him to stay over, take the test, and then drive back."

My guest broke into peals of laughter. "He won't. Nobody ever passes the test the first time. It took me five tries, and

I'm a good driver, I'm told. People who've driven for years in other states don't pass it."

"He will," I said, to be answered by more laughter.

"What I really came for," she said when she was able to talk again, "was to tell you I'm going to town tomorrow and will pick him up and bring him back. Where's he staying?"

I told her and said, "It's very nice of you, but you won't have to."

I heard her laughing as she walked back to her car.

As I waited for Ade the next day, I tried to figure out the reason for these consistent failures of a simple test. Perhaps it was nervousness or lack of experience with certain types of driving. Ade had thirty years of making his way through Chicago's jammed and often erratic traffic, much road and small-town experience, and could park any car in any space it could be slid into. And no uniform or officialdom would bluff him.

At dusk I heard a car pull up and park, and saw Ade on the path. It was my turn to laugh. Some one of the doubters would surely have seen him drive by, and the news would spread. It was a small triumph—but our own.

I was set for a short drive the next morning, but there was drifting snow, and of all things, ice fishermen, who must have driven up before the storm and did not want to waste their trip. Huddled behind shelters built with snow blocks cut from the pack on the lake, they looked like Arctic explorers making a last stand for survival. When the snow stopped they moved in to literally ring the shore by our cabin. Why there we couldn't imagine; perhaps someone at some time was rumored to have caught a big fish in that particular part of the lake. One of them, the Compleat Angler, wore a many-pocketed windbreaker, green alpine hat decorated with trout flies, and two cameras slung around his neck. He put a line in a hole and spent his time walking from one man to another. He did not catch a fish, and I do not think he took a picture. To this day I wonder what he got out of his stay in the cold.

Ade reconnoitered and came back, not smiling. "There's thirty-two of them, none more than a hundred feet from our water hole. And I don't see any toilet facilities. When the icicles run out we'll have to do something about our water. Have we any iodine or Clorox?"

"No. I used the last of the Clorox a few days ago."

"Then we'll have to boil it." He looked toward the lake. "Nice clean types."

The next day was sunny, the plow cleared the road, and we set out in our "new" car to see some more of our world. The forest was black and white, with deep-blue shadows, and here and there the tracks of a deer or moose came down a bank to follow the road edge, then go back into the secluded places. The muffled quiet that comes only with snow was broken only by the movement of trucks with the home-built enclosures that were the ancestors of today's campers. We counted twenty-one of them, coming or going in fifteen miles, which was an astonishing amount of traffic for that part of the Trail in winter. The fishermen had come in force.

When we got back to the cabin I looked at some tracks on our path and said, "These zigzag boot soles aren't ours. We've had visitors."

Ade looked toward the lake. "Most of those men are gone. I'll just check things."

Half an hour later he came in, looking disgusted. "Well, five gallons of gas are gone from the work building. It's a good thing I put locks on the drums up the hill. Whoever they were, they tried to be cagy. They came up from the lake through the woods to the east and walked down the road in the tire tracks to get here. The hasp on the door's been pulled loose, but it's set so they couldn't get it off. They stuck to our paths but they're real greenhorns not to notice that their soles were different and know we could see their prints when the snow is as fresh as it is now."

"But why?" I wondered. "They've got their own equipment and I don't see fishermen as vandals."

He shrugged. "Nosiness, probably. Some of them are a different breed from the ones who used to come here. I'd say they feel so far from civilization that they think they can do as they please and nobody'll know the difference. We'd better stick around the cabin until they all go. Somebody might get in and drop a match—and we aren't in the position of people who use a cabin just for a few months in summer."

On April 22, 1963, we made our first trip to town under our own power since November 1, 1954. It was exciting to arrange to get canned goods in case lots from our grocer, to help load the parcels and sacks of corn in the back seat, to be able to move where and when we wanted. And, best of all, we no longer had to feel that an emergency of ours might lead to inconvenience for someone else.

> get another car
> **clear small cabin**
> finish inside
> inside toilet
> fix roof
> take a vacation

────── May began with softly warm air, fruiting mosses, and thickly needled evergreens, recovering now from their siege of budworms. Blue jays talked in pleasant bird words in the cedars by day, and barred owls conversed in wheezes and squawls, roars and squeaks, clucks and hoots in the pines at night. The area that had once been buried under wood-chopping debris repaid Ade's patient clearing with a blanket of bunchberries, their white blooms opening slowly across the patch as the afternoon sun reached farther and farther every day. I found a secluded spot where fifty calypso orchids, rare in our area, were in pale-purple bloom, with some turning white as they passed their prime and prepared to fade. Nose came out early, and from her appearance, had had her young some time before. Gregory arrived a few days later, but came to the door only at night, so that I had to have one ear open for his scratching on the screen. I had cleared up editorial queries on my manuscript earlier, and Ade and I, with our transportation, prepared to get around and have some fun before the crowds arrived, but this was not to be.

The midmonth mail brought more editorial questions, and the rest of the summer was devoured by letters, trips to various lodges to make phone calls, and the rechecking of details relating to the book and its illustrations.

We did manage to squeeze in one picnic and went down the lake to a beach that edged the curve of a half-moon bay. The sky was faded amethyst, the water black sapphire, the breeze gentle, and the sand soft. We lay back against a drift-wood log and watched three gulls bathing. They hopped from low rocks into the water, splashing and spraying, then flew back to the rocks where they groomed their feathers. Seeing birds who lived in and on the water so enjoying their baths was novel and interesting, until a boat swung in toward shore and the birds flew away. This was the first of a dozen boats to come in as close as they could and peer at us as though we were bears. This reminded us that some pic-nickers on that beach earlier had left their lunch to walk along the shore and turned back to see a mother bear and two cubs enjoying sandwiches. Our relaxed mood had gone, so we ate and went home, having no unusual experience on the way except that a fast boat ran round and round us until we stopped and waited for it to leave. It was restful on our own bit of shore, though, and we stayed until so many mosquitoes began to rise from the still water that the darting, jeweled dragonflies could not catch them all.

And July had provided a treat—twin snowshoe-hare babies. They were small and brown and round, unlike cotton-tails because of their enormous eyes and hind feet. They played thump-thump in the grass and peek-a-boo among the interrupted ferns that spread above them like trees. And, when Bedelia was shut inside for the night, they slid through a small opening beside her gate and feasted in her corn pan.

When Labor Day was past and the summer homes and most of the lodges were closed, I was too exhausted and fratchety to relax. I was also disgusted because those never-to-return blue-and-green days were gone and we had had no chance to enjoy them. But, while I was deep in paper work, Ade had removed the trash from the storage building and hauled it, load by load, to the dump. With a vicarious feeling of accomplishment, I marked "Clear small cabin" from Ade's list, feeling that nine years to do it was not too long, considering the obstacles and more urgent tasks. I decided that the summer had not been so bad after all, and with only a small and transient pang for what I had missed, I turned my attention to the neglected earth.

Plumes of blue asters and sprays of white yarrow were scattered through the seeding grasses as I expected, but the goldenrod, bright above the browning ostrich ferns, was a new arrival. One of the abandoned garden plots was a mass of jewelweed, shoulder high and covered with brown-spotted orange trumpets. I caught the scent of mint as my foot crushed a stalk fallen into the path, and pushed through the grasses to look at a pink coral mushroom growing near the ditch in whose bank Gregory slept. I walked into the woods, picking at the burry seeds of tall buttercup that clung thickly to my pants legs and went on to find Indian pipes in their usual place under a big pine, whose roots gave food to them. Their ghostly shapes had come, lingered, and been transformed. Their stalks were dry and brown, and hollow cups, once their pipe bowls, turned upright and were covered by round, regularly ribbed open discs.

The next day, while Ade was getting the mail, I walked to the shore and watched a mother merganser with a dozen almost grown young, who were rushing across the water, trying to get up to takeoff speed for their first flight. I had not seen them when they were small and following their rust-crested mother in a string like bows on the tail of a kite. I had not seen their green-headed, white-throated father, either. Mergansers had nested somewhere on our shore every spring since long before we came—and I had seen the parents and then the young ones growing every year but this one. Across the lake I saw splashing and heard loons calling as a large group also practiced for their first migration. I had not heard their calls during the busy months just past and there was little time left for me to hear them before the lake froze and they were gone. Civilization disguised as publishing had taken my eyes from the forest's children and closed my ears to their voices.

In the middle of October, late warmth with fall rain brought a second spring. Wild rose stems leafed and produced a few of their transient flowers. Green strawberry leaves appeared among the maroon of those dying, and the fading cream of the violet plants was pushed aside by their new green. The raspberries were as thick with leaves as in the normal spring. Some white strawberry blooms appeared and a few of the many violet buds had opened before frost came at last, and took them away.

While the out-of-season green was still with us I looked out one day to see a grouse with one "chick," almost full grown but still being watched over. While her single child fed, the mother stood on the highest of some large stones and never stopped turning her head, searching for danger. At the same time a small doe slipped out of the woods onto the bank, with a single fawn who lay down and stayed motionless and almost invisible while the mother moved back and forth, watching our windows and studying the two grouse. Only when she felt all was safe did she lead the fawn into the yard to take some grain from the bench under the cedar tree. They were still there when I heard, faintly, the far-off sound of a shotgun. A grouse hunter. The two wild mothers listened but, when the sound was not repeated, went back to carefully watching their young. Both of these wild creatures were doing everything nature told them to do in order to safeguard their children, but they were completely vulnerable, neither having the slightest conception of pain and terror and death that could strike from a distance.

I felt that I had had enough of shooting around our home and sat down to write a letter to the local paper about it. It was a pretty stiff letter, but it was printed, and was so very successful that no one mentioned it to me except one summer visitor, who read it far away and wrote to thank me for writing it. It may also have been responsible for our not having any grouse hunters near us during the six-week season.

A late-October Sunday afternoon brought us one of the pleasantest surprises of our lives. We heard voices on the path and went out to greet one of the "grocery brothers," his wife, their two teen-age daughters, and his father, who had not been so far up the Trail for years. The lady had been reading "Butternut Wisdom," a column written by Gladys Taber for *Family Circle*, and had come on a plug for my book. They were all so eager to share it with us that they had made the long trip specially to bring it. I was touched and pleased, and thrilled because this was the first published comment on my work I had seen. I returned their kindness as best I could by showing them the first copy of *The Long-Shadowed Forest*, which had arrived the previous day.

Early in October, a photographer from a Minneapolis newspaper had visited us, giving us our first contact with the metropolitan press and a day of stimulating talk. In November, when the book came out officially, this matured into a feature story in the paper's Sunday magazine, illustrated with numerous photographs of us and a number of Ade's illustrations from the book.

We went to town a few days later and had the new experience of being recognized by strangers who had seen the feature. Most of them offered interested congratulations, but one woman stopped her car, got out, and said, "You're Helen Hoover. I saw your picture in the paper." She paused, looked me up and down, then asked, "How did you get that kind of publicity?"

That stopped me. I made some noncommittal reply but have always wished I had said something like "We bought fifty-one percent of the paper's stock." The only trouble with that is that she might have believed me.

Then it was the eve of the deer season, and even though no deer had arrived, I restlessly watched the yard. Ade suggested some target practice, which would be fine for steadying my shaky hands and at the same time warn off nearby deer. Whether it was the noise we made, my earlier letter to the paper, or the publicity attending the book publication, we neither saw nor heard hunters during that deer season.

———— Early in December Mama strolled across the snow with her well-grown new twins. She showed none of the nervousness of some earlier fall returns, and we decided that she had escaped harassment this year. Then the young mother and child who had come to the yard in October returned. We named her little buck Fatso for obvious reasons, but his mother remained simply Little Doe during the time she spent with us. But Pretty did not come, nor her fawns, and we wondered if they had run into an ambush some place far away. I spent many hours of anxious listening and watching for them, and for Starface, who, as the last of Peter's sons, was very special.

It was on Christmas morning very early that I heard the squeaking of hoofs on the snow. The sounds came from west of the cabin, and I looked out to see Starface, standing where we had first seen Peter. He had brought a friend. This new buck was tall, had an unusual dark-brown coat, and looked about with such an expression of hopeless yearning that we promptly named him Wistful.

Then, on the fifth of January, when thirty-below cold sent the birds and squirrels home early, Pretty came back at dusk, her fawns frisking beside her. She had been shot again, this time a graze from the rear along her left hip. She stepped carefully but did not limp. I wondered if her brighter-than-most coat made her an easy target. I also wondered about certain hunters who, talking to me in the past, had almost wrung their hands over the "cruelty" of wolves to deer and in the next breath told of snapping a shot after a deer running away. Pretty had been hit twice that way, not too seriously either time, but a shot at the poor target of a bobbing rump makes no sense. It is unlikely to bring a deer down, and if it should, would ruin much of the meat, provided such a shooter thought of a deer as food instead of just something to kill. If it did not stop the deer, but caused serious injury, the animal might recover and be crippled, or die slowly in sickness and pain.

Once our enlarged deer family were settled with us for the rest of the winter, a great wave of thankfulness for everything the forest gave us came over me. I had to express it in some way, so I sat down one afternoon and wrote the story of Peter Whitetail's coming. And that night, when it was snowing, I tried to put on paper my gratitude for all Peter had brought us and taught us during his short stay.

That winter with the deer was as rewarding as other winters but was full of apprehension because the wolves returned. Long before we heard wolf songs in the hills, the deer told us they were around. They gathered in the yard, restlessly listening, bodies tense and ears moving. Then they stomped for food. They did not move away when we took out corn as was their custom, but stood quietly and began to eat before we were back in the cabin. There was no arguing

over who ate where, only a steady filling of their first stom-
achs. When they had swallowed all they could hold, they
vanished.

They were gone for three days. At two o'clock on the following morning I heard a stomp and took out food. I carried
no light, made as little sound as possible. I was conscious of
deer very close to me in the dark, closer than they had ever
ventured before, and I could vaguely see shadows around me.
I piled up heaps of grain and Ade had brought in much cedar
earlier. When dawn came, the deer were gone, as was most of
the food.

So began a twenty-four-hour job which we divided between us and kept up until the wolves left near the end of
the winter, fitting in work and catching sleep as best we
might. We could not use shots to frighten the wolves because
this would also send the deer away from our food. Instead,
we reversed our policy of quiet and were as noisy as we
could be when we went outside by day. The deer came only
on every third or fourth night and we flashed lights and
shouted near the cabin on nights when we felt the deer would
not come. The wolves did not care for this and several times
we saw them pause on the lake ice, then run for Canada when
they heard or saw us. If we had not planned on staying all
winter we would not have fed the deer at all, because they
would have come for food at their accustomed place and
might have found the wolves waiting.

Our care in trying not to tame the deer paid off. They ran
from lights and noise, while deer fed at other places for the
entertainment of observers, and who were accustomed to
lights and numbers of people, were easy prey for the wolves.
(I believe that deer so tamed have too much trust in and dependence on man, and become less wary of natural danger.)
When the wolves found such a gathering of deer, unscathed
in the presence of man, they were emboldened, with fatal

results to the deer. The sad thing is that the people whose
deer were destroyed really wanted to help them, but did not
realize that in order to do this they must forget weariness and
put the needs of the gentle animals before their own.

On one of those nights when the deer were in whatever
place of safety their instinct showed them, the silence was a
tangible thing. Light struck from the bright, white disc of
the moon through incredibly clear air, so cold that its moisture
had frozen and fallen, to give back the moon's rays from the
snow in points of silver fire. A little lost wind rustled stiff
needles high in the pines and dropped down to rattle frozen
maple brush. A moaning rose, a chorded mingling of tones,
that swallowed the silence, swelled and faded, came from
everywhere and nowhere.

As I stood in the snow under the trees, the wolf song faded
and a great, gruff bark filled the air—a leader calling his pack
together. Howls from the road a hundred feet from me answered him. The tones were both high and deep, clear and
mellow, ringing and echoing as though the very stillness had
given tongue. Something stirred in me that was not of my
memory but was handed down from ancestors who knew the
dire wolf as a competitor for meat. I shivered from more than
cold, but I was not afraid.

The wolves howling on our road sounded like a large number, but the next morning their tracks showed that there were
only three. If I could have seen them they would have looked
like a wolf I once met on the path. He resembled a large sled
dog—a husky with perhaps some German shepherd—with
pointed snout and wide nose pad, rounded, upstanding ears,
and clear greenish-gray eyes surrounded by markings that
gave them a slanted look. His legs were proportionately
longer than those of the dog he resembled, and his feet, larger.
His thick tail flowed behind him as he, after looking me over,
ran away.

A few days after the howling on the road we saw a pack of seven running on the lake ice. There were a father and mother and their two young, perhaps an aunt and uncle, with maybe a stranger who had been permitted to join the family. The pups had outgrown the spiky tails and awkward, oversize feet of babyhood and were almost as large as the adults, but whirled off, wrestling and rolling, to investigate snow ridges, then gallop frantically to catch up with the others. One started to look into the matter of the wooden cover on our water hole, and had almost reached it when the father gave one authoritative bark. The nosy pup hastily left the man-thing and took up a place behind his sire and mother.

This discipline and obedience is characteristic of all such family groups, which are tight-knit. The females are ready for breeding only once in two years and they produce fewer young—how not being fully understood—when food lessens, and so they fall into balance with the animals on which they feed. The mother is so devoted that she leaves the den while her fuzzy, ungainly pups are nursing only to feed on meat brought to her by her mate or other family members. No animal works harder to provide for his family than the dog wolf, nor shows greater patience with his pups, even if they chew his ears when he is trying to enjoy an afternoon nap. Once I met on the road one of the vanguard of a new breed of "adventurers," who find amusement in courageously chasing animals with snowmobiles. He told me that wolves are dreadful gluttons because one he chased was so stuffed with meat that he had to vomit it up so that he could run. The truth was that he had forced a dog wolf to disgorge the hard-gotten food for his family, so that he might save his own life by running into land so rough his tormentor could not follow.

I received many letters from persons who had read my book

and some of the many articles on Minnesota's timber wolves, widely written about as endangered survivors of large numbers once found throughout the United States. A few of my correspondents understood the wolf-deer balance, but most said something like "How can you defend a creature as cruel as a wolf? I've seen pictures of how they gouge live deer and I can't bear to think of it."

Restraining the impulse to reply that such people seem mostly concerned with their own feelings, I answered all such letters more or less as follows:

"No wild animal is cruel because the word implies consciousness of inflicting mental or physical pain. Predators feed as instinct directs, and their killing is guiltless. Only man has the power to understand what he is doing, and so only man can be cruel.

"Many gouges and gashes borne by deer are not caused by wolves. A doe with frightful tears on her ribs once came to feed here. A game warden who dropped in later saw her recovering and told me he had seen a pet dog attack her. He shouted, the dog ran, and when he called on the dog's owner he was told that 'Fido' had been under the porch all day. Again, a young fawn was scraped by a scatter-bolt truck on our side road. The wound resembled claw marks, and was huge on so delicate an animal, half her side being raw and bloody. But the bleeding stopped, the gashes healed, the skin turned black with the start of new hair growth, and by the time she lost her spots I could hardly see where the injury had been."

———— We were planning for spring when the wolves finally left our area, and shortly after, unusually heavy snows began to deepen the layer on the ground. Such low deer browse as was uneaten was buried. The snow was fine and dry and shifted underfoot. It drifted but did not pack. The deer could have stood on packed drifts and so reached the lowest cedar boughs, which were well above their heads when they stood at ground level, but these soft drifts could not support their weight. Plowing shoulder-deep through the loose snow was too exhausting to allow them to go far in their search for food. Occasionally the does reared on their hind legs and brought down cedar branches for their fawns, but this was a dangerous emergency measure. Deer are not built for this kind of balancing, and the shifting, slippery snow was an added hazard.

Strange deer, who had come along the plowed road looking for browse, watched our deer moving around without fear, then came down to try to get at the food. There was a big red doe with pale-coated and lovely twins, another doe, then a yearling buck, and four adult bucks together. Then more came, and more, until it was impossible to keep track of them. Our deer fought to protect their food supply by rearing and striking with their front hoofs, and some of these blows drew blood.

Ade went to town and brought back a hundred pounds of corn, all he could get because many other people were feeding birds and deer through this bad time, so that feed stocks were low. We put it out in widely separated spots, hoping all our visitors would get a little, even though we could not offer them a square meal.

I prepared to dole out our cereal and as much chicken feed as Bedelia could spare, and wrote an emergency SOS to our ranger friend. He came up the Trail often, and being in town, would be able to get more feed than Ade, who might go in when there was none to be had.

The area around the cabin was full of deer when we heard

the truck pull up. By the time Chuck came down the path, smiling and burned by the winter sun, there was not a sign of them except tracks.

"I brought eight hundred pounds," he said, warming his fingers on a cup of coffee. "Too much?"

We assured him that it was not, while he looked out of first one window and then another. Finally he said, "They've really worked on your brush, but all I can see is tracks. Where are they?"

I laughed, and Ade pulled on his cap and jacket and went out, saying, "Watch."

He picked up the tree pruner, and as he walked up the path, three brown oblongs that looked like boulders lifted their heads, stood up in a patch of shadow, and stretched. Then the doe and her plush-covered fawns walked slowly from their resting place to follow Ade.

He stopped under the first big cedar tree and clipped a small branch from high above his head. The three deer were at the nourishing leaves almost as they fell on the snow. They did not even wait until Ade had walked on.

At the snap of the pruner, two pairs of ears appeared above a fallen log, and two does got up and set off after him. Three antlerless bucks stepped from under the big trees and moved after the does. As more branches fell deer appeared as if by magic, from behind trees, over little ridges, seemingly from the snow itself, and joined those already trailing Ade, his pruner, and the falling cedar. Some stopped to nibble branches already cut; others followed him along their hoof-packed trails to get a share farther on. The sound of the pruner faded. The neutral coats of the deer blended with the shadows and the beautiful animals passed from our sight.

1964

get another car
clear small cabin
finish inside
inside toilet
fix roof
take a vacation

———— The ice was still on the lake in the middle of May, gray and slowly melting, a dull contrast to the land where spring was dancing by in full regalia. Everything was early and abundant, the result of the slow thawing of the snow that had let the water soak into the ground to wake the roots. The absence of wind also contributed to the luxuriant growth, because most of our spring blows were northish and inclined to chill, if not actually freeze.

Sometimes people who see the forest only in summer, when its tallest evergreens are dark, its brush thick and full of shadows, find it somber, even depressing. I wish they could see it as it was that spring, when all its growth was touched with lightness and fragility. The little maple leaves were as serrated as snowflakes, and against their yellowish masses the new cedar looked more blue than green. The dark balsam twigs had inches of pale new growth, tender and aromatic, and their tops and those of the spruces shot upward with zest, as though delighted with the water and the sun. The ground was arrayed in varicolored green, whose multitude of shiny leaves moved in the mercurial breezes to fill the open spaces with shimmering.

Orange-and-black bumblebees hunted nesting places. Such hellgrammites as had not been caught by fish or used as bait by fishermen emerged from the lake as dobsonflies, with long transparent wings. Mosquitoes were thick, big ones whose bite was much less sharp than their size might indicate. The sheet webs of ground spiders, dew-covered in the morning, added their glimmer to the brightness, and a female fisher spider, elegantly marked in gray and black with touches of white, made the eave over our door her headquarters. Bats fluttered and darted in the dusk and every evening we heard a toad's shrill and monotonous love song from the ditch where water trickled slowly.

One evening I caught a whiff of skunk on the wind, absent in our forest since we had been there but as familiar to me from my Ohio girlhood as was, in these later days, the cool touch of a squirrel's brown-gloved fingers as he took food from my hand. And the next day brought a grackle flock, more than a hundred of them, squeaking like all the rusty gate-hinges in the world, and their iridescence was as bright as the spring forest—violet and blue and green on their heads, every shade of bronze on their backs and wings. They feasted on beetles and spiders and corn—and more corn.

Then the ice opened and a few boats moved on the lake. Some people who had driven up the Trail for the first time and turned down our side road, thinking it would lead to Canada, stopped for directions. While Ade was explaining that they would have to return to the Village and take the road along the shore of Lake Superior, the grackles swept down and the man said, "I never saw so many crows to-gether." So I pointed out that crows were half again larger than grackles, were less iridescent, and had black instead of light beaks. As he and his wife went up the hill we heard him say, "These backwoods people don't know a crow when they see one, and we'll just go ahead on this road. It's bound to go through to something."

And the woman said, "That woman seems intelligent. It's a pity she hasn't had our advantages."

Ade shrugged, picked up a can, and went up the hill for gasoline. He came back chuckling. "I walked to the road and saw that car going back from the dead end. It's from Chicago—has a city vehicle sticker on the windshield." He patted my shoulder sympathetically. "Poor disadvantaged Helen!"

"Well, we could go back—" I began. But he was already on his way to the work building.

The woman's appearance, though, had reminded me that I was a pretty dull-looking female, especially my hair after the long winter in the shadows. A friend whose hair had turned mousy from seawater bathing had sent me a bottle of something that she said had done wonders. "We're about the same reddish shade, and if you leave this on for five minutes it brings out the highlights and doesn't change the color. You might like to try it."

So, when Ade next went for mail I scrubbed my head and put on a small amount of the preparation. Five minutes later I discovered that I had used every drop of water in the house. I grabbed a bucket and, clad only in pants, headed for the lake just as a boatful of fishermen drifted to a stop off our landing. Not wanting to add toplessness to my already eccentric reputation, I dashed back into the cabin for a shirt, only to discover that the big washing hanging wet on the lines held every top I owned that did not have to be pulled on over my head. And I had too few towels to stain one with what I now thought an abominable concoction. Half an hour later Ade came back, and went to get me some water, crowing like a superior-minded rooster. When we went to town a few days later, the girl at the check-out counter in the grocery looked at my flaming mahogany head and said, "Whoever did that to you?" And no one could blame her. Henceforth, I gave up trying to make city improvements in backwoods me.

The morning after the hair fiasco, I poked my foot into one of my gray corduroy flats and felt what I thought was a sock wadded up in the toe. I reached my hand in, jerked it back in response to some reflex, gave a yell that brought Ade on the run, and dumped the fisher spider out of my shoe. Ade covered her with a glass casserole and we studied her a long time, legs spreading three inches and body to match, not dangerous but capable of a painful bite. She was in defensive position, body pulled back and mandibles lifted, ready to protect herself as best she could, even though her shortsightedness must have let her see only monstrous shadows. I felt pity for all small creatures who have such frail resources to use against huge animals like humans.

That afternoon a sharp-shinned hawk struck a cedar branch and broke his neck. We brought him inside to examine him before we gave him back to the earth—and that night we itched. I thought we were attacked by no-see-ums, but they, although small, are hardly invisible. Finally I took a magnifying glass and discovered a flesh-colored mite, no more than a hundredth of an inch at the widest point, on my arm. This creature and his relatives had left the bird to live on us. This meant washing every bit of cloth in the cabin and scrubbing ourselves and our house as we had never scrubbed before. Three days later we had lines of drying blankets, a shining cabin, weary muscles, and no more mites. Thereafter, we examined dead birds or animals outside and with rolled-up sleeves, and scrubbed hands and arms when we were through.

A few nights later I stood in front of the cabin, enjoying the feeling that I was not alone in the pitch blackness and listening to the wheezing voices of two young barred owls in one of the cedars, where their mother may have brought them for a mousing lesson. Then a dog began to bark and I heard the bawling of a baby bear, treed by the dog, no doubt. I was wishing that whoever owned the dog would call him in so that the terrified little one could run away when I heard a rifle shot and a sound of falling. I stood for several sickening minutes, while the dog growled and the bear cried his pain and terror; then, and only then, did the shooter fire again, three times before the silence came. But it was not the normal silence of the forest night, but one devoid of the faintest whisper, a silence filled with fear and wild things listening.

In the morning we saw boats coming and going from the location where the sounds had risen. Ade slid our boat into the water and moved out so that he could get a view of the shore. He returned looking sick.

The bear, not as big as sixty-pound Little Bear, who had slept high in a pine near the cabin in 1955, was lying in his blood, and people were coming, and bringing children, to see the corpse and hear the killer's story. "From comments I heard across the water, I gather he's quite a hero," Ade finished.

"No. He's civilized," I snapped, and wondered what would come next from city jungles to our forest's innocent life.

I was back to normal when, on a warm afternoon Nose arrived at the door, and Gregory scratched for food at a convenient, for him, two-thirty in the morning. I stepped outside to watch his departure across the clearing by following the waving plants that were faintly visible by starlight. A luna moth—that pale-green, swallow-tailed bit of night magic—drifted toward the cabin eaves. I snapped on my flashlight in time to catch the green glitter of tiny eyes and see the fisher spider jump, grasp the moth, and retreat into a hideaway.

I began to scratch, and as I ducked inside, thought of the mosquitoes that must have floated in while I was feeding Gregory. Well, another spider, a fuzzy brown individual who lived in a funnel web by the kitchen sink, would enjoy them. She had been there a long time, waiting patiently for food that did not come, when I got the idea of feeding her. I cannot bring myself to kill anything, but Ade had no compunction about swatting flies and mosquitoes, so I used his victims. In my efforts to put a fly in the outer mesh of her web, I touched it and she immediately appeared at the opening of her funnel. She ignored dead insects, so I took flies and mosquitoes that were still moving, touched the web, and held the food directly in front of her. She took every one. I had had no idea that one could hand-feed a spider. Incidentally, if any reader should want to try this, he should check a good reference and make sure that the subject is not a black widow or brown recluse. He should not touch the spider, nor use insects stupefied by insecticide or repellent, as their chemicals are not selective.

When I saw the wild strawberries blooming I went to look for calypsos, but there was not even a leaf. A young doe had nibbled there earlier, slim as a sapling, graceful as curling mist, red as an autumn leaf, beautiful as the forest itself. If the calypsos had to go, I was sentimentally glad that they had been taken by so lovely an animal. The forget-me-nots had seeded themselves from a high bank, and it was as though the forest had spread a pink-and-blue-dotted veil over the changeable green of our clearing. Bees hummed, and metallic-red damsel flies darted and lifted in a small cloud.

I saw Nose, lying comfortably flat on the mound in front of what had been Gregory's burrow. I wandered toward the road and saw a new burrow entrance in the side of the drainage ditch. It was half-hidden by cedar roots, and sheltered by a thick mat of overhanging mosses. Gregory stuck his head

out, then came forward to lie down on his "porch." It is hard
to think of a groundhog as philosophical, but Gregory seemed
to take being ousted from his first home in just that way.

The next afternoon, Nose was waddling around in a care-
free way, nibbling tasty shoots, when Gregory came running
down the path, burbling and ready to play. Nose let him get
near, then slashed her claws across his face. He backed off,
then returned, still burbling but less confidently. Nose rushed
at him like an attacking dog and sank her teeth into his
shoulder. He screamed and ran, with Nose hard after him
until they were both out of sight. She came back and settled
calmly under the shed to eat her oatmeal, but I felt it was just
that a squirrel who had challenged her right to the food
managed to give her a good scratch before he retreated.

I waited up for Gregory that night as usual but heard
squealing and growling, which meant that Nose had also
waited. I felt sorry for him, cut off from his cookies and carrots and occasional treat of a cabbage leaf, so the next day I
took the food and left it in his burrow entrance. He emerged,
sniffed at the carrot, lay down, and whimpered. He was not
seriously injured physically, and although a groundhog has
very little facial expression, there was something about him
that reminded me of a scolded child who had no idea what
he had done wrong. I sat in the path, making soothing noises,
and after a time he stopped his sad sounds and came to me. I
handed him a cookie. He ate a little, dropped the rest, and
went back into his retreat.

Each evening I took a ration and left it on his "porch" and
each morning it was gone. Then came a morning when the
cookies were gone, the cabbage was wilted, and the carrot
untouched. Three mornings later I saw a squirrel approach
the burrow entrance without caution and take a cookie.
Gregory was gone.

It was mid-June and the traffic on the side road was relatively thick, so Ade searched for signs of blood or perhaps a small, mangled corpse in the ditch, but there was nothing. With that off our minds, we stopped worrying about him, because he was such a harmless and amusing little wild person that we felt he would be enjoyed wherever he went.

Shortly after, Ade had to make a phone call and we drove to Conrad's Lodge. While I was waiting in the lobby I caught a high, penetrating male voice from the lounge. ". . . big black groundhog tried to sneak into my yard. I blew it in two. No groundhog's going to hang around and chew holes in my foundation." I was stunned. Poor Gregory, who only wanted to find a friendly groundhog to play with. And the foundation was like ours, concrete and stone buried deep in the earth, and the idea that a groundhog could chew holes in concrete was idiotic. The man who killed the little bear had racked up another kill.

———— A few days later, a newspaperman called me via Conrad's telephone. He was gathering material on the controversial question of whether or not the Boundary Waters Canoe Area should be officially declared a wilderness, and wanted our viewpoint. His time was limited, so he chartered a plane in a distant town and we drove to meet him and be interviewed at the harbor in the Village. He said he could hardly believe the height of feeling he had encountered during his interviews of residents of the main BWCA entry points, and was incredulous when we told him we had heard little of the uproar. He said that the extent of the agitation was excellently demonstrated by the owner of a very commercial lodge, who was so wrought up that he told the reporter lodges could never support commercialism.

Later, when a public hearing about this was held in the Village, Ade and I drove in. We had a hard time discouraging people who wanted to put a "multiple use" sticker on our bumper. One man, entirely overlooking the tourist business, said that logs were the only crop the people of the county got from the BWCA, and he did not seem interested when I said that there were vast acreages for lumbering in the rest of the Superior National Forest and that the full allowable amounts were not being cut. We heard false and conflicting statements that, if the wilderness proposal became law, there would be no fire control in the BWCA, and that no one would be allowed to enter except foresters to fight fire. Someone even told us that there was proof that the area would be kept solely for the private use of certain politicians! Considering the increasing interest of tourists in the forest itself, it was hard for us to understand the local opposition to the preservation of the wilderness character of the BWCA, because, if protected, this unique land would continue to bring business, even though surrounding areas might be lumbered or built up until they lost their attraction.

Although few spoke for the Wilderness Bill at the hearing and many spoke against, the bill was passed, in agreement with the wishes of the people of the United States as a whole.

———— Some weeks later as I stood in the clearing, not very happily noticing that the daisies and dandelions were blooming again in what had been Gregory's munching ground, Ade brought me the first royalty check from the book. I did a double take. I was right the first time—the check was several times what I had expected and the book was a reasonable success. I handed the check to Ade, who stared at it, looked upward, and said, "Roofing at last!"

We were headed for town in fifteen minutes, and on the way I had one of my most rewarding brainstorms.

"I'm going to call the movers in Duluth and have them send

a couple of men up here to move the piano into the log house," I announced.

"But where'll we put it? And Jacques and some other strong man could move it."

"I know where—and this is a grand piano, if a small one. Movers know how to handle it and are insured. What if it slipped and crushed some lumberjack's foot?"

"Well, it's fine with me, but where you'll put it . . ."

"Not to worry. There's always room for another piano, or something."

After the floor under the piano's new location was braced, Ade retired joyfully to the roof. To the sound of pounding and the smell of tar I sorted boxes of lists and notes, reminders of our struggles to make the cabin livable and attractive. They might give me an idea for another book.

I could see the cabin as it was in 1954 when we moved in —water- and smoke-stained Celotex ceilings; floor boards so rough and splintery they could neither be swept clean nor effectively scrubbed; walls water-streaked and unfinished; gaps around the floor edges, openings between the logs— everything dark and depressing. And that basement with a spring in it! Things had been changed in stages from the substantial beginning John Anderson had made when he filled the basement and made the little house solid. No one could have leveled the floors, though, and occasionally a stranger coming in reeled to the north as though he had stepped into a tilted room in a fun house.

I found a rough sketch of the original furniture's position and remembered a day when we sat in the living room on the softer of two old sofas, drinking coffee and looking into the woods through the west window. That was when I first grasped the magnificence of the white pine that stood like a sentinel at the edge of the clearing. I went to the window and looked up to its top, more than a hundred feet above me, with

its tufts of needles like thick, green fur, and began to understand why trees were among man's first gods. Then I became
aware of a length of rusty stovepipe that rose directly outside of the window, right in the center.

"What's that lovely thing?" I asked.

"Pipe from the furnace," Ade said reasonably.

"But it's right in the middle of the only view this house
has! You'll have to do something . . ."

He solemnly made another note on an already crowded
sheet of paper, a list of small improvements that might be
handled in odd hours. "What I need for this is a length of
wrapping paper. I'm beginning to have a notion it'll take
more than a year or two to get this place shipshape."

"Probably, but there can't be too many more things."

"Lots. That door, for instance." I turned to look at a tarpaper-covered opening in the west living room wall.

"What do you suppose it was for?"

"Another room. Cutting the door was as far as Johnson
got. He couldn't handle his outside job and work on the
house at the same time."

"I can understand that," I said with feeling.

It was during our second winter that a squirrel chewed
through boards Ade had nailed over this opening and trapped
himself between them and the paper. This meant loosening
the paper, opening the kitchen door, and gently shooing the
panicky little fellow until he found his way out. It was, as a
matter of course, a bitterly cold day. So Ade covered the outside boards with composition shingles, left behind by the
Larimers in one of the summer house's outbuildings. Squirrels do not like to chew on these, perhaps because the grit
affects their teeth. The door had not been changed after that,
but the present red denim curtain was an excellent disguise.

I tried to remember but could not the number of neck-
cricking scrubbings and paintings we had given the ceilings

before I had the brilliant idea of using glossy enamel, which was brighter and could be washed with a minimum of effort. Nor could I straighten out the number of changes in floor coverings before we put down vinyl that looked so much like pine boards that visitors occasionally complimented Ade on his beautifully laid floor. The gaps around the edges had been "temporarily" stopped with wood strips and corrugated paper in the early 1950s. Ade had been hoping for years to find time to put in regular baseboards.

Numerous local people painted soiled logs in light buff, saying this looked like new-peeled logs, but to me it was the brindle-yellow of the public washrooms in old-fashioned courthouses. I could even imagine the disinfectant smell. So we had covered our interior wood with undercoat and red-maple-color varnish. No flat finish could have so brought out the irregularities in the hand-hewn logs and beams, nor have been so cheerful, even on the darkest day.

How many times we moved furniture around in the cabins and exchanged pieces between the two houses I had no idea, but I would never forget the time we moved a heavy couch from the summer house.

I was pulling weeds when Ade came up with the wheelbarrow, saying that the couch was too heavy for me to help carry and the path through the woods too rough, anyway, so we could haul it along the road. (This was before I had demonstrated my muscles by moving logs.) I looked at the path, the product of years of walking along one trail—narrow, twisting, crisscrossed by roots, rippling with hummocks. It was hardly a service drive.

"Sure," I said, not sorry to leave the weeding.

"I'll get the couch crosswise on the wheelbarrow, and push and balance it. All you have to do is pull."

This sounded simple enough. What I did not realize was that the only way I could pull was to harness, so to speak.

Ade grasped the barrow handles as if he were about to start off through a field with an 1860 plow. The couch teetered precariously, I took a good grip on a pair of ropes that ran over my shoulders, and we were off.

We had only five hundred feet to go, but it was mostly uphill. Pebbles slid from under my feet, and every time I broke stride the ropes either went slack and threatened to dump our load, or tightened painfully on my shoulders and began to pull me over backwards. I finally leaned as far forward as I could without having four legs and began to make steady progress. At this point, a shining Imperial with people in the same style nosed over the hilltop and stopped to let us pass. I kept my sweat-stained face as low to the ground as possible and hoped they might think us refugees from a flood, or something. Ade gave the barrow handles a mighty twitch, flipped my "harness," and shouted "Giddyup, mule!"

We were speaking again by the end of the day, and henceforth furniture was carried along the path. This worked but proved beyond question that my métier is not furniture moving.

———— I was still sorting papers when the piano movers arrived, not in a small truck, which was all they needed, but in a medium-size van. This must have created a sensation, because for some time after we had people dropping in to find out how much we wanted for the cabin, which they had heard was for sale.

Once the piano had been skidded through the woods, I sorted music instead of papers, impatient for cool days when we would need the heat that would dry out and release the stuck keys. Then it rained and Ade left his roof to finish the last section of the bookshelves he had started in 1959.

Five years to build some bookshelves may seem unduly

long to people who have a lumber yard nearby, but Ade, in spare time, had cut and sanded each board by hand from lumber we salvaged after a building was torn down by friends. We had gone together in the boat, loaded the still-useful boards into it, and brought them home on a clear day of still waters—a very pleasant way to move anything.

While I classified and shelved the books, Ade built a storage cupboard in an empty kitchen corner. Once this was done and the wood cookstove replaced by a three-burner gas plate, with a large, heavy kettle that did duty as a Dutch oven, the cabin interior was settled.

The little house was convenient and comfortable, even attractive when I found time to keep the tops of things uncluttered, but it had taken ten years to make it so. It was with something like complacency that I crossed "Finish inside" from Ade's list.

———— This was the year when we first had mallards in the yard. A pair had come in April on a day when wind was ruffling new leaves and the space under the trees in front of the cabin, churned by the deer's hoofs, was a mass of muddy pools and rivulets. Both birds had their bills buried to the eyes as they strained insects and eggs and seeds from the semi-liquid.

I have a special liking for ducks because they waddle so comfortably and their plump faces wear such pleasant expressions, so was glad to have them even though neither Ade nor I favored the importation of alien species. There was a limited food supply for our indigenous water birds, and any large number of introduced birds could not fail to make changes. These mallards were tame, the descendants of ducklings sent some years before by a sportsmen's organization to be fed by lodges and individuals. We did not take any. The idea of rearing ducks as pets for the later benefit of hunters on the Mississippi flyway did not seem quite cricket to us. The corn-fed mallards thrived, and returned survivors of earlier flights now were spreading out looking for nesting sites. We missed our mergansers, who liked nesting privacy, and we seldom heard the whistle of a golden-eye's wings any more.

Our mallards had typical plumage, the male a gorgeous fellow with iridescent green head, white neck ring, royal-purple breast, white body, brown-shaded wings, and black-and-white tail. The female was a modest patterned brown. Both had a blue rectangle, the speculum, on their wings, the blue strongly banded with white.

When I opened the door to give them some corn, the male ran off a little way, leaving his lady to go on feeding. He appeared to be considerably less than brave, but was instinctively protecting her by attracting attention to his conspicuous self, so that she might go unnoticed. His tameness showed, though, when he came to the corn before I had gone back into the cabin.

The next day a second pair arrived, indistinguishable from the first unless one might have examined them closely for individual differences in feather markings. There were noisy arguments and tail-feather pulling by beaks, until one pair fled into the rising ferns near the house. The victorious pair settled to enjoy their mud while Ade and I looked for the other two. He spotted the male, standing at the edge of the ditch by the little bridge and peering into a tangle of last year's horsetails. The female emerged from them, quacking excitedly, and the male entered the ditch, to start his own quacking. They had discovered the trickling water there, with its own share of mud and food.

We distinguished the pairs by calling those who fed near Peter's tree Mr. and Mrs. East; those who fed under the big pine, Mr. and Mrs. West.

One morning Mr. and Mrs. East wandered past Bedelia's yard when she was taking the air. She promptly went into a fit of hen hysterics and could not be quieted until the ducks, looking back as though completely shocked at such behavior, were gone. This was peculiar, because she accepted the occasional ruffed grouse that came by with clucking, as if she recognized a friendly chicken. But it is useless to try to read the mind of a hen, especially one who accepted with aplomb the passage of a goshawk over her wire roof, but raised the echoes if a blue jay flew over.

The red squirrels, after deciding that the ducks might be large but only birds, challenged for the corn. We felt that the squirrels had prior rights, so, since the mud was drying and no longer interesting to the ducks, we fed them between the cabin and the shore. They liked this, and both pairs ate peacefully at separated piles of feed. When their big crops were full, they lay down to rest, heads tucked under wings, or went to sit on the boat skid, where they preened and slid into the water to paddle, then came out to preen again.

All was serene until the red squirrels sounded a frantic alarm one afternoon, then disappeared. The two female mallards froze at the sound and the males lifted and circled overhead. A great gray owl more than two feet tall was perched on a branch. As rare as this bird is in our area and especially in warm weather, I thought the ducks needed help. I walked toward the tree until the owl took flight.

That night there were scratchy footsteps on the edge of our roof. In the morning I found a flying squirrel tail lying near the feeding bench, where a venturesome member of the family who fed in our woodshed had gone for corn.

The red squirrels began to feed with caution in bright daylight only, and the mallards did not come. The flying squirrels stayed away until, four nights later, I heard their soft chittering in the shed. I went out with a large feeding of corn and grahams. There must have been twenty squirrels, crowded and piled on the narrow inner shelf, a tangle of soft fur with faces, feet, and tails sticking out at improbable angles. There was no room for food on the shelf so I offered crackers by hand. Heads popped magically from the fur tangle, and individual squirrels, cracker in mouth, jumped to the near log ends and disappeared upward so quickly they might have been released by tight-coiled springs. Others were coming, and as I turned to go in for more crackers, one landed on my back, climbed to my shoulder, discovered where he was, and complained as loudly as so soft-voiced an animal might.

In the morning the red squirrels fed normally, and the female mallards came alone for quick snacks. The owl had gone and the mallards were nesting.

I grew stale and cross in my futile efforts to get an idea for a book, and to clear my muddled thoughts, went to town with Ade. There were turning leaves—yellowing green and soft red—on the raspberries and willows, but the maples were almost bare. The pines were shedding tufts of needles like thin, tawny shuttlecocks. Hard frost had come early to shrivel most of the ground plants. And there were mallards everywhere there was water. At one point, where the road passed close to the brink of a small lake, a flock of mature birds and full-grown young started to cross from the forest to the lake side as we approached. We stopped and were surrounded—ducks in front, behind, on both sides, even ducks underneath.

When we got to the Village the harbor was full of ducks, and they crossed the road in long strings, going to the back door of a restaurant for refreshment. I asked a friend where they all came from. She said that the departure of summer people and the closing of many lodges had left the tame ducks to fend for themselves, and many had made their way to town, apparently looking for people to feed them.

We bought four hundred pounds of corn, all we could load into the car, with the intention of making sure that any mallards who came our way would be strong enough to take off when it was time. And when we got home, our yard was dotted with ducks. Three days later there were more than a hundred and Martha Conrad reported as many in their clearing.

It was a joy to go out with feed. Ducks came in a waddling crowd, to walk over my feet, stand on my toes, all looking up eagerly and quacking. The only way to get the corn to them was to scatter it thickly over their backs, from which some snapped up grains before they could slide off to the ground. There were black mallards among them, dusky of feather with a deep-violet speculum edged slightly with white at the rear only, and many mixed varieties. All were full-grown, and the lake was in an uproar all day as the summer's young splashed and paddled, lifted, and soared higher and higher with every trial.

Ducks eat a great deal, and four hundred pounds of corn is very short-lived when offered to so many. Ade got ready to go to town for more, since no one at Conrad's could go at this time. As he stepped out the door, a mother duck with six young, so new they were not yet past their downy stage, scattered from under his feet. He jumped sideways to avoid crushing any of them, missed his footing on the edge of the step, and fell into the dead ferns.

An hour later his sprained ankle was greatly swollen, and he did well to hobble around with an improvised crutch; he could not possibly manage the foot pedals of our car. It was one of the few times when I regretted that I had never learned to drive.

I walked up to Conrad's and called Chuck at the forestry office. The young lady who answered said he was away but would soon be back and planned to go up the Trail in two days. Meanwhile she would call and arrange to have corn held for him. Martha and I felt that by careful rationing we could keep the ducks at least partly fed until Chuck arrived.

Our little ducklings were the problem. They could not swallow coarsely cracked grain nor compete with the big birds, who drove them roughly away from the food, so that their hurt cries kept their mother fighting courageously for them. But she had no chance against so many. I got out an 1880 coffee grinder that we had once used to grind corn for juncos and reduced the big grains to little-duck size. Ade put a cupful on the step and stood in the doorway, protecting the helpless family by waving the pole he was using for a crutch. The mother stood threateningly between her duck-lings and the rest of the ducks, showing no fear of Ade, and ate nothing at all except some bits of moss and dead leaves she found near the step.

On the night before Chuck was to come we had a storm. Before dawn the sound of the rain and wind was so loud it woke me and, thoroughly alarmed at such an unusual racket, I got up and looked out the west window. Through a curtain of water turned greenish by the ugly light below a cloud of utter blackness, I saw the big pines and spruces whipping and bending like saplings. I had turned to wake Ade so that we could get to the strongest part of the cabin in case one came down on it, when the roaring began. It was the sound of trains in a subway, magnified to fill the forest; the voice of an elemental force, bellowing of its invincible power. Numb with terror, I forced myself to stand perfectly still and wait. I heard a tree cracking, the sound thin and sharp against the hideous background of noise. The roaring swelled and reached a limit of hearing, so that it did not seem to grow louder, as it moved from the west, almost overhead, toward the east—then dropped abruptly to an ear-splitting whine and was gone.

I did not know I was partially deafened until Ade pulled

at my shoulder and said something I could not hear. I relaxed all at once and he had to push me into a chair before I tumbled flat.

"What was it? What on earth was it?" I asked when I could hear again and speak without stuttering.

"A tornado. I've heard 'em when I was a kid in Missouri."

I considered this but found that I could not be more scared than I had been. "I thought they didn't have such things here."

"There's a change in the weather pattern. The storm line is moving farther north. Let's look outside."

The inky cloud was almost out of sight in the northeast, the rain cloud overhead was just a cloud, and blue sky showed above the western hills. The biggest spruce at the edge of the clearing was down and we saw a few other windthrows in the woods. The yard was almost flooded—and full of ducks.

"You'd think there'd be more damage," I said.

"I'd say it went up the lake as a waterspout. We're very lucky. All we got were the side winds. And so are the ducks. They'd be mostly dead except that they sleep on shore." He looked closely at me. "You're kind of pale."

"I feel fine," I said blithely, "maybe a little featherheaded. I'll just sit down for a minute."

I did, involuntarily on the wet doorstep, then went inside with Ade's help and fell instantly asleep from reaction.

Knocking at the door wakened me. That's Chuck, I thought vaguely, and sat up to see Martha coming in.

"The road's all fallen trees and the power and phone are out of service," she said. "I hope you have some corn?"

"Not much," I said.

"What can we do?" she said. "There're more ducks than ever."

"It's a guess when Chuck'll be able to get through now," Ade said. "We'll divide the fifty pounds we have left."

"And we can bake extra bread for them," I added.

He loaded the corn into her canoe and we watched her paddling home through water ornamented by ducks. As we walked back to the cabin Ade saw some green grass that had not been washed out. We gathered it for Bedelia. At the age of nine years and five months we felt that she deserved some pampering after such a disturbance.

———— Two days later the mother of the six ducklings was in very poor shape. Her feathers were limp and ruffled and her head drooped, but still she ate almost nothing and stood guard over her family with Ade's help as the babies ate their ground corn on the doorstep. We had nothing left for the rest and knew Martha had none, because her ducks had come clamoring to join those in our yard, only to go away disappointed.

The little family was just leaving the step, with the mother duck a few feet ahead, when a plane came over so low that it almost touched the tree tops. The ducks in the yard scattered wildly, the mother duck calling to her young as she ran away. The little ones crouched, then scooted under the shed as though evenly spaced on an invisible cord. Once sheltered, they settled to have a nap.

A few minutes later the mother came running back, calling loudly. She rushed back and forth, and finally stopped at Ade's feet, to look up at him as though asking help in finding her children. Her feathers were sleek now, and she stood very tall, her body shaken by her fast heartbeat and breathing. From under the shed there was a *peep*, and then another. She turned, visibly relaxing. Downy heads appeared along the edge of the shed floor and her family popped out, one by one. I handed Ade some bread and he leaned down, offering it to her. This time she accepted, and ate the first good meal she had had in days.

They left hurriedly at the sound of chain saws on the road, and shortly after Chuck came down the hill.

"We're checking damage to the timber," he said. "When I saw the state of the road into here I wondered if you people had been hit, so we cut our way in. The highway people can't be everywhere and a twister went through toward town. Thousands of trees toppled—one spruce as big as that one—" he pointed to our fallen tree—"twisted like a stick of candy and dropped without breaking off. Are Conrads okay?"

"Yes," Ade said, and stopped. Chuck's mouth had fallen open and he was staring toward the shore.

A solid sheet of ducks was moving toward us, the mother and her six ducklings in the van.

Chuck smiled. "It's a good thing I had your corn in the truck before the storm hit. My cargo will really be welcome, but those little ones'll freeze when the waters close."

"We could try to keep them in the cabin," I said.

Chuck shook his head. "Not too good. Got a box or a basket?" I nodded. "Fine. I'll take them to town. They'll have open water in the big lake until they're ready to fly."

While he and an assistant brought our corn, I caught Mrs. Duck and her family, and Ade settled them in a carton supplied with goodies. The rangers went on to clear the road to Conrad's and take them half the corn, and when they came back I met them at the top of the path and handed over the cloth-covered carton, from which came contented quacks and peeps. Mrs. Duck and her six were going to town under official escort.

———— As the days grew colder and sleet mixed with the rain, ice glazed the shore rocks and laid geometrically pat-

terned plates of crystal along the edge of the water. We could
hear the bell-like music of their breaking as the water moved
them against each other. There were fewer and fewer ducks
coming for food each day, I no longer heard crows, and I
had a queer, almost uneasy feeling. It always touched me at
the big seasonal changes, lingering from earlier years when
everyone within miles of us had gone away at the first snowfall and come back with the thawing. I had made all kinds of
changes in my life without a qualm—from job to job, from
town to city, from residence to residence, even the big jump
from Chicago to the woods—but this was a bigger change. It
had taken me years to learn why: the change from wild
neighbors to human was a change from a guileless world to
a sophisticated one. Though the weather gave warning, I was
never ready for it, and even in 1964, when I knew that people
would be near us all year and the innocent time would neither
come nor go, I still had that tremulous sense of a changing
world in fall and spring.

I sat at the typewriter one afternoon, listening to cars pass
occasionally and wondering who drove them, when I heard
mallards squawking on the shore and saw a boat lingering.

I ran down the hill. Two fishermen had tossed bits of bread
onto the water by our skid and were trying to catch themselves a duck dinner with a landing net.

I made noisy and suitable comments. They laughed. Then
I had an inspiration.

"Ade," I yelled at the top of my voice, "bring the bullwhip.
The long one."

The boat left in a rush of water, and Ade came to the
shore, saying, "Did you say bullwhip? What would we do
with a bullwhip?"

I told him what the fisherman thought I might do with it,
and explained that my Great-Aunt Anne, who had actually

driven an ox team, had taught me how to crack one when I was a youngster.

"That's another story to enhance the reputation of the crazy woman," he said, and we went happily to the cabin to find some food.

The growing volume of incidents demonstrating man's inhumanity to almost every creature that was unfamiliar to him and many that were familiar had made me uneasy, and the feeling of discomfort grew with the approach of the deer-hunting season. I tried to think of a book theme, but I was too distracted by every human sound to concentrate. My sleep was broken and I spent my days trying to hide my nervousness from Ade.

If I had not been so disturbed, I would have found the antics of the hunters on opening day amusing. They crept through the brush above the cabin, slipped from tree to tree in the old forest between the houses, even moved along the shore, bent over and slinking. They were perfectly conspicuous because of their bright-red clothes, but we let them prowl since the deer were not around. In fact, the more of them hanging around our cabin, the fewer out looking where they might "fill," which is the area's euphemism for "kill." When the darkness came, I marked the first of the nine days off the calendar as though I were counting the days to the end of a prison sentence. I tried to read during the evening, turning pages without knowing what the words meant, and I saw Ade watching me. I had not fooled him at all, but he said nothing. We turned in early and finally I got to sleep, to wake suddenly, sure I had heard Gregory scratching at the door. Then I remembered that Gregory was dead, and that Nose was safely asleep underground. But I had heard something, so I pulled on my robe and went out to stand on the step and look into the blackness of a moonless night.

Ice bells tinkled on the shore; needles trickled from a tree with a faint rustling. An owl hooted in a cedar, then flew as silent as mist. I looked at the tree that was Peter's tree, and remembered that he would not stand under it again, that Pig and Brother would not come back to this place where they had been reared by Mama and Peter, that Fuzzy was gone, and Little Buck. I was filled with pain as I realized that Ade and I would never have truer friends, and that Mama and Pretty and Starface were somewhere in the forest that was now unsafe for them. When they were gone we could have no more friends like them because of the approach of civilization and its influx of humans, who did not understand either the forest or its children, and many of whom would not trouble to learn. Then I felt a wave of hope as I thought of the growing education of youngsters along these lines—until I remembered that fifty-four of my allotted years had passed. I would not see the kinder world that a new generation might bring. Gregory, Peter, Pig, Brother, all the others we would see no more, were still part of the forest but as individuals they were lost, except in my thoughts and love—and in Ade's. And when we went they would, in a sense, die with us. I would not accept the going of so much beauty and gentleness from the world. I wanted others to know them and perhaps keep them in their minds and hearts as time left me behind, and I could do something about this. My next book would be the story of Peter and our special deer. In fact, I had already started it. My sketch of Peter's coming to us was the perfect opening chapter.

As I turned to go in, I heard a stomp, and knew what had wakened me. I looked but saw only the vaguest shadow at the edge of the thick dark. Our deer were now behaving as though the hunters were wolves. Brought back to the practical level, I went for feed.

Every night until the shooting was over they came in the darkest hours, ate, and vanished. On the next Saturday after the end of the bloody days the first staying snow came, as softly and gently covering the earth as a mother wrapping her firstborn against the drafts of winter. Ade saw deer tracks on the main road when he went for mail, not made by our deer, he thought, because these tracks came and went along a trail that led to other parts of the forest. Red squirrels were busy around our doorstep, and the next morning the doglike tracks of a fox crossed the yard. Ice was thickening along the lake shore, the ducks were gone, and the quietest time of the forest was near.

The hardier owners of summer cabins, who had stayed on to enjoy Thanksgiving under the big trees, left when the snow came. Proprietors of lodges that would be open during the winter were spending Christmas outside. There was too much new ice floating on the lake for the most venturesome boatman, and ice fishermen would not arrive until the lake was frozen over. Not many people are attuned to the great silences of the wilderness without man, but Ade and I loved these few weeks because they brought us the quiet that had been winter-long when first we came.

Mama slipped cautiously into the yard ten days after the end of the hunting season, followed by Pretty and Pretty's sister of another year, Eyebrows. Little Doe came with Fatso, rounder and more coppery than ever and looking very young for his spike antlers. And there were two young does with fawns, new members of Mama's entourage. Starface came every evening to watch from the path, and some days later joined his relatives and friends for the winter.

With the deer outside the windows and the stillness unmarred by man sounds, the days flew by and the pages of the deer story stacked up. By Christmas I had things well enough in hand to do something special. The day was clear and not very cold, and the snows had surrounded us with a Christmas-card forest. All of which said, "Go for a drive."

We idled along the empty road, passing through a forest entangled, tufted, swathed in glittering white. Some of the windthrows left by the big wind of fall were so buried in snow that they could hardly be distinguished from outcroppings of granite. A pileated woodpecker flew across the road in front of us. One cabin had three cars outside and a cheerful painted Santa waving from its clearing. People were inside and the denizens of the woods were minding their affairs away from our sight.

We came to the end of the plowed section, at the edge of a frozen lake overlooked by a bluff. There we ate sandwiches and drank coffee from a Thermos, while the clear sky misted over with mother-of-pearl and a slim moon appeared magically. Then a black wall of cloud rose in the west, to steal the color from the sunset mist, to silhouette the trees in white, and to engulf the moon.

We drove homeward through a dull-silver forest, where the yellow of our headlight beams sent milky-blue shadows running beside and ahead of us, while golden sparkles danced and disappeared on the gray velvet of the unmarked roadside snow. We arrived home in the dark, just as the big cloud began to deliver its snow—thick flakes, feathery, floating and gleaming in our lantern beam. And down the hill one small lamp had glowed all afternoon in a window to light us home.

The night after Christmas was windless, faintly lighted by the frost-dimmed moon, bitingly cold. I became aware of movement through the snow-muffled woods—rustlings as branches were touched, the faint creaking of steps on the snow. From the window I saw Mama nosing in the yard for grain. When I opened the door, deer moved all around the house, bounding into the brush, flowing in liquid grace through the shadows between the trees. These deer were strangers. Only Mama stood firm, stomping under a tree.

All night long the deer stopped to feed, led by those familiar with us and not afraid, and then moved westward. From their number and their wildness, I knew that most of them came from a distance. At five o'clock, when I and our grain supply approached exhaustion, the yard was empty.

On the fourth of January Ade and I drove to town. When we came to the end of our side road we saw many deer tracks crossing the Trail and continuing on to the southwest. The tracks were not fresh, and I thought that these must be trails left by the deer who had fed in our yard a week earlier. I had witnessed a mass movement of deer. This might be a migration to a wintering yard, in which case the herd would return to their original location in the spring. It might be a movement like those of the past, when the whitetails came northward into our region as its virgin forests were cut. I hoped it was the latter. The section of forest surrounding us was too old and tall-grown to supply good winter browse. A new home amid the brush of some recently lumbered area would be better for the deer.

We drove home at a crawl through such a snowstorm that I had to hold my door open and watch the edge of the road for Ade. It was the first of several heavy snows that during the next two months raised the snow level three feet and gave us a time to be treasured, because the animals who were used to us and our quiet cabin-yard showed us natural behavior we might never see again. Soon all the Trail would be black-topped and winter days could be as full of people as those of summer.

On a Saint Patrick's morning without any new green many deer came out of the forest, from the snow-covered hills and

the cut-over land and the swamps—Mama's far-flung descendants—back to the place where they had wintered as fawns, with strangers timidly following their trails. They trampled the snow into a playground where the fawns leaped and flung up their heels, while the does stood quietly watching and the bucks were shadows behind the clustered stems of the brush.

I took out the paragraphs I had written about Peter's legacy to us, and while the deer were all around me wrote them into the ending of *The Gift of the Deer*. I finished the last page when the squirrels' running up and down the maple stems told me that the sap was rising.

I looked up from my task to meet Eyebrows's interested gaze through the glass of the window box. The big trees had shadowed the snow beyond her, but it had melted in an open spot at the edge of the clearing. There, on a cushion of dried horsetails, Mama rested in the sun, and I had the feeling that she was gradually moving farther away with every year.

Then, with the melting of the snow, the deer went away as gently as mist on a summer morning—and the sounds of men were heard again in the forest.

1965

> get another car
> clear small cabin
> finish inside
> **inside toilet**
> fix roof
> take a vacation

———— The crows had returned before the sap was rising. The next spring sign, which seems to be set for the end of March, was the opening of the pussies on the willows. When April was three-quarters gone they looked like dark pearls against the browny-purple of the catkin-tasseled alders. The snow was almost gone when a big rain came to wash away what did remain. Then there were a hundred hungry juncos and sparrows to be fed before they went on to their nesting grounds.

Nose came out from her entrance under the shed. She nibbled here and there, sniffed under roots and logs, then gathered dry grass for a fresh bed and went home. We watched for several days, thinking to see her clearing out and replacing bedding for her youngsters, but she did not reappear for a month, and we concluded that her burrow was so secluded no male had found her during the early spring.

There were rain, and fog, and nights that almost, but not quite, froze. Some ice lingered on the lake in floes like relief maps of translucent black glass, with sharp new mountains and old ones worn down, valleys and river beds, cirques and lakes.

It was noisy ice, with its own vocabulary of sounds—rumbles, tankles, creaks, the noise of slamming doors, the moving of wood in an old, old house. It struck me that it had been more or less like this for ten thousand years, since one of the last glaciers scooped out the lake bed and water filled it as the melting ice retreated; and as I looked on it, there was no sign of man. I might have been the primitive woman who used the flake tool we had dug out of the garden plot some years before—a flint chip, worn at one edge and slightly shaped to the hand. Did that woman stop scraping a hide and come to this shore to watch for the ice's going as I did? I thought so, because open water to her would have meant good fishing, water birds to catch and roast, perhaps an easier and shorter way to get to hunting grounds than across the rugged land.

Two mornings later it was warm and the ice was gone. Mist formed in a layer above the water and fell in veils from the face of a cliff. Then a fast boat ripped the mist layer and set the water moving, the waves breaking, washing, changing over and over before they died. No part of the water or its shore was not moved or shifted or abraded a little. So any action creates a pattern and brings some kind of change. When someone writes that man, because of his mastery of a few natural phenomena, may very well no longer be considered a part of nature, I wonder that the writer and those of whom he writes do not realize that man's mastery is very limited. We use light without thinking about it, but lifetimes have been spent studying its nature and it still is not fully understood. I wonder, too, at the foolhardiness of those who plunge ahead on so superficial a knowledge of elemental forces that any use on so slight a basis should terrify them.

The birch twigs delicately arranged new leaves and tassels

against the robin's-egg-blue sky, marking the kind of days lodges would like to tape for tourists, and I learned that Alvin Tresselt, my juvenile editor, was coming to the woods to work with me on a book to be made from my children's nature stories. He was an Easterner born and bred, and everything around us would be new and different to him. He arrived, we explored the woods a bit, and the book grew almost without effort. Alvin titled it *Animals at My Doorstep.*

Ade and I were conscientious about reminding him to watch for bears, and I am sure he thought we were having fun until he opened the door one morning and said, "I think we have company."

A bear, almost full-grown, was strolling along the path from the storage building toward the house, looking larger than life and very black.

"Get the suet cage hanging on that wire, will you?" I asked. "I can't reach it, and he'll pull the whole thing down."

He went, bringing in the cage and watching the bear, who merely stopped to see what was going on. Alvin kept looking at me suspiciously for hours. I felt it would be futile to try to convince him that I had spoken without thought because it was routine for us to bring in the feeders when bruin appeared.

Our guest had no sooner gone than the fast boats, the water skiers, the mosquitoes appeared in crowds. Even the SAC jets had one of their active spells and came and went high above, making thunder in the clear sky. Automobile traffic increased greatly, and one of the small trailers brought us an old friend from my laboratory who had recently retired and taken to the open road. He stayed in the summer house, where he could stretch and move about as he pleased.

That night Ade walked over with him to be sure he had everything he needed, and shortly after they left I heard a squirrel at the door. I opened it to face, in the lingering twilight, not a squirrel but a middle-size bear, who turned away and took the path toward the west. I closed the door and would have thought no more of it, except that I saw Ade's light returning through the woods. He and the bear would surely meet on the path. I called to him from the west window and he promptly turned his back on the black beast and began to search the woods with his light in the wrong direction. The bear moved to one side, stopped, and by the time I had made myself clear to Ade, was goggling from Ade's light to me in the cabin window as if to say, "What's all the fuss about?"

One night Alvin's big bear bumped his nose against the door until I thought he would scrape its pad raw on the screening. He could effortlessly push in the removable panel if he discovered it, so at dark Ade hung a temporary door outside, three inches thick and resting against the door frame. Mr. Bear could push to his heart's content and I could stop worrying about the mess he would make of our groceries if he came in. For some reason he showed no interest in the windows, which he could have entered more easily than the paneled door. Because he was very fat and had a magnificently thick coat, we decided we might expect an early winter, although a diet of rich garbage had probably put him in such good condition.

We had a series of down-pouring showers. It was muggy, yet the air seemed fresh and sweet, and so pure that any unusual odor came strongly on it. Both the bears wandered past at intervals, advertising their coming on the wind. We were putting out no food that might attract them and—perhaps for this reason, perhaps not—they followed the path just outside of the glassed-in window box, not even glancing at the cabin.

Since we had not yet met a bear who liked oatmeal, I continued to give this to the flying squirrels, spread on a paper to keep it from falling between the shelf and the back wall of

the woodshed. They came and went at night, seemingly undisturbed by the big animals. Very early one morning I heard
a faint shuffling sound in the shed. Through the door panel,
by milky false-dawn light, I saw a full-grown male bear,
impressive for size alone. He was carefully pulling the paper
from the shelf, and when it fell and showered his face with
the remains of the oatmeal, he backed up in alarm. After
cleaning his fur and eyes he moved noiselessly to the shed
and used his nose to push a bucket he had knocked from the
floor to the ground into its original position. I could hardly
believe my eyes. Bears simply are not neat, but this one
seemed to want to leave as little evidence of his visit as possible.

He walked a few feet in a beginning drizzle and lay down
under the cedars, so relaxed he might have been a big furry
shmoo, and did not bother to move when the rain increased.
Why should he, with his thick coat? Instead, he rolled onto
his left side, a six-foot-long, barrel-chested storehouse of
power, stretched his four legs straight out and a little above
ground, and wriggled his toes!

Then he rolled on his back, as much at ease as a horse rolling in a meadow. After more of this, which must have given
his back a wonderful scratching, he flopped onto his side
again and dozed. Half an hour later he flipped upright,
combed his face and head carefully, and went away with a
bouncy walk that was almost a dance. He might have been
carrying a sign reading: *I am a happy bear.*

Friends a mile away on the lake shore came in for an afternoon and said they had also noticed the big bear's careful
investigations and, because he was such a polite bear, had
named him Gentleman Jim. Later, one of these ladies told
me she was out walking and turned to see the Gentleman's
huge bulk a few feet away. She squealed and fled. I asked
her what he did, and she said, "I didn't wait to see." I said

that he probably leaped straight up and ran in the opposite direction, on the grounds that if there was something to be afraid of, he had better go, too. To offset this, she had seen a cub, little more than a baby, eating at their bird feeder. He went away carrying a red apple in his mouth. And while we were talking a mother and her new twins and her yearlings walked in single file past the window—and five bears, even if two are lap-size, make quite a parade.

On another afternoon a cub sat down outside of Bedelia's run. She clucked as though she had met a new chicken, and the two settled on opposite sides of the wire as if exchanging confidences.

Bedelia was very sophisticated and democratic in her approach to the forest, so she remained poised and calm, even when the baby bear pulled open the run gate, put his forepaws and head into her house, and licked up her feed. Then, as though suddenly realizing her danger, she went into chicken conniptions. Ade, who had been watching for a chance to shoo the bear without sending Bedelia flying into a tree, ran to the rescue but was not needed. The little bear fell out of the run backwards and headed away from the sudden racket at full lope. Bedelia was so scared, though, that she needed comforting, and we settled her for a day or two in a box under the piano.

That night we heard a scrabbling on the log ends at a corner, and soft thumps on the roof, followed by heavy steps pounding across it. A bear had chased a flying squirrel. When there had been no sounds for some time, Ade and I took a lantern and opened the door. A young squirrel slid from under the dormer where she had taken shelter and crawled uncertainly onto the top of the open door. The lighted inside world of the cabin utterly confused her and set her quivering with fright.

Ade and I stood without moving, hoping that, as she crept

forward and then backed along the door top, she would turn around and discover that the familiar, dark outside world was still there. But she did not turn, and while the chill of one of those late-summer nights that may bring frost filled the cabin, she moved cautiously back and forth, peering over the edge of her narrow perch, trying to solve a problem she did not understand. Then she moved to the hinge side of the door, stood up, climbed onto the trim, and tried to go higher. Apparently one must go up, not down. But the varnished logs were too slippery. She managed to move diagonally by holding to irregularities with her claws and took refuge on top of a baking-powder can on a high shelf. Our efforts to reach her only sent her back to the door top, on which she was as effectively trapped as on a rock surrounded by water. (Flying squirrels, unlike their relatives, cannot swim because of their gliding membranes.) When we tried to urge her from the door top she crouched in a trembling heap, and gentle efforts to catch her only drove her again to the wall.

"The thing is," I said, "she's so very young and everything is unfamiliar."

Ade nodded, said "You've given me an idea," and went out, to return with a fragrant birch pole still covered by its bark. He leaned this against the door, letting it extend outside onto the step.

The squirrel immediately sniffed and turned toward it. After examining the top of the pole meticulously, she trusted herself to it, and began inching down backwards while keeping a wary eye on us. Eight minutes later she reached the step, from which she immediately hopped to the feeding shelf in the woodshed and began to eat her delayed supper of oatmeal.

When I opened the door in the morning, a medium-size bear dug his claws into the trunk of the cedar beside the

shed to stop his descent, and turned his head to look at me before he slipped to the ground and walked away. I doubt that bears, whose fastest movements are like slow motion beside the flashing leaps of flying squirrels, have much luck catching any—but they keep trying.

The only bothersome thing about this summer of bears was that one of them, quite large from the signs, selected an area not far from the cabin for his toilet. There was nothing we could do about this, but wondered how we might clean it up, the surroundings being solid rock. Then I noticed a cottony mold growing thickly on the droppings. By the time the bears had gone and the first skim of snow had melted, there was no sign of the manure heap.

This was definitely a "bear year," which people said was due to the good berry crop. I do not think anyone really knows though, except the bears, because we had had a similarly productive year when almost no bears were seen, and a silly rumor spread widely that resorters had poisoned them. As if they would destroy such a favorite sight of their guests! And well I recall a later "bear year" when wild crops were poor.

It began to rain heavily in March, and three months later there had been only a dozen days without at least a shower. Gushing water had cut channels to the lake, which was higher than when lifted by the snow water of early spring. The ground was so sodden it sprung and oozed beneath my feet.

The rains kept on, the greenery was lush, buds opened everywhere, and many insects drifted and darted, fertilizing the flowers as they paused to feed. By late summer, however, the continuing downpours were defeating the promise of the abundant blooming. The growth was still lush, but the prevalence of clouds obstructed the sunlight the plants needed to produce their fruit.

Then, when the time for frost was near, came the bears—not in their usual scattering, but by dozens. The failure of the wild berry crop had forced them to hunt for food in garbage dumps near lodges and towns, along with the "tourist bears." They did not find much, though, because the bad weather had reduced the number of human visitors and the amount of leftover food. The hungry animals appeared in towns along the north shore of Lake Superior. One yearling, named Frank by his admirers, found a good thing for himself at a roadside restaurant, where he went every evening to eat the leftovers and drink milk from a bowl. He even appeared on television, sitting up and eating an ice-cream cone. Conservationists, aware of danger to both bears and people in such situations, took food into uninhabited parts of the forest to help the animals, and hopefully, to draw them away from the towns and highways.

Bears had strolled along our shore all summer. That there were more than usual did not mean much to us because we were accustomed to their year-to-year variance in number. There were frequent but commonplace stories of bears, indifferent to broken glass, going into a house through one window and leaving through another, after licking clean the pan of bacon fat or fish-fry grease left where its delectable odor might drift on the breeze to the nostrils of any bear who happened to be passing.

When we saw a cub licking up the cracked corn we had put out for the mallards, squirrels, and chipmunks, Ade changed their feeding place to a spot some distance from the cabin. The next night the big garbage can where he kept the feed was knocked over; he moved it inside a small building. Two days later I opened the door and faced a full-grown female, sitting on the step within hand-shaking distance. The next afternoon I looked up from my typewriter to meet the eyes of a big male, four hundred pounds of uncertain behavior, standing outside my window. After dark he smashed a window out of the building where the feed was kept and ate some ten pounds of it. And so started the noises in the night.

Clang, as an oil can was tossed aside. Thump, as a log was flung out of the way. Bang, as our washing machine was overturned in the woodshed. And there was the hair-raising rustle of thick fur rubbing against the door, the snuffling of noses that left smudges on our windowpanes. We tried everything humane we had heard of to discourage bears, even ammonia, the fumes of which sting their eyes and noses, but they were so hungry they braved even that. It was only a matter of time until we should find ourselves in a dark house with a bear as dark as the night, and with no electric light we could turn on quickly to locate him; and leaving either oil or gas lamps burning was out of the question because a startled bear might strike one, setting the cabin or even himself on fire.

Both of us grew haggard from loss of sleep. Ade was trying to do the illustrations for *A Place in the Woods*, but could not draw with shaky hands. As the drawings were urgently needed and neither one of us would consider shooting a bear, we packed a bag and drove along the almost all-blacktopped Trail.

I remembered with affection the mud and ruts of yesterday. Then I wondered whether increasing traffic had made the old road obsolete or the road improvement had caused the traffic increase. I was thinking of the blacktop's part in the slow deterioration of the once-wilderness environment when we reached a motel by Lake Superior where Ade could sleep and work in peace.

I had time on my hands while Ade was at his drawing board, and walked along the rocky shore, watching the never-still waves doing in their big way what the wash from boats

did in a small way on our lake. One morning I saw a number
of people gathered back of a cabin and went over to see
what the excitement was. A bear had tipped over the garbage
can. Smiling to myself, I walked back to our unit and that
night, when all was quiet, I found myself listening, and knew
that I missed the big black things that went *boomp* in the
night.

———— The summer of 1965 was not all book-planning and
bear-watching, though. The influx of people increased steadily until the road was seldom free of cars, and boats passed
at all hours of day and night.

On the twenty-first of July I heard a squeal of brakes and
stopped typing, my hands motionless above the keys. There
was a shot. I felt the heavy beating of my heart, because we
had seen Pretty with her fawns pass through the maple on
the hill the day before. I went out just as the fawns bolted
into the yard. As the car drove away, Ade arrived from the
shore where he had been caulking the boat, and we waited a
long time, but Pretty did not come.

Then he went to the road and came back shaking his head.
"There's blood, but no deer. They didn't call the warden to
get her."

Sadly I remembered our beautiful doe, a victim of increased
automobile traffic after her five safe years at our once secluded spot, and I wondered then, as I do now, whether her
body was thrown on a dump, fed to dogs, or eaten as illegal
venison.

The fawns were as delicate and lovely, as slim and graceful, as their mother had been. They still had their white-
spotted red coats and had not been weaned, but they adapted
quickly and took some leaves, a little grain, licked some salt.
However, without their mother's milk they would be under-

sized, and without adult training would have little chance of surviving both the hunting and the winter.

Then I heard a stomp in the night and went out to see Mama coming toward me in bright moonlight. She showed her years in her swayed back and sagging skin. When she chewed the grain I gave her, her cheeks wrinkled; her teeth were so worn down that eating surely was hard for her. Perhaps that was why she had come to us at this season which she had not done since the year she bore Starface and Little Buck in our yard and when, later, Pig and Brother had been shot here. Then I wondered if she already knew, through her special senses, that Pretty's fawns were here and alone. I was never sure but I think this was the answer, because both fawns and Mama were gone the next day.

———— I tried to work, but strangers kept knocking on the door, usually to ask how come we lived in a national forest. They found it hard to believe that they were not within those boundaries but on private land at the edge.

One afternoon Ade went to the summer house to measure the sink, which we wanted to exchange with the one in the log cabin. It was quiet, and I was typing steadily when I heard an alarmed human sound. I opened the door to see a woman and two children huddled behind a man, from whose uplifted foot a red squirrel was flying through the air, to land heavily on the edge of our doorstep. I picked up the terrified, whimpering animal and felt for broken bones, while the man more or less jumped up and down.

Ade came around the corner as if on cue, saying, "What's going on?"

I turned my attention to the squirrel, who did not seem to be injured—only half-stunned and pitifully scared. While I quieted him I listened to the man, who still had his family behind him as if to protect them from assault. It seemed that they were exploring, and when they came on a cabin without a driveway, thought it must be deserted in such a God-forsaken place. The squirrel had attacked one of the children and tried to climb his leg. He had bravely shaken off this danger, which his father had tried to kill with a kick. However, he had merely lifted the squirrel with his foot instead of striking it with his toe, as he had tried to do.

Ade was stricken speechless. I gave the squirrel a graham cracker from my pocket and let him escape up a cedar. Then, suddenly, I had had it. I yelled louder than the man, the group fled as from a den of lions, and Ade and I tottered inside to gather our wits.

Ade did little for the rest of the tourist season but stand guard. I tried to keep my mind on my work, but was always listening for some disturbance. I managed to get a short version of the deer book in shape to sell to a British magazine for eating money, but gave up after that.

Little by little, my frustration and agitation built up, and near the end of August I woke in the small hours with a very sick stomach. I fled to the privy, not bothering to wake Ade, who I thought could do nothing to help. I was wrong, because my sickness was more than a minor upset. At dawn Ade found me on hands and knees at the doorstep, too weak to lift myself onto it and knock for help.

I woke around noon and Ade greeted my appearance in the living room with: "We are going to get an inside toilet!"

I did not argue, because I knew as well as he did that a sick spell such as I had had would have meant death by freezing if it had struck on a really cold winter night. I also had lost all illusions about the quaintness of privies. I did say mildly that the project seemed an impossible dream without piped-in water—which also seemed an impossible dream.

Ade handed me literature he had obtained earlier when

we heard about a gas-fired toilet operated by electricity, either 110-volt AC or 12-volt battery. It sounded fine, so we bought one. Ade installed it, a friend promptly named it "The Hot Seat" and I checked "Inside toilet" from Ade's early list.

It was very satisfactory. Bottled gas supplied its fuel. Ade bought an automobile storage battery for it, and a charger— long-wanted for the car battery in winter—so that his little power plant could keep the batteries up while supplying light. The vented vapors were minor, and waste was reduced to a small amount of dry ashes and salts, which could be disposed of without mess or polluting anything. Ade was able to cope with the complexities of the toilet's construction, so that we had no serious problem when, for example, a switch stuck. If he had not been able to read electrical circuits we should have had to call an electrician, not easy in our isolated place but simple anywhere not too far from a town. We bought our gas-fired toilet from one of the large mail-order houses, and got information on repairs and servicing from the manufacturers, whose name and address we obtained from our supplier.

Ade came back from the mail one day in September with the news that a phone cable was to be laid along our road. We had not wanted or needed a phone in the days when our isolated place was almost inaccessible, and therefore safe. But the Trail's improvement had made our area accessible. We decided that since the outside was reaching us, we should be able to reach the outside.

I wrote immediately. A prompt reply gave prices and said that the cable would not be installed until the next summer, but that we could have a phone any time by the placing of a drop line from the main line along the south edge of our property. For a minute I thought I had misread the letter, because so many had told us we could not have a phone without taking the power. Ade went to Conrad's Lodge at once and called the office, the manager arrived the next day to talk it over with us and view the ground, and by the end of the week we had a telephone.

Even though it was on a party line where conversations might be overheard and which might be busy when we wanted to call, it brought back the feeling of being able to cope that I had enjoyed during earlier woods years. I went back to work and was ignoring an unseasonable wave of ninety-degree heat that made typing a sticky process, when I noticed that the sky, as much of it as I could see through and above the motionless trees, was a peculiar, glare-faded blue. I stepped outside to see what was happening.

A light covering of patchy, dove-gray clouds was hurrying across the zenith from the west. I was thinking that we might get a sprinkle that would cool things a bit, when blue light flared from behind the clouds and the simultaneous crash set my ears ringing. I went inside—fast.

It turned as dark as the hour before dawn between flares and the noise from the passing electrical center was deafening. Rain and hail pounded on the roof, and some miles beyond the lake, another storm center moved in Canada, bluish bolts that looked like tree boles marching along the hilly horizon and adding their light and noise. Ade came dashing in from the work building, saying that a tree had broken off in front of its window and he wondered if I was all right. Needless to say, I was glad to have him for company. Once the time between the flash and the crash had lengthened enough to tell us that the uproar was more than a mile away, he returned to whatever he had been doing and I went out again, just as the clouds opened in the west to let the golden light of sunset slant across the water and through the woods.

All at once the clouds, lighted from below, were dusty copper, and the lightning, now south of us, sprayed in showers like bursting rockets. Their color, against the glowing sky, was what one might imagine ultraviolet looks like to a bee, a luminous rose-tinged blue. The upper sides of the leaves on the small willows and birches near the cabin were shining as though newly gilded. The last drops of rain fell like gold beads. The lake, past the black tree trunks, rippled in molten gold. The upper parts of the balsams were gold-brushed wherever the light could reach them, and the under-sides of the high pine branches were a deep red-bronze. I looked up the path and saw a cow moose with her calf, standing quietly and watching me. There was something about that tall, awkward forest mother that was like the forest itself—quiet, steady, violent only when there was need. I watched her lead her calf away and stayed by the step until the enchanted light began to fade. As I turned to go in my eyes fell on the small metal box, stamped "Bell System," that was attached to one of the cabin logs. Nothing could have been more incongruous. I told myself that the hectic summer just past was probably no more than a coincidence of crack-pots and there might never be another like it, or a need for the phone.

———— Jacques, who had been working in the woods since spring, dropped in on a flaming October day. He told us that he would be working near a distant lake all winter, which was bad news, and that the man who killed Gregory had sold out and gone, which was good news. Ade mentioned that our *No Hunting* signs were being used as guides for out-of-the-area hunters, and when Jacques left, went up to the road to remove them and put up a couple of *No Trespass-ing* signs. These would at least indicate to strangers that this was private property, and most of them would know it was illegal to hunt on such land without the permission of the property owner—for all the good it might do.

I dug in on the book, going ahead through the falling of the leaves and the rains that wet things down before the coming of the snow. My stomach felt as though inhabited by bats as the deer season approached, but when two days of it had passed without incident and there was no sign of our deer, I began to relax. Then, late in the afternoon there were two shots next door.

Ade picked up a pair of recently purchased binoculars, went up the path, and returned with a license number. He picked up the phone, listened, hung it up. "There's a phone off the hook."

Three days later, after numerous trials of the phone, we knew that the line was being blocked. To know that anyone near us was so callous to the needs of others as to deliberately isolate them frightened me. I thought of fire, serious illness, of an accident to Ade, of my inability to drive, and the fear exploded in panic.

When the sun had gone down six days later to end the season, I was disgusted with myself for giving way to fearful imaginings, and told Ade I needed to get my balance again. I walked to the road in the twilight and leaned against our car. I had only been there a minute or two when there was a shot so near that I saw the brush shake as the deer fell and the hunters ran to it. I heard four voices, then the slam of our door and Ade calling "Where are you?"

I answered, and pushed away from the car to sit down and lower my head against growing dizziness. At that moment there was another shot. The bullet passed so near my head that my right ear rang and I heard the slug thunk to a stop somewhere back of me. Ade dropped down beside me.

"I'm all right," I managed. "Are they gone?"

"Yes. I heard them run back into the brush."

I was holding my hand to my ear, trying to get rid of the continuing noise in it.

He said, "Was it that close?"

I nodded.

"Where did it go?"

I turned to look at the gravel pile. "There," I said, pointing to the telltale hump where the slug had gone in.

He dug with his fingers and exposed the .30-caliber bullet. He looked at me, at it, then upward in the direction from which it had come, his face distorted by fury and horror.

"Great God! If you'd been a few inches to the right—or standing—"

"I was," I said flatly. "Both. I moved just as the shot came."

He put the bullet in his pocket, held out his hand to me, and without another word we went back to the cabin.

We sat close together on the sofa, and after a long silence he said, "We can't stay here through another deer season. We might as well be in a war."

I shrugged, having been so thoroughly shocked that I was indifferent, then said: "I don't like to turn and run. And we'd miss the first snow maybe."

Ade shook his head. "You don't seem to realize that you came within inches of missing all the rest of the snows."

"I know. But what if the deer come at night for feed?"

"They'll know we're gone and stay away. They can smell, can't they? We go."

I knew finality when I heard it. "Okay," I said. "But we can't go far, not in the old car. It's fine for the back road but—"

"We can drive to town, take a bus somewhere. Anywhere'll be safer than the woods when the hunters are in it."

Perhaps I am not very brave, because I was so relieved that we would not go through another deer season in the woods that working on the book became easy, and was helped as our deer returned. Mama arrived first, bringing one of Pretty's fawns, a lively, dark-furred little doe we named

Orphan Child. Eyebrows introduced a fine, strong buck fawn. Fatso was gone, but his undersize mother, who seemed to bear only single children, brought another small buck, very handsome, with a pale and delicate face. Starface was even more an image of Peter. And I must not forget Friendly, a doe who had been with us before in winter and was so tame that we thought she must be someone's summer pet.

I had just finished typing my manuscript on the bitter cold afternoon of New Year's Day when two ladies came down the path, whose snow was fortunately so beaten down by the deer's hoofs that they could walk without trouble. They had read *Forest* and had come from the Village to see us and the locale. Ade showed them around outside, and as they were coming back to the cabin, Friendly ambled out of the woods to them in her best manner, and stood and cocked her head as though she understood every word they said to her. They were thrilled and we were pleased, and I think Friendly had a good time, too.

It was a good way to start a new calendar year, but did nothing to help me with the problem of marketing the book I had just finished. I had written it as a labor of love and wanted it to be changed as little as possible lest some of my feeling for the deer be lost. I mentioned my quandary in a letter to a writer friend, who sent me the name and address of her agent. I sent the script to New York and some weeks later had word that the book was sold.

Then the days began to warm and we woke again to the problems at hand, like considering when to open the under-house ventilators—not too early because of the cold, not too late because of mildew. The deer began to leave by ones and twos, and while we looked with pleasure on the part of the roof that was finished and leaked no more, the part that still leaked had Ade fidgeting for weather warm and dry enough to permit him to go to work on it again.

I was inventorying our remaining canned goods when the phone rang. I heard the operator putting me through to my agent's office, then: "The Reader's Digest Book Club has taken your book." I said nothing, because I could not make a sound. "Can you hear me? The Reader's Digest—" I began to splutter unintelligibly but the noises must have made sense at the other end of the line because there was laughter and "It's so much fun to call and tell people things like this. You'll get a letter right away." I think I said "Thank you" before the phone went dead.

"What's the matter? What's wrong?" Ade was asking.

I finally got hold of myself enough to say, "Would you like a new car this summer?"

"Well, the Chevy takes a lot of persuading to shift gears— what are you talking about?"

I explained more or less. "It's the biggest book club in the world—it goes into a lot of foreign countries—millions of people are going to read about Peter and Mama."

He looked out to where Starface was nosing in the snow for corn. "Bread on the waters," he said, picking up the corn can and going to the door. "You know, I don't think it would have worked out this way if we'd fed Peter for any reason except just to help him."

> *get another car*
> *clear small cabin*
> *finish inside*
> *inside toilet*
> **fix roof**
> *take a vacation*

1966

——— The news of such astounding good fortune seemed to addle our brains. When Ade next went for mail he had to walk because of another late snowfall. At the main road juncture he met a woman who had come from the Village in a Jeep to get something from the Lodge. They waited by the Trail—and waited. Then she recalled that just before Ade arrived, a car had gone toward town pulling a trailer-house (never just a trailer up here). Ade decided that the trailer entourage and the mail truck had come to grief on the road, which was not yet plowed. As they were wondering whether they should go to the Lodge and call the sheriff in case the accident had been serious enough to cause injury or a fire that had destroyed the mail, the mail truck appeared on its way *back* to town. It had passed through early, and a glance at the fresh tire tracks in the snow should have made everything clear to Ade in the first place. I reacted by sitting down and writing a silly mystery which ended up as a newspaper serial.

Shortly after I completed this piece of foolishness, arrangements were made for me to meet my agent in Duluth. On the appointed day I arrived at the hotel, disheveled from the ride on a crowded bus and exhausted from listening to the life history of a woman who sat next to me. I scrubbed, combed, rang my agent's room, and walked down the hall, expectant and uncertain.

I shall always treasure my first sight of her—tall, slim, elegant, and gracious. Momentarily I wondered what she thought of me, wearing the only old dress I could let out to fit me—patterned and adding inches to my girth, of course—and with my hair, skin, hands, and shoes all showing the scuffs of the hard years. Then I knew, before a word was spoken, that these externals would not matter to her if the internals were right, and that we were going to get along not only as business associates but also as people. The only sour notes during my stay were a foghorn that kept her awake all night and an electrical storm that did the same for me.

——— Ade met me in the Village when I returned. He had picked up our mail, and while we waited for lunch I opened an envelope and took out my share of the book-club advance payment. I looked at it, then at Ade, whose eyebrows were raised in question.

"Have you given any thought to the kind of car you'd like?" I asked.

"Well, yes. There's a car in the window of the Ford place —good lines but smaller than anything we had in Chicago. They call it a Mustang."

I handed him the check. He looked, whistled, and said, "We've just time to eat and put this in the bank. Then you can see the car."

I looked and was lost. So, without knowing anything of

the Mustang's popularity, we went home laden with specifi-
cations, color charts, and accessory listings.

When we arrived at the cabin I expected to be pleasantly
surprised by the contrast with Duluth, but was not. I had
been in the forest long enough for it to have impressed itself
so deeply on my mind that I would never find it strange.
I was astonished, though, to realize that the long-unfamiliar
pavements and traffic and general din of a city had passed
without my doing more than watch lights when I crossed a
street. The city years had left their pattern in my mind as
solidly as the forest had, and I had not even thought of the
trip's being my first beyond the Village in eleven years.

The one new thing, and that unexpected, was a heightened
consciousness of the forest scents. The overriding smell made
of evergreen resin in the sun and fungi working in the earth
was there, but I was aware of other odors, some fragrant
and some unpleasant, that blended with the main scents to
make up that "woodsy smell."

The next morning I caught the fragrance of anise as I
stood on the doorstep, as I had caught it shortly after we
came to the cabin, before I learned that it rose from decaying
aspen logs. I walked on to lean down and learn that the leaves
of jewelweed and of dandelions are as distinctively scented
as those of geraniums and cabbage. I paused on the path and
caught a whiff of old-fashioned fly spray—from the red
and deep pink and pinkish-white flowers of my painted
daisies. As I proceeded up the path I found that the greenery
of yarrow, interrupted fern, ostrich fern, mountain ash, maple,
and all the other plants each had its own faint and separate
scent. The aroma of one kind of honey came from the purple
tassels on a thistle, of another from late-blooming trumpets
on a honeysuckle bush.

I turned into the little trail across the hill, where, under the
high-spreading branches, one-flowered wintergreen and blue-

beads, wild sarsaparilla and twisted stalk were preparing their fruits and adding their breath to the atmosphere. In a damp place there were mosses, smelling like earth and water. In a tiny open space grasses and pearly everlasting gave off their special scents. Sweet williams smelled of cloves, and the large-leaved aster greenery was sweetly aromatic. I stopped to watch some sulfur butterflies drifting above a patch of daisies and was scolded by a young chipmunk, who seemed to think I was trespassing.

I was near the road when I caught the charnel-house stench of decaying flesh. I looked for a dead animal and found a stinkhorn surrounded by carrion flies, who would carry its spores when they went. Ahead was a wild-rose bush, blooming a second time, whose fragrance removed the unpleasantness of the fungus from my nostrils. I sniffed the dank, generic tang of a swamp on the breeze, then a perfume that recalled a bushy plant common in gardens in my home town. We called it simply "a shrub" and it bore brown flowers whose petals, when crushed, released an exquisite scent. Something near me now smelled almost the same. I did not locate the source, because a car rushed by on the road, raising the dust and filling the air with the acridness of exhaust from a badly tuned engine. This deadened my nostrils to the delicate odors around me. Disgusted, I turned homeward, wondering why people did not bother to keep their cars in shape and cease to offend others with this unnecessary stink.

While I was exploring with my nose, Ade had made his list of colors and accessories for the car. We agreed on everything but the need for an air-conditioner. Ade said we had no use for such a thing in Minnesota. I agreed, but thought that since we had decided to go out during the hunting season we might as well see some of the country while we were gone, and it could be plenty hot in the Southwest, which I, for one, wanted to see. I lost the argument, but have been tempted to bring up the subject a few times since, such as the day we crossed the desert along the southern border when the thermometer stood at 110 degrees in the shade. But we stood it all right, and would have missed something if we had not felt that blasting heat and smelled the dust-laden wind.

It was during this summer that we noticed a marked difference in the behavior of birds and animals. Strange whiskey jacks and blue jays accepted us at once and were reckless in approaching in comparison with those we had fed when we first came to the forest. They were being fed in many places now, and were becoming too tame for their own safety. We did not see a fox or weasel from thaw to freeze. Bears nosed around our cabin every day and showed no fear, half-tamed by people who fed them in spite of the Forest Service's warnings.

Nose was not happy with what she found when she first emerged, all her bolt-holes being either full of water or blocked with ice, and those *huge* deer everywhere. We fed her and she disappeared, to reappear late in May, when the woods were thawed and the deer gone.

We noticed that the daisies, her very favorite greens, were blooming all over the clearing for the first time in years. She did not even venture out to eat them at night. And we wondered why she no longer drank from the mossy ditch west of the cabin. Then Ade saw her hanging precariously onto the slippery wet rocks of the lake shore, trying to snatch a drink from the splashing waves. He watched her lumber at full groundhog gallop to a newly dug burrow doorway between the lake and the cabin, and realized that she feared the bears and was avoiding the paths, which they used.

She was thinner than usual for the time of year. She rarely ventured further than her doorway under the woodshed, which was also protected by the cabin and its doorstep. If she came even as far as the step we felt that the bears must be far enough away for their scent to be weak to her snub nose. All in all, her fear was keeping her from getting enough to eat, and without her thick layer of fat she could not live through the coming winter.

The next time we saw her peeking out, I gave her a big feeding and added a dish of water. After looking at it and me with more than her usual suspicion, she tried it and drank heartily. We wanted to give her some peach juice but decided against this, because it might attract one of the bears to the spot.

Thereafter, she scratched on the screen at night for her food when she felt it was safe, then ducked under the shed to eat. She hid from the quickest flash of my lantern's light, and it was only on nights when moonlight reached the edge of the woodshed floor that I caught glimpses of her nose, wiggling as she ate. If she did not come to the door, Ade slid her food and water far under the shed floor, where she might eat without exposing herself.

She had produced two fascinating children, whom I saw playing together on a fallen tree that lay beside the path between the cabins. One was coal-black except for frosting on nose and eyelids; the other a clear gray, like the rabbit-gray that once was common in men's felt hats. They were thickly furred, and showing no trace of the rusty sleeve and belly color of most groundhogs, were distinctive and very handsome. I watched them for a while, wrestling and playing like puppies. Then they saw me, stared with the wondering eyes of all young animals, and scurried away.

We had no further sight of the gray one, but Little Blackie came around the cabin in spite of strong discouragement from his mother, who grew more possessive about her territory as she grew older. On some days, when we saw no bears and assumed that Nose smelled none, she came to the door for an oatmeal cookie. Little Blackie tried this, only to be promptly chased by Nose. He lay in wait under thick jewel-weeds and managed to get a small share without mishap, but finally settled for coming at first dark on evenings when Nose was safely out of his way.

I gave him a cookie one night, and had just returned to my chair and my book when I heard a scamper, then a bump against the corner of the cabin. A bear! I rushed out, thought-lessly ready to chase the big fellow, but there was no sign of either Little Blackie or his assailant. There was only a half-eaten cookie lying beside the cabin wall. And that was all for our handsome little friend.

I felt unhappy about this for a while, thinking that all would have been well if Little Blackie had not come to the step to be fed. Then I realized that he had to eat, and no matter where he might have gone in search of greens he would have been just as vulnerable to the bear, once he was at any distance from his burrow entrance. I was thankful that we still had Nose, our crotchety but lovable old reliable.

In July Mama slipped into the yard on the afternoon of a sunny day. She looked much as she had the summer before, but she stepped slowly and was much less agile than she had been. She stomped for corn just as decisively, though, and we went out together to feed her. From the window we watched her eat and then go to her favorite spot on the bank to lie down, chew her cud, and lower her head to sleep. I hardly left the window until it was dark, because I felt that we would not have old Mama's company much longer.

Late in the night we heard her stomp, and Ade gave her another meal by starlight. After she had eaten she vanished in the brush on the hill. Then we heard a thud and a tinkling sound.

"She's been hit," I said, starting toward the road. Ade ran ahead of me, muttering as he passed, "Keep quiet. It's funny we didn't hear the car."

A man's voice said, "It's a damn deer. I've smashed my grille. There's a piece out of it. Let's get out of here before somebody spots us." And another said, "Bring the deer. It might have the piece of grille stuck in it."

Ade had almost reached our entrance when the car backed past, a dark, heavy sedan, running without lights and with its powerful engine tuned to whispering perfection. No wonder Mama had not taken alarm. There could have been a number of reasons, all of them bad, for these motorists' secretive behavior, but none of them mattered to me. I only knew that Mama, our dear, faithful Mama, was gone.

The galley proofs of the deer story came in the next mail, and with Mama's death so soon past, I checked the proofs with a tight throat and tears behind my eyes. I heard every car that went by, and knew that where once in the summer there had been one, there now were a dozen. Human voices from the road, the lake, the yard—for strangers still wandered through—competed during the day and into the night with the sounds of breezes and birds. Our once-safe haven for the deer was safe no longer.

Numerous visitors came to thank me for writing *The Long-Shadowed Forest*, and to talk to Ade about his drawings.

I remember one couple very well because the woman accidentally helped lessen my depression. She stood in the clearing, looked around, and said, "So this is the long-shadowed forest. It's just like the rest. Why did you call it that?"

I pointed to the shadows streaking across the clearing and explained that shadows are long in all northern forests, that even at high noon on Midsummer's Day the spears of shade from the spruce and fir tops reach out toward the north. Then I told her that if she studied the section of forest around her summer home, and opened her heart and mind to it, she might find her own long-shadowed forest.

"But," she said, "it wouldn't be the same."

I agreed. No two people, even though they stand side by side, see things in the same way. No two parts of the forest are alike, nor two minutes or days or seasons in any particular place, but basic values remain. The sun shines, the rain falls, the winds blow, the earth crumbles—and everything else comes from these. What one finds reflects from himself.

Then she asked how I could write so serene a book when there were so many causes I might take up, and it occurred to me that she had become so incensed at outrages against the earth and its life that she had forgotten the ultimate goal, "Peace on earth."

After they had gone and I turned again to my desk, I was in the agitated state of mind that gripped me whenever I began to work on the story of the deer, who had almost all been killed by men. I decided to practice what I had been preaching and went outside to sit at the base of a big pine and let the forest's timeless values remind me that nothing is gained by trying to change the irrevocable.

When Ade went after the new car a month later, I was stuck at home waiting for a foreign phone call. I knew the wait might be long, because there were now eight connections on the party line and the line was constantly in use. Indeed, the call had not come some hours later when I heard a strange auto horn blowing Ade's initials in Morse code. I rushed up the path to view our purchase, and Ade ran down to monitor the telephone.

After I had admired the burgundy paint and black upholstery, got in and out a few times, sniffed the newness, and regretted that I could not go for a ride in case the still-delayed phone call came through, I locked the doors and carried the keys back to Ade.

He greeted me with, "You remember that fellow who used to ask us over and then say, 'But you haven't got a car'?" I did, emphatically. "Well, I met him outside the post office. He looked at the Mustang and said, 'I'd have thought you'd buy a more conservative car.'"

I snorted. "Some day I'd like to rent a red Jaguar and drive over to see him. Hearing his comment would be worth the trouble."

At six o'clock I knew it was too late to expect a call from a location seven hours ahead of us, but there is always a way. At three A.M. I put the call through, without even the minor interference from those people on every rural party line anywhere who listen in to pass the time and to keep up with local news. I took a childish satisfaction in knowing that the next day's gossip would not include details of my conversation with a friend in Oslo, who hoped to visit us on a planned trip to the United States.

Power and phone problems rose shortly after from high winds that dropped trees on the lines. We watched a forestry plane scoop water from the lake and pour it on small fires along the power line south of the cabin, and thanked goodness that we did not have the power and so the worry of a warming freezer full of food. Then the wind died, and with this came tragedy. Someone decided to reconnect his own power and linked up the 14,400-volt main line—to electrocute a lineman on a pole. The whole area was shocked, and people said over and over, "Nothing like this ever happened here before!" No, but there had been no high-voltage line in earlier days, when people had cut off their private low-voltage power sources and repaired their own lines. Nor had there been so many people, among whom was one who undertook to do a dangerous job he knew nothing about and so bring death from amateur bungling.

Then a young man came to the cabin to ask if we would

sell him the 1937 Chevy, which he had inspected in the carport. He was not the first person who had wanted it, but
he was the first who had a real feeling for old cars and did
not think of them as something to be used only to make a
fast buck. Our discussion broke off when it started to pour.
I made a pot of stew and dumplings for all of us, after which
our visitor rushed home during a lull in the rain, saying he
would stop in the next day.

While I washed the dishes, Ade leaned against the fridge
and stared—at me, at the ceiling, back to me, again to the
ceiling.

After some minutes of this, I put down a plate and asked,
"What *is* the matter?"

"Nothing, except that this is the only heavy rain we've
had for months and you aren't very observant."

This made no sense to me and I said so.

"The roof," he said. "I finished it when you were in
Duluth, and I've been waiting for a downpour ever since.
Do you realize that this is the first real rain in twelve years
that hasn't dripped down our necks every time we went
through an inside door?"

After I finished the dishes and marked "Fix roof" off the
list, we talked about the old car. It had been to us something
like a faithful horse, to be curried and given sugar lumps,
so to speak, while it was usable; to be put out to pasture after
its accident; and now, when it was nearing its thirtieth birthday, to be passed on to someone who would feel somewhat
as we did.

When we left Chicago for the two-month stay that had
become permanent, the Chevy's trunk, top, rear seat, and
both running boards—if you remember what they were—all
carried heavy loads. We were less than two hundred miles
from the city when there was a bang and a lurch as the right
rear tire gave up the ghost. Luckily we could coast into a

roadside service station. It was hot and dusty, and I was digging into the soft-drink dispenser when I heard the attendant say to Ade, in an apologetic voice, "I'm sorry, but I'll have to charge you for fixing the tire." I looked at the car, old in years even then, covered with dust, laden with household goods. We might have stepped straight out of *The Grapes of Wrath*.

Ade was making some notes on the Chevy and Mustang gear ratios when I said, "I think my father was a lot smarter than I thought he was when I was young."

"Huh?"

"Well, he told me once that the way to take the measure of a man was to limp up to his back door in your old clothes. We did, without intending to. And we learned, didn't we?"

"We did." He finished his notes and said, "We'll give the Chevy to that young man."

I nodded. "He's the right one for it."

So, in October, when the leaves were bright and sun showers sparkled on gray water, we stood by the road to watch the old car being towed away, to be renewed and eventually join the parade of antique cars. I sighed and Ade said, "There's another loose end tied up. Do you have the feeling that a lot of things are balancing out? Changing for us in one way and against us in another?"

I nodded, and we walked past a mountain ash tree with berries like massed garnets, past the red-stemmed maples that waited for winter above a carpet of their fading gold leaves, past a trail worn by the hoofs of deer who would walk their trails no more, to the cabin where a few lingering raindrops glittered on the vining stems of the false buckwheat I had transplanted when we made our first garden.

———— The publication date of the deer book and a publicity trip to Minneapolis and Saint Paul were scheduled for mid-November. We made arrangements for a friend to feed Bedelia and keep the oil stove going so that the house would not freeze if a sudden cold spell came. Then, after some warning shots for the deer, we drove away on the afternoon before the hunting season opened. The deer, if they came at all, would not hang around once they knew we were gone and there was no feed. The prognosis was as good as we could expect, and I even felt relaxed about the coming publicity—until I remembered that one of the teeth I had lost during the bad years was an upper front incisor. I spent most of the day practicing how to face a TV camera with a missing front tooth and not look as if I had a paralyzed upper lip.

The busy days in Twin Cities were exacting and exhausting, satisfying and fun. It was with a feeling of having successfully crossed another river that we returned to the Village, and stopped for groceries and mail. There was a note saying that our friend who was looking after things had had to leave two days before but had arranged everything. That was all right, because the stove would run for three days when set low and Bedelia's pans would hold food and water for a longer time. It was dark when we felt our way down the hill, having forgotten to bring our flashlights. Ade stopped to look in on Bedelia while I went on to light up the house, which was pleasantly warm.

I was looking at the kitchen counter when he came in saying, "She's been fed this afternoon. Someone must have given a hand."

"That's good," I said, "but look at the droppings on the counter. Black, brown, and green. We never had mice, voles, and lemmings in here before." I picked up a grain of wheat. "Did we have any wheat?"

"No. We haven't even scratch feed that would have it in."

I tasted the grain and spat it out. "Whoever helped our

buddy must have seen signs of mice and put out poisoned grain. That's what attracted so many small animals. But I can't imagine who would. People know we don't use poisons!" I stopped, appalled. "My tame mice! And I was going to do a children's book about them."

Ade made a queer sound in his throat. "They were cute, coming for their suppers every evening. Well—there isn't anything we can do but clean out all the damn stuff we can find. We'll go over the place with a fine comb, but there'll still be some in the ceiling and carried outside."

I sat down, flipped pages in a book, got up again. "I think I'll go to bed."

———— In the morning I looked out of the window. Light snow had fallen while we were away, and the yard was crisscrossed with human tracks. Ade and I went out to see what we could see. Apparently a slight thaw or freezing rain had coated the thin snow with ice after the tracks were made and had preserved them perfectly. They covered the clearings, the hill, the woods between the houses, the swampy land near the brook, but did not extend beyond our property. There were also lunch boxes with lodge napkins that had been used to wrap sandwiches, empty shell boxes and cartridge casings, beer cans and broken whiskey bottles, and other less savory souvenirs of the people who had come to this place where there was not a deer track to be seen. I felt only contempt, and we did not say a word. I went to get something to hold the broken glass, which I wanted to collect as completely as I could before either one of us or some animal was cut by it. Ade went up to the road and drove off. I had dumped the glass and was back in the cabin when he returned.

"There's not a deer track within a mile on either side of the road." He laughed between his teeth. "I guess that tells

us off, doesn't it? But they don't know why we went out.
They think we just ran from the hunters. Wait till the news
of the publicity trip and the *Reader's Digest* sale gets around."

I was not much concerned about either intruders or books
because the first mouse casualty was creeping feebly across
the floor. I picked up the pitiful little creature and held it
while it shivered and squeaked and died. We dropped everything else to search the house for the poisoned grain. We
cleaned it from behind books, from beneath my desk drawers,
from between phonograph records, while the tame mice who
had stored it so carefully died one by one, crawling into my
lap while I was reading, creeping across the kitchen counter
to the hands that had fed them. And others died in the roof
and under the floor, so that the cabin was filled with the
sickening and sad smell of death and decay. I was miserable,
and felt that no matter how many books we had sold while
we were away, it was not worth this.

A week later the mice were all dead and the stench was
fading. Ade brought the mail, settled to read the local paper,
then announced that he was taking me to the movies for
Christmas. The show in the Village had an advance ad for a
special children's program, *Bambi* and *Tarzan*, and we would
go along with the rest of the kids and forget the tiresome
adult world for an evening. I liked the idea, and said we
could eat in town for a change.

Ade had been right about the book news, because just after
this the invitations began to come in bunches. It would have
been impossible to accept every one and bad manners to pick
and choose, so we refused them all, including one from someone who had known us through our hardest years, but had
not thought of inviting us to dinner before. Ade burst out
laughing when I told him about it and said, "At last I have
a chance to say 'I told you so.'"

We drove to town late on Christmas afternoon, with a couple of sandwiches in case we got hungry after the show. We found every eating place closed, sat in the car in a below-zero wind by the harbor to eat the sandwiches, went to the show, where we added candy bars and popcorn to our dinner, and had a marvelous time.

There had been a little snow while we were inside, and we started home over a surface covered with virgin white. The moon was sliding toward its setting through a dimly luminous sky, and the treetops by the road glittered faintly in its light. Then the moon was gone and stars twinkled on the sleeping forest, while the aurora lifted its misty green and white in the far, far north. When we turned onto our little road, the big trees sheltered us with their snow-heavy branches, and I was half asleep when Ade stopped just before we reached our entrance. I looked up and he pointed to the snow ahead. There were deer tracks, a lot of them in various sizes, crossing the road from the thicket and going down our path.

We followed them slowly and quietly and came into the clearing to see Starface standing under Peter's tree, patiently waiting for his corn. And behind him were others, shy and new to us, whom we would see clearly when they felt it was time.

There is magic in the forest, magic to heal the wounds made by men.

———— When I went out to check Bedelia's lantern-heater on a night in late January, I found her awake and coughing. I covered her against the cold, brought her inside, and fixed her a box in the kitchen where she would not be exposed to drafts and we could keep an eye on her.

By early morning she was wheezing and coughing so loudly

that she woke me. Her comb was hot with fever and I could hear gurgling in her chest. Pneumonia—or something very like it. I woke Ade to help me search for a bottle that I thought held one penicillin tablet. He found it, but there was only some white dust from its former contents. We dissolved this in water, which Bedelia was drinking in quantity, and it eased her some.

I called a druggist, who said I must have a prescription. "For a hen?" I asked. He hung up. I caught a doctor who was just leaving for a medical convention and who thought I was playing a practical joke. I tried the druggist again; this time he understood what I was trying to say and said he would get something into the mail, which would leave the Village in an hour.

Ade picked up three tablets of an antibiotic, but by evening we knew they would not help. Bedelia's breathing was as bad as it had been before we gave her the penicillin dust. Then I thought of a Chicago friend who knew how we felt about Bedelia and who was employed by a world-famous pediatrician. I reached her, explained, and she said she knew "her doctor" would help. I called the local postmaster, who said he would phone us as soon as the medicine arrived. We waited while Bedelia did her noisy, painful best to get enough air to stay alive. Two days later the postmaster called and Ade went to town. He returned with an antibiotic that was specifically for pneumonia and other respiratory diseases, with careful directions for administering it.

Within hours Bedelia's breathing was easier and the strangling cough had lessened, but it was too late. Like an elderly person, weakened by severe illness, she faded until her heart stopped.

We put her outside in an animal-proof container to be buried near the Prince and Tulip in the spring, but we kept forgetting that she was not still around. I found myself saving bits of apple for her, and every time Ade went outside he started to check on her and her heater. She had been not only a living link with our first spring in the woods, but during the nearly eleven years of her life she had been so totally dependent on us that caring for her had become an integral part of our lives. Remembering not to do all the little things we had done for her was difficult and distressing.

We were still depressed as winter moved toward its end. There was no way to stop listening for Bedelia's conscientious attempt at crowing in the morning, no way to avoid seeing the little house and run that now were empty. And tearing them down would have left a bare space, which would be just as strong a reminder. Ade thought that if the rising pressure of what is called civilization should eventually force us to leave the area to find a new writing and drawing place, it would be a good idea to make a scouting trip as soon as the vegetation was in condition to keep our deer comfortably full without supplementary grain. The other animals would not need our help by then. We could return before the end of May, refreshed by a look at the Southwest, which he wanted to see as much as I did. He did not mention it, but it was understood that the best way to get out of our doldrums was to get away. After all, we had not had a vacation in thirteen years.

However, the early spring was such that, if you did not have a sense of humor or at least of resignation, you would think that a city apartment was a pretty good place to live in after all. Aside from the general drabness and chill, it was cloudy for long periods, which we did not appreciate because the ground cannot warm up without sunshine, and the vegetation must wait.

In early March it dropped to twenty-five degrees below

zero. The snow was thirty-three inches deep, which was not exceptional, but the cold snap brought deer we had never seen before to the yard for food. And due to the perverseness of things in general, the grain supply was low. I might, by stretching it, make it last three days.

It was a little warmer two days later, and we drove to town to buy feed, seeing less and less snow as we approached Lake Superior until, in the Village, there were only brown remnants left. The day was warmish and sunny there, and people thought the back of winter was broken.

It did thaw a little in our border area, but it was nothing spectacular. It was enough, though, to bring us the pleasant sound of water drops from the roof plunking into the little basins they wore in the packed drifts. It also brought an influx of snowmobiles, whining and roaring and rumbling as their drivers took advantage of the soon-to-go ice and snow. The crows arrived on schedule, but I would not have known it if I had not seen three of them, because the engine noises drowned even their cawing. I was reminded of a remark I had once heard a woods dweller make after he returned from a visit to a city. "I couldn't wait to ride my snowmobile through the woods for some peace and quiet."

Then it dropped to fourteen below at night, but the crows had said it was spring and I was willing to go along, even though the ice on the lake was as solid as it had been in January and snow was falling again. That day brought the Incredible Adventure of the Frightened Snowmobilist, or maybe I should call it the Frightening Adventure of the Incredible Snowmobilist.

This man pulled up by our boat skid and came running to knock at the door. I opened it.

"Have you seen that rabid deer?" he blurted as he came in and hastily slammed the door behind him.

"The *what?*"

"The rabid deer. I was chasing him with my sled and my engine stalled and he tried to bite me. Those big teeth could snap off a hand!"

"Relax. The deer turned on you because you were running him to death. They get winded in a hurry, especially at high speed. And in this cold they'd soon frost their lungs."

"A fellow up that way—" he waved toward the east, "told me that, but I thought he was kidding."

"He wasn't. And a deer couldn't snap off your hand if he tried, which he wouldn't, because they have no upper front teeth or canines. What he could do is strike with his front hoofs. You can see from the tracks outside—we've deer all over the place. Just leave them alone for their sake and yours."

He was still excited when he stepped outside. "I'll let 'em alone, all right. And remember—I've warned you." He turned on the doorstep to add: "There's some woman up on another lake who's written a book about a big buck and his family. It'll tell you! You ought to read it."

He went, while I wondered what he or someone else had seen in *The Gift of the Deer* that could have been so incredibly misinterpreted.

By the end of March a warm air current had brought us three days and nights well above freezing. Big drifts in sunny spots were down to two feet, and bare ground was beginning to show where the wind had picked up the snow to make the drifts during the winter. I had never seen our snow level drop so fast, and we began to plan our trip—until the temperature fell just enough to give us freezing nights again.

Slowly, slowly, the remaining snow melted. Then more hours of the twenty-four were above freezing than below, and by early April three-quarters of the ground was bare. The strange deer had gone back into the forest, and those we knew were spending most of their time wandering through the woods, eating the bits of fallen cedar, the ruffles of moss on the tree bases, and such ground evergreen as they found tasty.

Starface, six years old, spent a lot of time with Wistful. Both showed the first rising of their antlers and would leave us soon—provided the weather continued to progress toward summer on schedule. There were four does and six fawns, one of whom was an orphan adopted by a returned visitor we called Big Doe, who had identical twins of her own. The twins seemed to move on cue, heads turning together and at the same angle, forefeet stepping out as though they were about to dance a duet. Big Doe was a careful mother, although she paid no attention to Wistful, who, from his behavior and appearance, might have been her three-year-old son. Only Mama, of all our does, had mothered all her children, no matter what their size or age.

The weather at mid-April was simply awful. It rained steadily and heavily for twenty-four hours before a north wind brought sleet. Ade started for the mail, saying he doubted that he could make it if the road were not bare of snow. He returned to report that the road was washed out completely halfway between our cabin and the Trail. The car was stuck in a hole where he had tried to turn around when he saw the washout, and he had walked back. He thought a mountain goat with ice creepers could get along just fine, because he had had to jump from one water-covered icy surface to the next and wade boot-top deep through pools and rivulets. After he got his breath he took an ax and a shovel and went back to dig the car out.

I checked over the larder, reduced because we had expected to leave before the end of the month. We could eat with care for two weeks. The grain supply for the animals would not last that long.

The next day, when the deer came in, Big Doe was lame. We did not see any injury and thought she must have slipped on the ice and strained her right shoulder. She stayed close to the cabin with her fawns, confident that we would supply food. All we could think of were the almost empty corn cans and the impassable road.

Two days later the yard was a slough, plowed by hoofs and full of ponds that we crossed on planks. Big Doe found it so difficult to limp through this that I began to feed her small rations in the woods, where thick duff made the walking easier. Ade was out of the picture with neuralgia, brought on by his digging the car out of the mud in the sleet storm. But what else could we have done?

In the afternoon, our ranger friend came down the hill with two sacks of corn, saying he thought we would have a lot of hungry customers in such weather, and although the road was more or less patched up, he did not think we should try to use it without a four-wheel drive.

Two days later we had an inch of snow and it froze again. Migrating birds were arriving, mostly juncos and sparrows, all in fine condition except the only hermit thrush I ever saw near the cabins, who twitched as though poisoned and died. I thought of the beautiful song lost to the world, of the insects she would have eaten, and of the stubbornness and greed of men whose chemicals were destroying so much of the earth's living treasure.

Early in May the temperature rose into the fifties and the lake ice was softening. Only small patches of snow remained. Nose was doing her spring burrow cleaning. The elder buds were swelling day by day and the willows wore their pussies like silver jewels. Some of the deer had left us, including Big Doe and her fawns, so we assumed that she was enough recovered no longer to need help in feeding herself and her family.

A week later the sun and the soft wind had come. Three does and two fawns were still with us, lying comfortably near the cabin on the springy fallen grasses of last summer. The earth grew greener day by day and soon the last deer would retreat into the forest.

It had been one of *those* springs. We had not enjoyed parts of the weeks just past, and it was too late for the trip, but we were members of the animal family and could not have rolled happily along the freeways if we had not done our best for our wild relatives at home. After we decided against going, we were not sure whether we had really wanted to go or had only convinced ourselves that we did.

get another car
clear small cabin
finish inside
inside toilet
fix roof

1967
TO FALL

take a vacation

———— When greening time ushers in the new forest year I am always optimistic. This time I felt that, although we missed Bedelia, she had lived a long time for a hen and had given us both eggs to feed the body and laughter to feed the soul. We should be grateful that we had had her so long. As to the general situation around us, although the number of people coming into the area would increase, it seemed reasonable to assume that they would learn how to live with the forest instead of endlessly trying to fight it. They would surely understand, after a little backwoods experience, that the only way to conquer a forest is to destroy it. They could hardly want to do that, since they came because of it. I told myself, "Everything will come right," and pushed aside a doubting whisper that said, "Or will it?"

At about the time when we had planned to return from our vacation, a high wind brought down another of our big spruces, a very tall and dignified tree that had stood almost alone with only an aspen shimmering at each side as though in attendance. With the wind trying to push me off the path,

I walked up the hill to look at the splintered stump, three times my height, and saw that the aspens, which had appeared small beside the spruce, were actually some seventy feet tall. Nose came out from under a small forest of ferns and headed for the cabin. I followed to feed her, and as I turned to go into the kitchen, smelled smoke. It was too strong to come from a nearby fireplace chimney but I could not locate it in the wind. I tried the phone and found it dead—a tree on the line, no doubt.

Ade came in with two buckets of water and I asked him if he smelled it. He led me outside and pointed toward the south, where heavy smoke was now plain to see, rising south-west of us and rapidly spreading eastward.

"It looks close," I said. "Should we go to help?"

"If amateur fire fighters are needed, someone will give us the word. It's not as near as it looks and it isn't coming this way, but there's a forty-mile wind behind it, if the blow is like it is here."

The fire did not burn long, thanks to the efficiency and hard work of the foresters, every experienced fighter in its area, men from the Duluth Air Force base, the Coast Guard, and surely others I did not hear about. They trapped it between fire breaks on both sides of its course, and, although it could easily jump a small lake, there was, providentially, a big lake directly in its path. But it turned nine hundred acres into blackened desolation during its brief life, and it was started by sparks produced when a tree fell on a power line.

We had a great many visitors that summer, and at last having time we could spare from cabin repairs and gainful activities, we found our callers stimulating and entertaining.

A few encounters were embarrassing, as when a newspaper-man arrived with his wife and son and found us still asleep. Others were hilarious, as when two couples caught Ade, black as for a night guerrilla raid, cleaning the oil stove. Now and then there was an awkward meeting, when the visitors and the Hoovers could find nothing to say to each other and sat in one of those awful silences.

Some contacts were thought-provoking, as that with an elderly lady who was worried about increasing restraints on all people, instead of only on the irresponsible. Just before she left she summed up her feeling: "Maybe some day human beings'll face the hard problem—making boys into men, you might say. Then they can stop yapping for laws that only pass the buck."

And there was a woman who, after glowing comments on the beauty of forest and water, said, "But I was shocked to see an American flag flying at a lodge. Such poor taste, with the Canadian Centennial going on, to emphasize that this shore isn't Canadian." I have regretted ever since that I did not tell her that there ought to be flags flying on both sides of the long, unguarded border all the time, to remind visitors here and the world in general that two great nations can live at peace with each other.

On a late-August morning we said good-bye to a sociology professor whom we had not been able to persuade that our published backgrounds were real and not fabricated to add interest for sales purposes! He felt that no one would give up so much for so little. I was feeling sorry for him, or anyone who found only sterility in living close to the prolific earth, when I was almost deafened by the roar of a bulldozer. It sounded as if it were working in our clearing—and it almost was.

A driveway was being built from the side of the road to the lake across the land that adjoined ours on the east. It passed little more than a hundred feet from our cabin door, and there was no brush on the land between to give privacy to our wildlife. Except for the flying squirrels at night and

red squirrels by day, any animals in our vicinity kept themselves discreetly out of sight during the disturbance. Nose
moved her feeding to the silent dark hours and seemed very
much afraid, probably from the effects of both the noise and
the vibrations in the ground. These things were, of course,
temporary, but the opened land would remain, and it was
opened still more when the shore was cleared and a trailer
parked there.

Ten years earlier this would have been merely something
new next door, because the owners of the land were not the
kind of people to annoy anyone or to disturb the wildlife.
However, in 1967, considering the growing number of
strangers visiting the area and the astonishing behavior of
some of them, it meant that the log-cabin clearing was no
longer safe from intrusion and thus no longer suitable for
studying wild animals. Having no nearby driveway into the
forest had been a safeguard for those at the cabin during the
years just past, but once a road is built, curious strangers will
enter it—by car if it is open, on foot if it is gated—and roam
around the immediate area.

Ade and I talked over our situation. When we bought our
place, we knew that power, phone, and a blacktopped road
were in the offing and that the old ways of life could not last
long after they came—but it seemed to both of us that the
alterations had come sooner and with farther-reaching effects
than we had expected. We went over the changes, and saw
the gradual loss of wilderness by attrition.

Power, phone, and road together attracted more and more
people, which meant more and more building. This necessi-
tated clearing, which increased run-off water and silting of
the lakes, and the installation of many cesspools that released
an effluent which stimulated algae growth in the clear water,
as the privies of the old days had not done. More planes and
boats to accommodate the larger number of people added

their oil films to the lake. With the opening of lodges in winter came not only more fishermen but also snowmobiles that left oil on the ice, to go into the lake body at breakout time.

Power had brought, along with convenience, increased run-off below the line clearings, fire from fallen trees, flood-lights at docks so that boat motors could be heard at any hour of the night. The telephone improved communications, but not in the degree hoped for. Its rings shattered quiet hours, and one had to listen and count the rings in case the call should be for him. Both power and phone were often out of service in storms, so more clearing was done in an attempt to prevent outages, and this brought more run-off. The improved road made it easy to go to town but had led to an almost total stoppage of a good freight service because of loss of business to people who thought it cheaper to do their own hauling.

Instead of a smattering of people who thought the forest so far removed from civilization that no rules of sanitation and behavior applied in it, crowds of this type zipped along the Trail, to pollute the water, cut trees for the fun of it, leave campfires burning, and litter their trails. On the other hand, some newcomers were so pollution-conscious that they saw smog in an exudation from the forest vegetation that showed as a blue haze on hot days, and declaimed about "detergent pollution" when they noticed the lines of thick, yellowish foam formed on the lake from natural debris after a day of rough water. Some even thought pollen dropped from the aspens was man-made dust, which was like calling bird songs "noise pollution."

We were aware that only a few highly commercialized establishments had so changed their locales as to destroy the wilderness character there, and that people who visited the forest for the first time in this year of decision for us would

not be able to grasp what had been lost during the years since
we had moved into the cabin. Also, most newcomers looked
upon the abundance of water and trees and land as inexhausti-
ble, and if they did not learn that it had taken many centuries
to produce the forest and that all of its parts were necessary
to its preservation, the creeping blight would continue to mar
one of the most beautiful places on earth. If so, twenty years
ahead these newcomers of 1967 would look around and feel
some of the pang of loss that was ours as we sat in our hard-
earned home, discussing our uncertain future.

Ade looked at me, sighed, and said: "There's only one thing
to do if we want to continue our work and life with the animals. Get out and look around. We've agreed to go out
during the hunting, and there isn't anything to stop us. With
Bedelia gone—and I wish she wasn't—and a good wild crop
for the squirrels, and the chipmunks probably crowded out
of their burrows by corn, and Nose almost ready to hole up.
Martha and Oscar are staying the winter, and she told me
when I met her on the road the other day that she wanted to
try feeding some deer. The cabin roof is done so we won't
have to worry about water damage. And we've a car good
enough to take us anywhere for as long as we please. It's
strange. How it's all worked out together."

"Yes. All we have to decide is when to go." I thought
briefly of the years when Labor Day had meant the beginning of the quiet time—but there was no point in looking
back. "We thought we'd figured everything when we came
in but we couldn't know we'd become almost a part of the
wild animal kingdom. It'll be a long time before I get used
to not having Mama or somebody stomp for food in the middle of the night."

"We aren't going forever, you know."

"Of course not—but something *has* gone forever from
here, as far as our lifetimes are concerned. And we only know

we're going to try to find another place for ourselves. When we looked for this place we had a picture and a location in our minds. Now there's nothing, and we may never find anything." I paused to steady my voice, then went on. "I'm thinking of John Donne. He knew that every man is involved in mankind, but not that mankind is involved in all other life. We didn't know it until we managed to save Peter. We touched the whole living world through him." I hesitated, then: "We've said it all. I'm going out for a while."

I stopped as I rounded the corner of the cabin to look at the slender seed pod of a jewelweed. It was half an inch long, pale green thinly striped with red, with five slim segments joined at the base and under tension, like springs. When it was fully matured it would explode at a touch, scattering the seeds. I remembered taking one of these ripe seeds and peeling off its outer coat, to find a robin's-egg-blue inner coating. Nose was lying on the mound in front of what had been Gregory's first burrow, her black-satin hands crossed. She glanced at me and yawned as though to say, "It won't be long." I looked up at the big pines and knew that I would not trade one of them for all the electrical gadgets known to GE. I remembered them covered with the kind of snow that fell like feathers from a burst pillow, and wondered if we would return in time to see the snow on them during the winter to come.

I was paying no attention to my feet, so tripped over a firmly anchored raspberry runner and went sprawling, to the acute alarm of a spotted frog, who leaped for his life. I sat up and yanked at the offending plant with no result except to fill my palm and fingers with tiny thorns. I gazed thoughtfully at the prickly stem. If one stubborn plant could so resist me, it might just follow that the earth would eventually stop man's presumptuous efforts to remake it. In any case it would renew itself, even though this might not be in the days of mankind. At that moment a fundamental truth crystallized in my mind. People are part of everything—stones and storms, mice and mammoths, lichens and linnets. We are what the ancients said we were: Earth, Air, Fire, and Water. But when we fidget, and tamper, and play with great forces, we destroy only our own tomorrows. We cannot mangle Eternity.

———— The time of the turning of leaves had come, and with it our departure date. I opened my desk drawer, crossed the last item, "Take a vacation," from Ade's list, and wrote "13" for the years. What we were doing now was not the rest and recreation he had meant when he wrote it, but it would have to do—and the list had ended along with so many other things. I stepped outside while Ade made a last check of the cabin.

The clear light of the sunset picked out every needle of the pine and spruce tops against the paling sky, and rayed through the trees to brighten the faded leaves of the raspberries and the shattered seed heads of the grasses. I looked up the path toward the road. I could locate the Mustang by reflections from its taillights, touched briefly by a line of light that picked its way through the bright-yellow maple leaves. It waited for our bags, already packed, and for us. It was a late hour for our start, but we did not have a time schedule and I had not wanted to leave until this perfect day was over.

A red squirrel dashed to my feet, sat up, and chattered hopefully. I went into the cabin to get him a piece of graham cracker, watched him rush up a tree, and knew that I would miss the squirrels' lively antics. I walked very slowly down the moss-edged path to the lake. The twilight spread lemon and Nile green and mauve across the sky above the hills, and the water moved only enough to have the changeable-silk look it had held when we first saw it from Petersons' dock.

The water and the squirrel might stand as representative of things that had not changed during our years in the forest. The forest—the shelter, the nourishment, the life of all its children.

As I stepped across a gap in a flat stone that extended out into the lake, the faint melodious voice of distant loons reached me, to be immediately drowned out by the roar and splashdown of a plane, returning from some fishing lake in Canada. Waves rushed from its pontoons, breaking up the patterns in the water, splattering against the rock where I sat, and pushing through the gap behind me in the stone. Exhaust gas crinkled my nostrils until a kindly breeze from the south replaced the stench with the clean, familiar scent of sun-warmed balsam resin.

I sat quietly, waiting for the disturbance to pass.

Slowly the water grew still, the sky dimmed into graying violet, and the good-night song of a late-staying robin rose like a hymn from the forest behind me. Faint rustlings told me that small animals, frozen in their places by the sudden loud noise, were again going about their business under cover.

I touched the water. It was faintly warm, although I knew it would be frigid in its greatest depths. It had a faint odor and taste, so faint that no one who had not drunk it when it was free of these would notice. It was still clear, though, and there was light enough for me to look down at the drowned rocks in front of me. They were covered as though with brown fur, long enough in places to drift slightly. This was algae, and I saw no small creature moving. Any coating on those rocks when I first saw them was transient, made of mud and plant debris, and there were many little water animals, but the mallards had taken care of those in their hunt for food.

I ran my fingers over the rotting surface of the granite on which I sat, turned to look at the wide break in what had been one slab when first I had come here to watch the sun set thirteen years before. I stood up and the stone rocked under my feet. It must be broken underneath, too, for the top fragment to be light enough to move so easily. The earth was patiently making soil from its rocks, undeterred by the actions of man.

A loon splashed to a landing a hundred feet away. Although it was too dark to see the bird clearly, his voice rose in a rich, three-toned call that has rung through the North from the earliest days of its lakes.

The light went out in our kitchen window, and I heard the cabin door close. Ade had moved the bags to the step and was ready to go. I called, and he answered and started ahead. I stepped off the stone, then waited until a dark bulk between me and the cabin had passed. Black bears have the right-of-way in their own domain. The notes of the robin showered like a benediction as I started up the slope.

I picked up my share of the bags from the step, then set them down again to look into the forest through air like silver mist. And some touch of magic let me see my old friends again. Starving Peter Whitetail staggered over snow turned rose-color by an aurora to his first meal of cedar under his tree. Mama stood watchfully beside her newborn fawns, who were no higher than the bluebead lilies of spring. Crippled Mrs. Mouse came back from something like despair to sparkling life when she found her lost babies on an old sock under our wood stove. Walter Weasel flashed over the drifts past the tracks of his threatening big cousin, the fisher. Little Bear slept high in his pine top, rocking, rocking in the wind. Big Cat dropped from the cedar beside the door and walked, with his lionlike gait, to the safety of his den under the storage building, where his bobcat companion's eyes glowed like fiery emeralds at night in the beam of my lantern.

Then there was only darkness in the arches of the trees,

and I knew that nothing civilization might give us could ever replace what it had taken away. But for a moment all things had been as they were before—for that one precious moment.

I hurried to the car, handed my bags to Ade, and walked back a few steps while he was warming the engine, thinking that if we had not been so alone in our beliefs—but we had been. Few of those who think they believe in preserving the integrity of the wild earth can give up their comforts, their companions, their prejudices, and their fears.

I could still see the little cabin, lonely and almost hidden by the shadows; it would be waiting for us amid its winter snow or its summer grass and flowers. I looked up at the great trees standing tall against the dim sky, the guardians of our very special place. I commended our wild friends to the care of the forest, whispered "We'll be back," and got into the car.

We began to move.

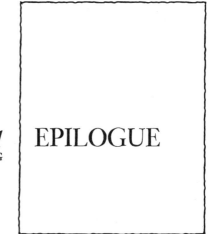

1971
EARLY SPRING

EPILOGUE

——— There was so dense a fog in the Village when we came back after our sixth trip of exploration that turning into the Trail was like taking a road into limbo. I rolled down my window so that I might better see the edge of the blacktop in case Ade needed guidance through the obscurity. Ade rolled his down to yell at the driver of a car without lights. We both laughed, because we had so many times gone through the same sequence on this stretch of road.

"I'd forgotten fog," he said, "except the kind that comes up like smoke in the morning between mountain ridges."

So, in the midst of a detailless world, we talked of places we had seen in our searching.

The Plains, rolling and vast—golden with wheat, banded by alternate planting, dotted with cattle, yellow and green and fragrant with sweet clover. *The Lower Sonoran Desert*, blazing with heat and rich with life—watched over by the saguaros, accented by scarlet-tipped ocotillos and the sunshine-colored flowers of the paloverde tree, tracked by peccaries and horned lizards and sidewinders, filled with the music of Gambel's quail. *The Rocky Mountains*, monuments to Creation, whose peaks might truly house the gods—green with forests, dancing with crystal waters, white with lingering snow; inhabited by old friends—whiskey jacks and black bears—and new—magpies and mule deer. *The Canyonlands*, a forest of stone; dangerous, harsh, beautiful, and incredible —cliffs and color, arches and monoliths, slickrock and gorges, with heat in its canyons and snow on its heights, with great rivers winding and arid sand blowing, and life as varied as its terrain. *The Painted Desert*, horizon-wide and rainbow-dusted—slashed by arroyos, sprinkled with rocks, its land only a base for its stupendous sky; where restless dust hides last night's tracks and unveils the stone-preserved footprints of dinosaurs. *Monument Valley*, silent, ancient, overwhelming—thousand-foot pillars of sunset-red stone, spaces that stretch into limitless haze; where all man's years have seen only a trickling of rock to the monuments' bases, where the cries of his struggle are lost in the wind, and time waits for him to go.

We had seen marvels but had found no place for ourselves. The Plains were cultivated or in grass for pasture. Many people were moving to the Rockies and the Sonoran Desert, and their towns disrupted the natural rhythms. There was no such thing as a representative location in Canyonlands, and to locate a suitable place in that maze of rock would take us years. The Painted Desert and Monument Valley, the latter to me the most wonderful place of all, were in the Navajo reservation, and since neither of us was fortunate enough to have one quarter of our blood from the People, we could not stay there—and this was as it should be.

"Well," Ade said, "something'll turn up. Anyway, the fog's thinning."

I looked out to see the entrance to a short loop of the old trail, used now to give access to some cabins. "D'you remember when the steep hill in there washed out and they put planks up and down to get you through?"

"How could I forget? I'd hate to have driven over it in a fog like this. The new road has the normal number of chuckholes, though. I've been feeling them. The frost up here would break up concrete, let alone blacktop."

He swung into our side road. It had been widened a few feet and the moss and ferns of the south bank had been bull-dozed away in the process, leaving bare and eroding earth. If, I thought, they don't widen it again for a few years, the forest will cover the scars.

After we passed the Lodge, we saw small roadside clear-ings with power poles, freshly opened driveways, piles of cut trees and brush, transformers lying on the verge where new clearings for poles and new driveways would soon be made. The change seemed to have gained size and speed like an avalanche. I had known it would happen, but seeing it was depressing, and the drizzle that began added to my state of gloom. I hardly looked around when Ade pulled up at the familiar cut-in and parked beside our second faithful, and now retired, Chevy. I remembered when Jacques had given it to us, and wondered where he was now and what he was doing.

"You stay here while I get the cabin door open," Ade di-rected. "It'll probably be stuck again, and you'd get soaked waiting down there. *I* brought my raincoat."

"Take your time," I said, wondering why the dampness in the unheated cabin caused the bottom of the door to jam against the floor but affected no other part of the building.

I waited, trying unsuccessfully to shake off my depression. Then I heard thuds, silence, more thuds—heavier the second time. The door must really be stuck. I had time to kill, and I refused to sit and brood. I sorted out twenty-four fan letters and slit the envelopes with a nail file.

Eleven writers discussed my books and four asked for an autograph. An old gentleman thanked me for stirring memories of his youth, and a twelve-year-old girl, for giving her an understanding of the wild world. A hospitalized woman, a man in prison, and a blind man who had read *Forest* in Braille told me they had used my eyes to see beyond their respective walls. A couple with a wild-country cottage had solved a problem by using one of our methods; another wanted advice on toilets. A university student named Gary C. Brown wrote: "War, hate, death. That is all I seem to read today. All this news about how man is *not* relating to his environment. What I want are positive books, books that tell how man *can* relate to his world. Books that tell how man has—as you have. Not bending the world to fit man, but bending man to fit the world."

Gary had said quite a mouthful, and I read it again. Just how *had* we done this? After considerable pondering I decided that, first, we had not thought we were any more important than the flora and fauna around us. We differed from most people who live away from towns and cities in that we did not try to live off the land. We caught no fish, as we killed no game, because we knew that man can take freedom and life from living creatures, but he cannot give these birthrights. Aside from the produce of our small gardens, we ate only certain leaves and mushrooms, whose gathering did not injure their plants. We cut no living tree and removed no plants except those that were so widespread and expanded so rapidly that the portion we took out did not endanger the whole.

Second, we had tried to leave as little trace of our passing over the earth's surface as was possible. The path I would walk down had been a driveway when we bought, but shortly thereafter a cloudburst had washed it out. We did not rebuild it but let the forest cover its rutted gravel and mud with greenery and flowers. The tall trees around me reminded me of the new power installations along the road and of our less contemporary lighting. Cleaning the chimneys of oil lamps and filling their little tanks had been a nuisance, to be sure, but a small price to pay for virgin pines just outside a window. And now when we did not want to use our power plant, our gas-mantle lamps gave plenty of light for reading and typing. Our only problems with them had risen in very cold weather, when the outside tank regulator might frost. The sign was a slow fading of the light, which sent Ade out to hold his gloved hands around the regulator until I yelled that the light was okay again. Since this happened every half-hour or so, it not only disorganized our evenings but half-froze Ade, and me when I took my turn. Then I had the idea of warming a strip of cloth—old fleece-lined cotton underwear was perfect—on the edge of the oil stove, where there was no danger of its catching fire. When this was wound firmly around the regulator, all was well for a couple of hours. Then at the first dip of the light, an alternate strip, warming meanwhile, could replace the first one.

Thinking that the trick was to find the simplest way of handling not only such pesky little things, but also the larger necessities of living, I opened the next letter and began to boil as I read it. The writer stated flatly that anyone who thought the U.S. of A. was still a land of opportunity was either a fool or mad. Thus, since I seemed to be reasonably intelligent and probably sane, what we had accomplished must have had some base outside of our own efforts.

Being called a liar hardly fazed me—this was not the first

time—but I was fed to the teeth with people who wore a defeatist attitude like a laurel wreath. And this particular fellow would examine his front lawn and generalize about the Great Plains. Ade and I found opportunity as people have done, are doing, and will continue to do as long as they are free to pursue happiness. There was no guarantee that we would find either happiness or success, but we knew that neither could be had without trying. We also knew what we wanted and had capital, without which no independent venture is possible, in the form of drawing and writing ability. We exercised our right to try, with full knowledge that we must make sacrifices and that we might fail. We did not, although there were many times when we thought we would, but even then we knew that we had gained something intangible and lasting by trying.

The sounds from the cabin had ceased. I slid the opened letters into the big envelope that held the rest of the mail and was ready to go when Ade poked a plastic raincoat through the open car window. By the time I was waterproofed and had lifted my bags out of the car, he was halfway to the cabin with his larger load. I followed slowly through a woods so brown and leafless that it might have been late fall instead of early spring. Except for the sogginess and the diminishing mist, the surroundings were as they had been on the afternoon ten years before when I had returned from a walk on the road to our "green pastures." I stopped where I had then.

The bank and the clearing were empty of deer. There was not even a track on the fading trail that crossed our path. The door of the tiny chicken house was closed, and the run where Bedelia had once dust-bathed had been dismantled two years before. I wondered what had become of the feed pan Ade had been holding in his hand on that past and lovely day. And suddenly the old feeling of shock and sorrow and disillusionment came to increase my feeling of emptiness, as it did each time we returned from our wanderings. I wished that we had not come, that I might find an excuse to leave—and Ade's voice came across the clearing: "Pete's sake, hurry up! I'm hungry."

I gathered my wandering emotions and hurried, envying him his recuperative powers, for he had loved our peaceful, gentle time as much as I had.

I sidled through the partly open door—a bulge in the floor kept it from opening fully, dragged the bags through one at a time, and tried to close the door. It stuck, I yanked, and Ade yelled, "Don't close it!" I paused and he said, "You can't open it from inside once it's shut. I'd have to go out a window and batter it open again. I had to use a log as a ram."

"What do we do? Leave it open?"

"Sure—until I take it off the hinges and plane the bottom."

This brightened my mood. As long as opening the cabin was uphill work nothing had changed inside, at least. Even the blended smell of wood, mildew, and mice was comfortingly familiar.

I lighted a match and turned on a stove burner. No gas. I sidled out and stepped into the woodshed where the cylinders were standing. I reached toward the handwheel of the shut-off valve, listened, shook my head vigorously, and opened the valve. I must have imagined I heard a deer stomp within a few feet of me.

As I turned to go in I looked toward Peter's tree—and saw him standing in the shadows beside the little heap of bare and broken cedar branches, left from his first meal with us. I was frightened, for I knew that Peter was dead and could not be there. Then the deer stomped again, and as he stepped forward, the clouds parted, both in my mind and in the sky.

Sunlight fell on him and I saw the white spot on his forehead. This was Starface, Peter's last son, so like his father that he had made me think I was seeing a ghost. Starface, ten years old, and still remembering his first feeding place, although there had been no corn under the tree for four winters. And the earth around the bole was trampled rough and the cedar's lowest branches nibbled free of leaves—nibbled when the weight of the snow had bent them down. Starface and no doubt other deer had come to eat the cedar and to rest here, in their own place.

I knew at that moment that this was still, and always would be, our place, too. No amount of surrounding changes would take it away, because such a place is more than a piece of earth, and its environment may be anything from the tallest trees to the highest towers. It is where you find the fulfillment of your deepest needs, and you find it only once, if you are lucky enough to find it at all. But once you find it, you never leave it entirely and you never lose it, because it has become a part of you. During all our wanderings it had been with me while I was looking for it in mountains and deserts and plains. From this time on it would be both here and with me wherever I might be, as long as I should live.

Starface stomped again. I leaned toward the doorway and called softly to Ade. He looked out the kitchen window, smiled at me, and rattled cans as he got one to fill from the small store of corn we always had waiting for our return. He handed me the feed and I looked up, past the sparks of colored fire struck from the raindrops by the sun, past the cedar and balsam and spruce and pine, to the spreading patch of blue in the sky. I smelled the sharpness of the forest's spring earth, saw a squirrel watching me as he groomed wet fur, heard a loon laugh far away on the lake.

As I took the can toward Peter's tree and Starface stepped back a discreet distance, I knew that I had found what all men seek—my place in the world of my time.

Helen Hoover, author of *The Gift of the Deer* and
A Place in the Woods, was born in 1910 in Greenfield, Ohio, and attended Ohio University, where
she studied chemistry.

During World War II, when her husband was in
the Navy, she studied biology at the University of
Chicago in her spare time. Before 1954, when she
and her artist husband took to the woods of Minnesota, Mrs. Hoover was a research metallurgist for
the International Harvester Company in Chicago.
Since then she has been a free-lance writer, con-
tributing to such magazines as *Audubon, Defenders
of Wildlife News, Gourmet, American Mercury*,
and also to many children's magazines.

————— A NOTE ON THE TYPE

This book was set on the Linotype in Janson, a re-
cutting made direct from type cast from matrices
long thought to have been made by the Dutchman
Anton Janson, who was a practicing type founder
in Leipzig during the years 1668–87. However, it
has been conclusively demonstrated that these types
are actually the work of Nicholas Kis (1650–1702),
a Hungarian, who most probably learned his trade
from the master Dutch type founder Dirk Voskens.
The type is an excellent example of the influential
and sturdy Dutch types that prevailed in England
up to the time William Caslon developed his own
incomparable designs from them.

*Composed, printed, and bound by Kingsport Press,
Incorporated, Kingsport, Tennessee.*

Typography and binding design by Clint Anglin.